SIR
SAM
FAY

SIR SAM FAY

JOHN NEVILLE GREAVES

The Book Guild Ltd

First published in Great Britain in 2018 by
The Book Guild Ltd
9 Priory Business Park
Wistow Road, Kibworth
Leicestershire, LE8 0RX
Freephone: 0800 999 2982
www.bookguild.co.uk
Email: info@bookguild.co.uk
Twitter: @bookguild

Typeset in Adobe Garamond Pro

Printed and bound in Great Britain by CPI Group (UK) Ltd, Croydon, CR0 4YY

ISBN 978 1911320 937

British Library Cataloguing in Publication Data.
A catalogue record for this book is available from the British Library.

MIX
Paper from
responsible sources
FSC® C013604
FSC
www.fsc.org

To my father, (John T. Greaves, 1900–1954),
who served the Great Central Railway and its sucessors from 1915 to 1954

CONTENTS

PREFACE

Several attempts have been made over the years to write a biography of Sam Fay, including one intended by himself, and I have been aware of the difficulties: his life was so long and so full and colourful that the highways and by-ways have proved absorbing. But it is strange that one of the greatest of Britain's railway managers has not so far received due historical recognition.

The Great Central Railway, London's last main line to the North, has not come down in histories as a resounding success, partly due to the continuing odium heaped (quite unjustly) upon its promoter, Sir Edward Watkin, by a succession of writers. But that has been proved to be a very myopic and distorted view. The true picture, which I hope emerges from this account, is that because of the exceptional abilities of the Great Central's Chairman and his General Manager, it demonstrated all the characteristics of a modern, beautifully engineered and economically operated railway, as compared with any in the land. Sam Fay's overall contribution to the principles of management of a large and complicated business was immense. His capabilities were recognised by the Government in 1916, when he was 'conscripted' to take charge of the overwhelmingly important business of ensuring the smooth operation, to and from the Western Front, of transporting troops, supplies and ammunition and the return of the wounded. As Director Movements – Railways, Roads, Inland Waterways and Docks – he did a first-class job, as was recognised by politicians, generals, and by King George himself.

At this time of recollection of the trials of the First World War, the hope is that Sir Sam Fay will receive a greater recognition of his place in history.

ACKNOWLEDGEMENTS

I am deeply indebted for the full support I received for this study from Andrew Dow (1943–2015), and after his untimely death, that of his wife, Dr Stephanie Dow. They were unfailingly generous in pledging help with the Great Central Railway (GCR) photographs of George Dow, and in their warm encouragement throughout. I received unstinting cooperation from Sam Fay's relatives: his sons Edgar Stewart Fay and John Yeo, both of whom I was privileged to catch before they died; John's wife Monica; and from John Samuel Fay and William ('Bill') Marvin Fay (grandsons), without whose steadfast kindness the journey would have been much more difficult and protracted. Fareham Local History Group were friendly and co-operative.

The National Archives at Kew were useful and helpful: all credit to them for their service to the nation in what they do. Gladstone's Library at Hawarden, North Wales proved, as always, a perfect resource for study and writing. Finally, the patient support of my wife, Iris, has been invaluable during the whole time.

None of the above splendid enablers is in any way responsible for shortcomings of conception or execution, which are entirely my own.

1

Early Days; 1856-1902

Samuel Fay was descended from a Huguenot family, Protestants who were persecuted in France by the Roman Catholic Church after the Reformation. An Edict of 1535 ordered the extermination of these 'heretics', after periods of toleration, and the Massacre of Saint Bartholomew's Day, 24 August 1572, was a forerunner of such slaughter. Thousands were killed – 8,000 in Paris alone. Many, however, escaped to other countries, notably to Prussia and England, and became valuable members of society in their new homes.[1]

One of those families was called 'Fay'. The name, in various senses, comes from Old French '*fei*', modern French '*foi*', as in quasi-oaths, such as '*moi foi*', or '*by my fay*', meaning 'by my faith'. Sam (as he always preferred to be known, even after his knighthood) was born on 30 December 1856, at Hamble-le-Rice, Hampshire, the second son of Joshua Fay (1824–1902), and his wife Ann, née Philpott (1819–1900). Joshua was a bailiff and gardener for the Rector of Hambledon, and later a farmer, a descendant of farmers at Awbridge from the late seventeenth century. Sam was educated at the village school, and then, from 1867, at Blenheim School on West Street in Fareham; it was founded originally for Huguenot refugees, and he is recorded as a fourteen-year-old pupil there in the Census of 1871.

In 1872 he started work as a Junior Clerk at Itchen Abbas Station on the

---

1   Some achieved great prominence, like Sir John Houblon, Governor of the Bank of England from 1694 to 1697; and Philip Cazenove, founder of the highly successful and respected House of Stockbrokers in London.

1

Mid-Hants Railway, which was worked by the London and South Western Company, who bought it out entirely in 1884. In the mid-nineteenth century railways were the most exciting industries to work for, and in his youth Sam 'thought it was fine thing to wear a uniform and say "Right Away" to the guard and engine driver'. But there was stiff competition for jobs, and at fifteen he was lucky his father knew an auditor on the L&SWR, and through him received a nomination for a clerkship from Lewis Ayre, a director of the company from 1835. Depending upon his passing a simple examination, he was swiftly selected. After only three months he was appointed as Station Clerk, and one of his duties was to operate a bell-signal between Itchen Abbas and Winchester Junction. This involved giving the signal to the box at the junction and releasing the down starter signal at the ground frame on the platform. On two occasions he forgot to give the signal, and as this was a serious offence he received a lively rebuke from the District Inspector, Mr Hills. Fortunately, in view of his future importance in railway history, he was not dismissed.

In April of the following year he worked briefly at Arlesford, and then Stockbridge, as Station Clerk until 1874. His Station Master at Stockbridge was often under the influence of drink, and although Sam was not a teetotaller, he was aware of the dangers of excess. In February of 1875 he became part of relief staff, at Turnham Green, and in December at Southampton. He was appointed, in the July of 1876 as a clerk at Kingston-upon-Thames Station, becoming, a year later, the Chief Booking Clerk there. From January 1878, following his twenty-first birthday, he began to keep a diary, an exercise which lasted only three years, but left us a series of insights into his character and activities at that time.

As early as the entry on 1 February 1878, he recorded the signs that he was looking for a more demanding position, noting a company instruction that 'Duties are to remain as they are till the end of the month', and he hoped that 'something would turn up worth going for by then'. After six years of varied experience he wanted greater challenges and responsibilities, having noticed that many staff changes and promotions were taking place on the L&SWR. A week later, a more personal note was sounded in that he was going up to London on the 2.55 pm to buy a birthday present in Oxford Street for 'Trottie'. That was the nickname for Frances Ann Farbrother (1857–1946), who was later to become his wife. After this visit to the emporia he went round to the Press Entrance of the Palace of Westminster, and saw Lord Beaconsfield arrive and Lord Derby depart, to a cheering crowd. He went several times to see and hear the proceedings in the House of Commons (his father was able to get him passes), recording at length the various subjects debated and the speeches made. But he does not appear to have felt the same attraction to becoming an MP as had many railwaymen of the day.

On Tuesday the 12th he was entrusted by Mr Pettit, his boss, to get £900 worth of Railway and Tramway shares at Birkbeck Bank, Southampton Buildings, which must have done no harm at all to his desire for more trust and responsibility. That evening, he and Trottie went to a concert in the drill hall. On the following day, the Feast of St Valentine, he received two cards – one of them from Trottie, but the other sender is not recorded. Trottie's brother, William, worked at Kingston Cemetery, and on the 14th Sam helped him take an old woman in her coffin up to the burial ground, recording in his diary that she 'looked very nice, though 84 years old'. The next day's entry recorded that Mr Adams had been appointed as Locomotive Superintendent in place of Mr Beattie, who had resigned.

Sam's diary revealed a wealth of information about his interest in various sporting activities. On Saturday the 16th he played rugby football at Kingston against the Clarendon Club. 'They got one try the best of us, getting ducedly[2] knocked about – a good buck on the shin, a bloody nose, and various other goodly knocks and ugly tumbles.' His main athletic indulgence, apart from energetic walks in Richmond Park, 'not keeping to the paths, but the rougher the park the better', seems to have been rowing – singles, pairs and fours – for which he trained quite hard. The sessions seem to have been particularly frequent between 7 and 27 May 1878 because Trottie expressed dissatisfaction that it was keeping them apart. He was elected a member of the rowing club on 20 March and by 10 October he was on the Committee. By 13 December of that year he had added ice skating to his leisure activities. In later years he took up golf, which he liked, though his handicap was recorded as 'astronomical'.[3]

On 25 February 1878 he had asked Mr Pettit if he had any objection to his applying for Queen's Road Station, where he had heard that the Chief Clerk was about to leave, but his boss poured cold water on the idea, saying that he had no plans for making alterations to his office. Undaunted, Sam

2   'Devilishly'.
3   Edgar Stewart Fay, 'Memoirs', page 67.

records that five days later he went to meet Mr Goffe, of Mr Scott's office,[4] 'to arrange a partnership in the South Western Time Table with him, but he did not turn up'. This sounds like a much higher grade than that of Chief Booking Clerk, but clearly the time was not yet ripe, and Sam does not elaborate.

There are regular mentions of going to church, usually with Trottie, sometimes twice in one day. He was obviously not an unwilling worshipper, sometimes making comments on the officiant or the sermon. For example, on 10 March 1878 he recorded that at the Evensong service at Ham, 'Mr Hough preached a beautiful sermon; he must be a good man. I would that I could live with such a man as he is, then perhaps my good resolutions would not fall to the ground so quickly as they do now.' Trottie remarked that she had not enjoyed a Sunday so much for a long time. 'It was a beautiful moonlight night, and I seem to love her more and more, not so passionately, perhaps, but with a purer love than of yore.' He also reflected on hearing 'a very nice sermon' at the second of two services in Ramsgate on 22 September 1878. On Sunday 6 October he went to church in Porchester in the afternoon, to his uncle's in the evening, 'sang a few hymns, smoked a cigar or two, done a glass of whiskey [sic]', and home to bed at the late hour of eleven o'clock. That outing had been to Longstock, near Stockbridge, on 1 October, spending the next day and the 4th, 5th, 10th and 12th out shooting – rabbits, pheasants, partridges and hares.

In a long entry for 11 March 1879, he was in reflective mood:

Read *Harold* again[5] this morning. Methinks my nature is somewhat the same as his, at least to ambition, but we are all ambitious there surely can be no sin in it, my fancy takes very high flights at times, building castles in the air I know never will be realized; in sober moments my thoughts plan out my future – they make me chief clerk at some good station, then, with my darling Trottie, in charge of a small country station, and eventually a large one: 'Man proposes, but God disposes.' However, unless it pleases him to alter altogether the course of my life,

4   Archibald Scott, General Manager from 1870 to 1885.
5   He had mentioned on 6 March 1878 reading *Harold* by Lord Lytton, and *Tancred* by Disraeli. *Harold, the Last of the Saxon Kings* (1848) was a eulogy to greatness and chivalry; later an opera by Verdi. Tancred, a novel based on the twelfth-century Crusades, was about Tancred, King of Sicily, a good soldier, idealised as one whose aim was the reconciliation of Judaism and Christianity; it was made into an opera by Rossini in 1813.

and if it please him to spare me, that seems a rational *castle in the air*.
Time will show! But my earnest prayer is that come weal or woe I may
'Meekly bear the storms of fate, and duty be my polar star.'[6] May I
never cause a pang to the one who loves me so dearly, may I ever be
a joy and honour to my Father and Mother and a blessing to them in
their old age; then when death comes at last may I be able to look back
on a well-spent life, from this day, for bad it has been hitherto, and be
glad to go to the place which my Redeemer has prepared for me.

In later life, Sam was to write extensively on themes philosophical and
spiritual, as well as on practical matters. A disproportionate number of the
descendants of Hugenots retained a strong awareness of such subjects, and
the ethical implications of them.

With due financial probity, he was in no mood to be married in haste:
on 2 April 1878 he mentioned receipt of a letter from a colleague in Exeter,
by the name of Brown, saying that he had got married ten days before. Sam
observed that he was 'a year younger than I am, and only in receipt of £70
[a year]… it is rather a bold trick'. However, on 16 May he revealed that
Trottie and he had become engaged. At the party in the evening, he had
several dances with 'Miss Tilbury, Miss Hall, Miss Louie Gardiner, and Miss
Dawn. Trottie said she could not dance, but rather annoyed me by doing
a step with young Gardiner'. Considering that he had spent the morning
rowing, and did not arrive at the dance until 9.33 pm, when Trottie had
been there since 6 pm, her attitude might be better understood.

Trottie seemed to have lapses of health from time to time: she was
bedridden on doctor's orders for four weeks from 12 July 1878. This
appeared to make Sam a little more attentive: 'I see her every day now at
some time or other', he recorded on 20 July, though it is notable that he had
started to refer to her as 'the Old Lady'. On her birthday, 16 February 1879,
he gave her an engagement ring (pearls and rubies).

---

6   A quotation from the German poet Goethe (1749–1832), his *Poems of Sentiment*, Book
    VI, 'Without Haste, Without Rest', lines 20 and 21. The full quotation bears out Sam's
    train of thought: 'Rest not, life is sweeping by/ go and dare before you die/ leave behind to
    conquer time,/ something mighty and sublime… rest not, calmly wait:/ meekly bear the
    storms of fate!/ duty be thy polar guide… conflicts past/ God shall crown thy work at last'
    (lines 13–16, 19–24). ('Polar guide': William Wordsworth describes in *The Excursion*, line
    694, as a guide for conscience, the Polar Star – the English nautical term.)

On the busyness of the L&SWR, he wrote that from midday, Monday 23 April 1878 to midday the next day he booked at Kingston 1,480 passengers; on 17 May between 2,000 and 2,500; on 10 June, 1200 after half-past one. By 31 July he noted the best month ever at Kingston: 25,000 passengers. The harsh winters of that time caused several traffic problems: On 24 December 1878 he recorded, 'The fog was so thick that one could scarcely see one's hand before one's face... Two engines failed through the bursting of the pipes with frost.' He wrote with obvious approval on 14 January 1879 that the L&SWR Manager, Archibald Scott:

> had been solicited to add the Government Duty of 5% to the Season Ticket fares but refused, saying that the fares were as much as merchants could pay in these hard times... The other Companies wished Mr Scott to join in reducing the wages of the staff, but he said he had got some good men and he meant to keep them.

By June 1879 Fay's only entry was to report that 'Nothing was moving out of course', but he did note that 'Poor Prince Napoleon was killed on 1 June in Zululand, when on a reconnoitering expedition, having been cowardly left by his comrades.'[7] On 12 July, he recorded going to Chiselhurst by the 8.17 am train, and saw the funeral of Prince Napoleon: 'An unforgettable sight':

---

7   That was the view of the great majority at the time. There was a court martial of the Officer in Charge, Captain Jaheel Brenton Carey (1847–1883), of the North Staffordshire Regiment. He had led a scout party of eight men, including the Prince, which set out early, by the enthusiasm of the Prince and without the protection party ordered by Lord Chelmsford for the Prince's protection. They encountered unexpectedly a large group of Zulus. Carey commanded a withdrawal, in view of being seriously outnumbered, but the Prince took charge and went forward. He was badly wounded, but fought on until he was eventually killed. He had worried his commanders in the past by his dash and daring (he always carried into battle the Austerlitz sword of Napoleon the First). The Prince was born in Paris in 1856, and at baptism his godmother was Queen Victoria and his godfather Pope Pius IX. He was 23 when he died. The court martial found Carey guilty, and sentenced him to be cashiered from the British Army. It emerged that the court martial membership was illegal, and in London the Judge overturned the findings: there was the matter of the disobedience by the Prince of his commanding officer, and the latter's deference, despite the superiority in rank, to the historical status of the Prince, which had to be taken into account. Carey was pronounced not guilty of the charge, and was allowed to go free. But his reputation and treatment thereafter suffered. He was posted to India, and died there of peritonitis at the age of 36.

A squadron of Lancers headed the procession, then came the bishop of Southwark and other clergy with an immense gold cross; the gun carriage with the coffin was drawn by eight horses. The Prince of Wales, Dukes of Edinburgh, Connaught and Cambridge, and Crown Prince of Sweden acted as pall bearers. M.Rouber acted as chief mourner for the Empress followed by Prince Jerome and his two sons, many deputies, including Paul de Casagnac, and then officers of our own army and a great number of French deputations, and finally another squadron of Lancers.

He 'caught a train nicely' and got back to Kingston by 1.7 pm.

4 December 1879: Mr Osborne had been transferred to Windsor, and although Mr Pettit had asked the Manager for a clerk to replace him, no one had yet arrived, and Sam had been required to take on the extra duties. No one had arrived by the 11th, but on the 13th Sam received notice from the Manager that he had been granted a rise to £80. On Christmas Day he wrote that he had worked 'duce hard' with the extra parcels work.

Saturday, 27 March 1880 saw him revealing his party-political inclinations at the time, when he recorded that as the Liberals had gained a great majority in Parliament 'it was goodbye to English Patriotism and England's supremacy throughout the world'.

The entries in the diary for April and May were dominated by further staff vacancies and speculation about replacements. On Wednesday 12 May, he was told that no more agents would be appointed at salaries exceeding £100 per year. On 7th, 8th and 10th we learn that Trottie had cut her thumb badly, having it sewn up, that she was 'very queer' on the 8th, and the wound had gathered, making her very bad in herself, though by the 20th she had 'gone with Milly to Castle Hedingham for a week', to see if it would do her any good. On 5 June he went to Castle Hedingham for Trottie, who met him at the station, though her thumb was still very bad. They stayed with a poultry dealer, Tom Westrop, and went to church morning and evening on the 6th. While there, Sam helped out at the local school on the Monday, before leaving on the afternoon train, reading out dictation to the youngsters: 'The young beggars evidently took me for a foreigner – they could not understand what I said.'

In September 1880 he and Trottie went for their holiday in Devon, where he himself found the local accent difficult to understand. To enlarge on this subject, though it means a leaping forward of the narrative, a portrait of Sam by 'Spy' appeared in *Vanity Fair* describing him:

> There is no nonsense about him, but there is an American accent, or to be exact it sounds an American accent. It is not. Given the chance he will assure you that he speaks the true Hampshire tongue of which the great American language is but a base and colourless imitation. That tongue, he contends, went to the United States from Poole Harbour and Buckler's Hard;[8] and the Great Republic has striven in vain to live up to it.

His son Edgar added that in the 1920s Sam's accent had softened, from years in the board room and at the War Office, but his 'R's (sounding Irish rather than American) survived to his dying day; not so much 'Hampshire' as 'New Forrest'.[9] Edgar came across later a surprising confirmation of his father's surmise in a book by A.F. Tschiffely,[10] entitled *Tschiffely's Ride*, describing a horseback journey from South America to the United States. Tschiffely came to England and wrote a sequel, *Bridle Paths*, detailing his rides in this country.[11] He relates how he hired a horse in a place in the New Forest, which could not have been far from Awbridge, and commented that 'the few men he stopped to talk to spake with an accent of the kind which I had heard in the hills of West Virginia. I have often wondered if the original settlers of that part of the New World were people who had emigrated from Hampshire'.

---

8   'Buckler's Hard': a famous ship-building operation on the banks of the Beaulieu River in Hampshire, and the site of emigrations to America in 1645.

9   Edgar, *Memoirs*, page 425.

10   Sometimes spelled in the literature with one 'f' and two 'l's.

11   Aimé Felix Tschiffely (1895–1954), Swiss-born Argentinian adventurer, teacher, footballer and boxer. He left to teach in England, but his book *Tschiffely's Ride – 10,000 Miles in the Saddle, From Southern Cross Argentina to Pole Star, Washington, USA*, was published in 1933 by Hodder and Stoughton (reprinted in German, French, Finnish, Polish, Spanish and Swedish in 1952). He started in April 1925 and arrived two years later to a ticker-tape reception, and being received at the White House by President Coolidge. Later he was a National Geographical Society Lecturer. His English 'Ride through Rural England', published in 1936, was entitled *Bridle Paths:* published by The Travel Book Club Ltd, 1936. Re-published Hodder and Stoughton, 1947.

Sam and Trottie enjoyed the West Country very much. On the 11th they went up the River Tamar on a steamer as far as Calstock, and they walked up to Gunnislake, 'one of the steepest and longest hills I've ever climbed. The scenery was very grand at Gunnislake, the banks of the river in some parts being almost perpendicular. Tavistock has a railway station of the West Cornwall Railway, but it is not used for passenger traffic.' He noticed some very peculiar points there, and made a rough sketch of them: 'the points were merely the rails cut off square and fitted closely against the other rail when pulled over, making merely a joint of it'. In the afternoon of the 12th they walked to the Great Western Docks at Tavistock, where, 'bye the bye, they charge a penny for admittance'.

On 14 September he set off to Ilfracombe by first train from Plymouth North Road Station, and 'managed to upset Trottie before leaving her', despite [because of?] their having been more than happy on the previous day. He learned of 'a very bad accident on our line at Nine Elms', five or six killed and many injured, a Kingston man among those who died. He left Ilfracombe, 'a beautiful place', at about 2.30 pm: 'The line is very queer, the gradients being steep the pace is merely a crawl for some considerable distance. Got home about half past nine.' He went to church in the morning of Sunday the 20th, and Trottie came home with her father by an evening train from Plymouth on Monday 21st. They went to church together on the following Sunday, and again on Wednesday 1 October for the Harvest Festival, where he 'enjoyed the singing and the service very much'.

On 11 October he applied for a Secretaryship of an Oddfellows Society, for which the salary was £12 per annum. On the 14th they went to a wedding at Teddington with a dance in the evening, arriving home by the last train, and the following day Trottie seemed 'knocked up' by the exertions, though by Sunday 17th she was well enough to go to church in the evening.

20 October, Wednesday: 'An empty train from Clapham Junction ran into a goods at West London Junction, blocking the Up and Down Windsor – trains very much delayed. It was said to be caused by the snow blocking up the signal arm so that it would not work.'

In November 1880, Sam changed his lodgings at Kingston. 'Things had been going on very rough there lately – bad dinners, worse cooking, late hours by other inmates keeping us awake, and the most objectionable feature, the conduct of the landlady's niece.' He was lodging, *pro tem*, at Shanklin Villa on the Richmond Park Road.

On 1 February 1881, he recorded that:

We had a tremendous fall of snow on 18 January, blocking up the lines and snowing in the trains all over the country. It was accompanied by a strong wind and caused great drifts. We were busy all day long keeping the lines clear; many of the trains did not run. Brown at Exeter tells me he was at work almost day and night and had 4,000 messages during the week.

9 February, Wednesday: 'The proposed Guildford to London Railway is meeting with a deal of opposition on the part of the Wimbledon and Putney people. The Kingston people are very much in favour of it.'

16 February: 'Thick fog again, causing a crash at Woking. The Exeter Fast Goods ran into the Southampton Goods, and smashed up a rare lot of trucks.'

In the entry for Wednesday 23 March, Sam wrote one of his infrequent prophetic observations on international politics: 'We have managed to come to terms with the Boers… thus laying in a plentiful crop of troubles in the future.'

On Bank Holiday Monday, 18 April: 'Traffic very good; managed to pull through it pretty well, the usual delays and faulty arrangements of the Suburban District notwithstanding. We want a double set of rails on the Windsor line as far as Twickenham and the same to Surbiton or Woking on the Main.'

Tuesday, 19 April 1881, saw the death of one of Sam's heroes, Lord Beaconsfield (Benjamin Disraeli), at four o'clock. He was:

76 – a good age, but we can ill-afford to lose him even now. His loss is irreparable to England, especially at this time when it is fashionable to run down British supremacy and influence. If we go on as we are with our colonies we shall shortly have no colonies left and England will sink to a second-rate power such as Spain or Portugal. Lord Beaconsfield's life shows what a healthy man may

achieve in this country, and his career must act as a stimulus to many young men trying to rise in the world. It is said that children craved to be near him and that women worshipped him. He said before his death that 'he would rather live, but not afraid to die.'

Two days later, Sam went to a sale in Teddington and bought a picture, *Young England*.[12]

Intimations of the end of his daily diary recordings, in favour of a more public literary venture, came in his entry for Thursday 28 April 1881: 'I have an idea that a paper called *The South Western Gazette,* devoted to matters affecting the South Western Railway, and giving the promotions and staff changes, would take off well if the profits were handed over to the [L&SWR] Widows and Orphan Fund.' He shared his idea with his colleague Goffe, and he had enlisted his fellow clerk, Dyer, in the General Manager's Office, who was the Secretary of the South Western Institute and Club. They set out a programme, and wrote to various agents in the country for their ideas. By May, help was being offered from all directions. 'We print at Drewett's in Kingston Market Place on very good terms... 500 should do for a start.' By 18 May, 700 orders had been received, and three days later the figure was 1,100, which Sam hoped that it was at least 1,500 as several large stations had yet to reply; 2,000 were ordered by 31 May. A further 350 copies had to be printed on Monday 6 June. The Directors 'were very pleased with it'. A total of 2,450 copies had been sent off by the end of that month.

After a few domestic notes, the last entry in his diary was on Saturday 16 July 1881, when he recorded that he 'Went down to Basingstoke in the morning to act as a reporter for the *Gazette* at the Widows' and Orphans' Fête held in Hackwood Park, the seat of Lord Bolton. Came home when the speeches had ended at about 6 o'clock.'

The *South Western Gazette* was clearly meeting a need for the L&SWR, and its abundant success an example of Sam's development in staff communication, which was to bear fruit in his managerial years. It was published from 1 June 1881 to 3 December 1887. The first Editorial set out its purpose, declaring that:

---

12 'Young England' was the name of a Disraeli-led party of Social Toryism, a hierarchically idealist feudalism, but politically egalitarian. It generated a strong support in its time.

No service, trade or profession is complete in our day without its newspaper: railway periodicals there certainly are, almost innumerable, but they do not represent the interests or opinions of the particular line we have the honour to serve. It is to supply this that the *South Western Gazette* is published. Written by South Western men for South Western men, in the pecuniary interests of the Widows' and Orphans' Fund, it deserves the support of all classes in the service, not on account of any literary merit – it has no pretension in that direction – but because it will assist a most deserving institution. Our object is to promote peace and goodwill among all classes in the Company's employ… and reserve the right to refuse any communication which is negative or of a political nature.

The articles ranged from Staff Promotions and Changes,[13] Music and Drama activities, Poems, news of Social Gatherings on various occasions, Staff News (marriages, deaths, deaths, promotions, etc.), Developments on the South Western Line, Gardening Hints, and the results of the SWR Cricket Club Matches, News from other Societies including the Widows' and Orphans' Fund, and the SWR Temperance Society.[14] There were also tales from other lines, from the Railway Guards' Society, and Railway Police News.

By the end of the first quarter, 31 August, by which time the circulation was 2,500 copies, the Balance of Accounts showed an excess of income over expenditure of £12 0s 5d, receipt of which was acknowledged by the Widows' and Orphans' Fund 'from Messrs Goffe, Fay, and Dyer'. The second balance sheet, for the period 31 August to 31 December, showed the circulation at 3,150 copies and a profit of £20 3s 2d for the Fund. By the end of March 1882, the circulation having been in January 5,000 copies at 1d each, with a slight drop in February and March, the Fund received £13 6s 9d. The expenditure figures included 900 free copies sent to the Somerset and Dorset Joint Line, and the advertisers in the Christmas issue. The editorial team was not averse to publishing

---

13 This item is under the heading (by way of encouragement!) 'Qui non proficit deficit', which might be translated as 'He who does not progress loses'.

14 A speaker at one of these meetings was credited with the following observation: 'A camel will work for seven or eight days without drinking. In this it is different from some men, who will drink for seven days without working.' The same speaker asserted that, 'The only man who actually needs a glass in order to work is a glazier.'

an Evangelical Hymn.[15] The influence of the Mission to the British Isles of the evangelists Dwight Lyman Moody and Ira David Sankey was pervasive at the time.

The *Gazette* carried regular reports of the authorizing of new lines, and the fact that the Great Western Railway was vigorous in opposing most of them. This was outspokenly commented upon in the issue of May 1882, page 4: 'It would be interesting to know how many thousands the South Western have been compelled to spend in opposing the encroaches of that Company... From the very first projection of the Great Western in 1834 up to the present time, it has been an endless cause of expenditure.' The writer continued, 'It was originally the design of the promoters of the South Western to make a line from Basingstoke to Bath and Bristol, and when the Great Western was promoted in the year named it was considered imperative to oppose it.' Other examples are quoted, but he felt it was:

> very gratifying to South Western vanity... to observe that where the GW and SW are in competition the latter Company manage to secure the lion's share of the traffic... The explanation of this is, we believe, to be found in the fact that the staff generally look upon loss of traffic as a personal reflection on themselves, and no effort is wanting to secure its diversion from a competing line. If the Great Western gets into Southampton, we have no doubt but that the same satisfactory state of things will exist.

The issue of August 1882 (page 4) dealt with the same subject, involving the GWR Windsor and Ascot Bill, the District Company's Bill for Running Powers from Twickenham through Kingston to Norbiton (both aborted), and the L&SWR Swindon, Marlborough and Andover Extension Scheme, which opened up L&SWR access to Southampton and a shorter route to the Isle of Wight... However, the Didcot, Norbury and Southampton Junction Bill had granted the GWR a route to Southampton. At the half-yearly meeting in August 1882 no fewer than 75 bills had been introduced to Parliament, all more or less affecting the South Western. But the Chairman was able to report an increase of receipts for the Company, over the figure for the same period in 1881, of £28,666.

---

15   March 1882 issue, page 4.

In November, the Leader Writer of *The Gazette* expressed his regret that in the consequence of the large amount of money owed by the advertisers it was not considered advisable to issue a *Gazette* balance sheet at present; this decision had the approval of the Secretary of the Widows' and Orphans' (W&O) Fund. The advertisers' deficit, on 1 July, was £40.19s 10d. Nevertheless, the W&O Fund was paid £13 2s 0d, and it was recorded that the Fund had received so far £125 17s 10d.[16] Page 5 of the July 1883 *Gazette* carried a notice of Sam Fay's book, promised in the Prospectus of the *Gazette*: *A Royal Road – History of the L&SWR from 1825 to the Present Time*, price 7s 6d; 6s to South Western officials. The July 1884 *Gazette* recorded a half-yearly balance sheet of an income of £197 12s 5d, despite an advertisers' underpayment of £39 17s 5d.

Sam relinquished his editorship on the *South Western Gazette* in June 1884, having been offered a position in the office of the Superintendent of the Line, E. W. Verrinder. In the following year he was appointed Chief Clerk, an office he held for seven years. Sam's successor as Editor congratulated him on his promotion, commenting that 'Mr Fay's history and promotion had been rapid and well-earned'. His highly regarded *History of the L&SWR, A Royal Road*, indicated that his leisure time had been occupied on a large scale, and his literary skills had developed considerably during the *Gazette* years.[17] The reviews of the book were highly favourable, and four of them are worthy of quotation here:

---

16   As a note to the work of the Widows and Orphans' Fund, an orphanage for the children of South Western employees was opened in 1885. The committee had organized concerts and collections for fund-raising, with the support of The Revd J.S. Pratt and Canon Allan Edwards, they had raised, in a surprisingly short space of time, £300, and a large house – 78 Jeffrey's Road, Clapham – was bought to accommodate children bereft of parental love and guidance. The opening took place on 11 March 1886. (The orphanage was moved to a new site in Woking in 1909.) It was clearly a work of charity close to Sam's heart.

17   Richard A. Powell, in his 'Introduction' to the reprint of the book in 1973, wrote that 'Sam Fay was essentially a practical man, but he was one of those few remarkable men who put his own thoughts into practice as well as making other men's theories work. He has not received the praise or recognition that he justly deserves and is now one of the forgotten men of the hey-day of railways… His technique was not to restrict expenditure and close unprofitable lines, but was based on the rapid expansion of business, both passenger and freight, by speeding up journey times, increasing passenger services, more effective control of traffic, and by using the most up-to-date equipment available.'

The writer has the good sense not to attempt that fine writing which the inexperienced are apt to mistake for the graces of authorship, and he [has] told his story in a plain, businesslike way, which makes it all the quicker and easier to read. (*Bristol Daily Mercury*, 18 October 1883)

This handsome volume professes to be a history of the L&SWR, but it... embodies a narrative generally of railway enterprises in England from 1825 to the present time. (*North Devon Journal*, 25 October 1883)

The work is well-written and in a highly-interesting style. Truth is... stranger than fiction, and the facts contained in this work are stranger and as entertaining as many of the popular works of fiction of the day. (*Windsor and Eton Express*, 27 October 1883)

A record of the struggles, triumphs and defeats of one of the oldest and most important of the railway companies in England. (*Dartmouth and Brixham Chronicle*, 13 October 1883)

Sam Fay's opening chapter of the book begins, magisterially for a 26-year-old:

Early in the present century, when England was recovering from the Continental wars of which the Battle of Waterloo was the termination, British shipowners, smarting under the losses inflicted by the enemy on their vessels, together with the frequent and tiresome delays caused by Easterly winds, which sometimes sealed up the passage of the Downs for weeks, heartily longed for a certain and expeditious means of transporting their ships' cargoes from the Southern Coast to London... With this end in view, an extraordinary scheme for a ship canal from Spithead to London was projected, at an estimated cost of £4,000,000. An engineer was appointed to survey the country, but the idea was abandoned, and the hopes of shipowners, which had for the time been raised, were dashed to the ground.

In 1825, reports reached Southampton of the completion and success of George Stephenson's line of railway from Stockton to Darlington. A few enterprising men in the neighbourhood appear at once to have been seized with the idea that such a railway from Southampton to London would answer all the purposes of a canal and prove the salvation of London merchantmen... The promoters of the line from Southampton to London, being the first to propose a railway in Southern England, were as a natural consequence met with ridicule in all directions, and that scheme was regarded as the outcome of disordered imaginations... Time was out of joint; trade was bad; the political world was in a state of excitement, and the Stock Exchange was seized with panic over Greek loans. So the scheme fell through.[18] Six stormy years passed away. Trade was still bad, and the distress, especially among the agricultural classes, fearful. In Hampshire during late 1830, the labourers, declaring their sufferings to be past all endurance, rose *en masse*. Meanwhile in the North the Stockton and Darlington and the Liverpool and Manchester Railways were paying good dividends. On 26 February 1831, the MP for Southampton held a meeting to re-open the discussion of the London and Southampton scheme, and the prospectus, issued on 6 April, of the 'Southampton, London, and Branch Railway' was issued with a capital of £1,500,000. This was launched as the L&SWR.

Fay gives an account, in astonishing detail, of the financing of the line and docks, the tonnages of fuel and cargo, numbers of passengers and of trucks and carriages and locomotives.[19]

A Royal Road contains many passages showing Fay's acute observation of facts, and an acerbic manner of expressing them in a humorous way. A good example of this is in Chapter IX, pages 53–57, on the 'Railway Mania' period:[20]

A great uprising in the railway world was imminent, and the original idea of railway men was that nothing more was to be done

---

18 *A Royal Road,* pages 3 and 4.

19 For the information he acknowledged his indebtedness to Colonel George Henderson (1783–1855), Royal Engineers (veteran of the Peninsula Campaign), of the engineering company Hamilton & Henderson, of Southampton, who had chaired the first meeting.

20 1845–46.

than lay down a line and all the traffic within fifty miles would be drawn upon it, was exchanged for a theory that 'every village ought to have its railway, and every village *should* have its railway.' On the Stock Exchange an excitement set in, soon to be worked into a 'Mania.' Throughout the year 1845 surveyors were overrunning the country in all directions, some of them being paid at the rate of fifteen guineas a day. They lived like lords at country hotels and played practical jokes on all and sundry... Engineers, lawyers and newspaper proprietors also reaped a rich harvest, and it was stated that an eminent QC was offered a thousand guineas for a speech, and that his clerk's fees in one session exceeded £3,000... Tradesmen left their counters and merchants their offices to gamble on scrip with other speculators in the open street... The vagabonds of society were let loose, knavery reigned supreme... newspapers abounded, with numerous 'supplements.'

So did railways: 'The Brighton and Cheltenham Direct,' 'The London and Holyhead Direct,' 'The Grand London and Dublin Approximation Railway,' 'The Bristol, Bath and Dover Direct,'... and hosts of smaller 'Directs' and 'Grands,' with their opponents – for each had its rival... It was subsequently discovered that the promoters of one line were not infrequently the advocates of its opposing scheme. As 30 November drew near, the day on which plans were to be lodged...

(continued Fay, obviously relishing his subject):

extra pressure was put on: solicitors and engineers had no bed for a fortnight... and special trains steamed into London from all quarters... special trains were refused to parties promoting lines in opposition to existing railways... Of 1,263 projects – three fourths arrant bubble – only 775 – many of these at their last gasp – managed to lodge their plans in time. A regular scramble for Bills took place, where the most unscrupulous were successful. The utter rottenness of these bubble schemes soon became apparent... Poor dupes took alarm... embarrassment or irretrievable ruin stared them in the face, and a panic ensued. Of those who were drawn into the speculating vortex few escaped, and the year 1847 was a dark one for many a home in England. An investigation of these precious schemes laid bare a state of wholesale speculation, bribery, and fraud unequalled before or since.

The central figure around whom all this madness raged was one George Hudson… who was left money by some relative or other, and speculated successfully in railways shares. He accumulated vast wealth, bought estates from dukes and lords, and found admission into the House of Commons as MP for Sunderland. The evil results of his 'reign' were too widespread for sympathy to reach him. His kingdom was swept away, the crown fell from his brow, and George Hudson, upon whose 'Yes' or 'Nay' fortunes once hung, died at last in abject poverty.

So much for history. In Chapter XIX (pages 125–131), Fay gives evidence of his grasp of the basic engineering of the L&SWR, rolling stock and track, including detailed descriptions of locomotive types, the companies that built them, and their designers. His history of the company is full of revealing information, all expressed in a lively and engaging manner, with a surprising depth and breadth of research on his part. It is not surprising that he said in his Memoirs that 'this little book was responsible for my subsequent career'. It was certainly a *tour de force* for a very young man in full-time employment.

Sam was not happy with his work as Chief Clerk under E.W. Verrinder, who by all accounts was not an easy man to work with, but he persevered for seven years. Things came to a head, however, when one of Sam's subordinates was promoted as a District Superintendent. Sam appealed against the injustice to the General Manager, Archibald Scott, who promptly appointed him to the position of Assistant Stores Superintendent at Nine Elms in 1891. In the following year he was elected as a Councillor of Kingston local council, but that was not to be of a lengthy duration. In 1890 he had made a tentative application for the vacant position of Manager of the Waterford and Central Ireland Railway. He was interviewed by the Directors at Kilkenny, but he did not see any prospects there, and he declined the post. 'Glad to escape', he wrote later, 'from an uncomfortable position.' After nine months at Nine Elms, his managerial experience was to start elsewhere.

The Midland And South Western Junction Railway

The M&SWJR was a cross-country line, running from Andoversford, north of Cirencester through Swindon and Marlborough, to a connection at Andover with the L&SWR line to Southampton. Built across the grain of natural traffic flows, it catered for the local traffic of the countryside, and its development met with strong opposition from the GWR, in whose heartland territory it was, and it always had a problem in balancing its books. The company was formed in June 1884[21] by an amalgamation of the Swindon, Marlborough and Andover Railway and the Swindon and Cheltenham Extension Railway. It had a working arrangement with the L&SWR to Southampton Docks Station. The GWR was not moved by requests to lower charges for the use of its station at Swindon, and unable to pay its creditors, the railway was declared bankrupt. On 20 December 1884, a court order was made that the company's Chairman, Lieut. Colonel Francis Douglas Grey, be appointed as Receiver. The Board of Trade sanctioned the opening of the planned Cheltenham to Andover connection in 1891, but the receipts therefrom failed to make a significant improvement in the overall operation.

In January 1892 the Directors of the M&SWJR asked Charles Scotter, who had succeeded Scott as General Manager, if he could recommend someone suitable to take over the post of Secretary and General Manager of their company, and Scotter suggested Sam Fay. Not long before the opening of the line from Cheltenham to Andover, a letter had been received by the company from Sam Fay, dated 11 February 1891.[22] It read:

> With reference to our conversation... upon the Managership of the Midland and South Western Junction Railway, I see no reason why the line should not be worked somewhat on the same principle as the several districts into which, for traffic purposes, the South Western and all other large railways are divided. That is to say, the

---

21 It was the second company of the title, the first being the line from Cricklewood to Acton Wells Junction, incorporated in 1864, which was absorbed by the Midland Railway in 1874.

22 The date is significant: Fay had applied for the job eleven months before Charles Scotter had recommended him.

Manager should have under him for traffic purposes, one uniform inspector whose duties would embrace a general supervision of the staff, the signalling arrangements and any other outdoor duties that may be found him. For the loco and carriage and the maintenance of the permanent way, two practical foremen – one for each department – acting under the instructions of the Manager would be needed, but I do not consider a highly-paid professional engineer is requisite, seeing that no large construction of stock or way works is contemplated. If the secretarial duties are added to those of the Manager, and I should be quite prepared to take this if so required, one clerk should be allocated to this branch of work, and probably one of those now employed… could do this without any additional cost.

He went on to propose salary rates for the three posts of uniform Inspector, Loco/Stock Foreman, Permanent Way Foreman, together amounting to only £312 per annum, exclusive of the salary of the Manager. Eight days later, at the Directors' meeting on 19 February 1891, Lieut. Colonel Grey reported that the appointment of a Manager be dropped. On 13 January 1892, Grey, as Receiver, called a Managers' meeting and the decision was taken that all its salaried officers be given notice. A representative was authorized to see Charles Scotter of the L&SWR, and this resulted in Sam Fay being appointed General Manager for a period of five years from 1 February 1892. He was granted a fixed salary of £300 per annum, with an additional payment of £100 for every £2,000 of net revenue. From 1 July 1895 the M&SWJ made a new agreement with Fay, when he was given a contract of £300 per annum 'plus a commission of £5 per cent of any balance to the credit of Revenue Account No.9'. The Locomotive and Carriage Superintendent had a salary of £600; this was reduced by Fay, soon after his arrival, to £200 (as a Consulting Engineer) – something less than the 45 shillings per week Fay had proposed in his letter of 11 February 1891.

He negotiated greatly more favourable terms than hitherto with W.H. Smith for advertising at stations and bookstalls, and with a firm for advertising in carriages and the company's timetable. He had, during bad weeks for revenue, to go out to various stations and debtors to collect enough money to pay wages. He sold off a troublesome engine, No. 4, and much useless rolling stock. He obtained a cheaper supply of coal, reducing the total expenditure by £2,974.

On 28 February 1893, the Board removed Colonel Grey from the Receivership, and Fay was appointed in his place, without any extra remuneration. He had to sell surplus lands for the repair of carriages, and some of the line was a mass of weeds.

Nevertheless, in due course, Fay showed a boldness well beyond anything seen before on the line: he developed long-distance traffic, with through carriages from Sheffield and Birmingham to Southampton in 1893, and later from Bradford, Leeds and Liverpool. These initiatives were continued later, with services from Manchester and Whitehaven to Southampton for immigrants from the depressed ironfield in West Cumberland. An important measure, with the consent of the Court of Chancery, was to secure a loan of £56,000 for a rolling stock fund. This enabled the purchase in 1896 of a goods engine, two mixed traffic engines, and new goods and passenger rolling stock. The Company was taken out of the Court of Chancery, where it had been for 13½ years, in May 1897. Between 1894 and 1898, traffic had increased by 73%, with only an 18% increase in expenditure.

The secretary of the line, E.T. Lawrence, had met Fay off the train when he came to take up his appointment, and he said 'Do you know this line is nearly bankrupt and there is not enough money in the bank to pay the staff at the end of the week?' Fay replied, 'Don't say that. I see great possibilities in this line', adding that he intended to go out in every way to build up traffic. He had fulfilled his visionary promise.

After several tussles with the GWR over traffic workings and delays, Fay negotiated with them in 1899 to double its Landsdown Junction to Andersford Junction within eighteen months, and to undertake within six months extra block posts from Andersford to Notsgrove, and Landsdown to Churchdown at places to be named by the M&SWJR. This agreement was signed on 14 March 1899 in return for the withdrawal by the M&SWJR of its scheme for an extension northwards to Ashchurch. This was the last thing that Fay did for the M&SWJ, as he resigned to take effect from 15 April 1899. The Directors paid Fay 'no more than he was due' when they expressed:

The deep obligation which they personally and the whole body of Stock and Shareholders are under him for the skill and energy with which he had managed the affairs of this Company for the last seven years, whereby its future prosperity has been assured... They desire gratefully to recognize that this result is largely due to his foresight, and skilful management, of the affairs of the Company.

Fay recommended his own successor for the M&SWJR. During his regime, receipts had increased by 63%, and expenses by only 13%; this was no mean achievement. He much remedied the railway's basic equipment, and great attention had been paid to improving the stability of the permanent way. In his leaving speech, reported in the *Gloucester Standard*, Fay gave fulsome praise to the railwaymen, managers, and directors for their unity and cohesion. One of his great abilities as a manager was to put together a good team and support it, an ability to be seen again in his career.

In a local paper in Cheltenham, reporting his departure from the M&SWJR, the editor commented that Fay had 'Made an empty sack stand upright.' He himself said that his 'Seven years in Cirencester were amongst the happiest of his life, and that if the days of his youth lasted up to his M&SWJ years, they certainly ended with them.'[23] He had married Frances Ann Farbrother in 1883, and they had raised five of his six children there.[24]

During the Great War the M&SWJR proved its worth through its geographical situation. It carried 181,683 officers and just under 3 million men, running 6,452 specials, in addition to 1,488 ambulance trains; it carried 134,852 horses, nearly 8,000 guns, 5,730 cycles, 15,176 tons of luggage, and 9,021 ammunition trucks. The 1916 engine mileage was 1,118,255. When absorbed by the Great Western on 1 July 1923, the M&SWJR owned 60 miles 55 chains of route mileage, worked the 2 miles, 33 chains of the Tidworth Camp Railway, and exercised running powers over 37 miles, 22 chains of other companies' (L&SWR, GWR, and Midland) lines.[25]

During Fay's absence, E.W. Verrinder had died,[26] and his successor, E.G.

---

23 Quoted, George Dow, op, cit, *Great Central*, Volume III, page 27. Dow added that Fay maintained a youthful, even boyish outlook in many directions thereafter.

24 Vincent David was born in 1901.

25 Colin G. Maggs, *The Midland and South Western Junction Railway*, David & Charles, 1967, passim.

26 In July 1893.

White, had died also, in March 1899, and Fay returned to the L&SWR as Superintendent of the Line, at the age of 42, under the General Manager, Charles Scotter. During his stewardship of that office, he introduced imaginative improvements, both technical and managerial. In 1899 he displayed his zest for competition; in his desire for speeded-up services, he ran a trial train from Waterloo to Bournemouth, to boost its attraction as against the London Brighton and South Coast service to Brighton. It completed the 108 miles in 110 minutes. On the following day the Chairman sent for him. 'Don't do it again, Sam,' he said; 'Not in my lifetime.' Apparently the Chairman had been on the train and had been rather shaken by the hard riding. Another anecdote from Fay's time as Superintendent of the Line appeared fifty years later in a Fareham (Hampshire) local paper:[27]

Fifty years ago, when the Meon Valley railway line was being laid, Sir Samuel Fay, Superintendent of the then London and South Western Railway, came down to inspect a section where the track had to be built over a very muddy stretch of land. His clothes were spattered with mud, and because he had to go to a meeting afterwards, he got someone from the Fareham station staff to clean them. He watched the young lad, then in his early twenties, at work for a bit. 'How many days holiday do you get in a year,' he enquired. 'Three Sir', came the reply. 'And where do you go?' – 'Moreton-in-the-Marsh, in Gloucestershire.' 'Who goes with you?' – 'My parents and sister.' The lad had a pleasant surprise not long afterwards, when he received a pass for one whole week off, and railway tickets to Moreton-in-the-Marsh, for himself and the rest of the family. This week, the 'lad,' Alderman V.T. Keen, 'father' of Fareham Urban Council, told a council meeting that with his memories of the Meon Valley line, he would be sorry to see it closed down. The closure is now proposed by the British Transport Commission, who intend [1954] to replace the service with buses on the Fareham-Alton Road.

Later in the year, 1899, the South African War began,[28] and Fay had to work closely with the War Office; most of the troops and equipment were shipped

---

27   Press cutting, unattributed and undated, in Edgar Fay's Memoirs.
28   11 October to May 1902

from Southampton. The L&SWR gave a good account of itself. The railway transported 212,330 officers and men, 27,000 horses, and 1,186 wagons and other vehicles. The experience was to stand Fay in good stead when he was co-opted for such operations in the 1914–1918 War.

As the London and South Western Railway progressed from the late nineteenth century to the early twentieth century, changes were afoot, not only in terms of locomotives and rolling stock but also in the way that the company was administered at Waterloo. 'Probably the finest General Managers the Company ever had were Sam Fay and Herbert Ashcombe Walker, both of whom contributed greatly to the advancement of the Company during the period.'[29] A new publication, the *Railway Magazine*, reported in July 1897 (page 90), that:

> the L&SWR had made very extensive arrangements for Queen Victoria's Jubilee traffic... the Company had a very liberal scale of excursion fares to London, such as from Plymouth and back, a distance of 468 miles for 12 shillings and from other stations in proportion. The Naval Revue on Saturday, 26 June brought an enormous traffic onto the system, the whole of which, needless to say, was most successfully dealt with by the staff, acting upon the carefully elaborated arrangements drawn up by the management for the occasion.

In the year 1900, at the Paris International Railway Conference, the subject of automatic and power signalling was in the air. Not long before that, a system of working points and signals by an electro-pneumatic, or 'low-pressure pneumatic system' was tried in the USA. The President of the Low-Pressure Pneumatic Signal Company had been in London in the summer of 1900, and with a New York State Senator, Charles Owens, met the General Manager of the L&SWR. Owens told them Sam Fay, the LSW Superintendent of the Line, was going to the US for a short holiday, and it would be good if he could study the system in use there. On Fay's return from the US, the *Daily Telegraph* interviewed him, reporting on 2 November 1900 that the Board of Directors of the L&SWR, at their last meeting, had

---

29 John Scott Morgan, *London and South Western Miscellany*, Oxford Publishing Co., 2003, pages 10–11.

adopted his recommendation to hold a trial of the system. In the interview, Sam said that:

> Gradually, it will apply to the whole line... No longer will immense signal boxes be required, the marvels of the great structures of, say, Waterloo, Cannon Street, and Liverpool Street with their complicated levers, will become things of the past, for it is certain that no railway company can be behind another.

He said, 'I am certain that we are approaching a revolution all the way round in our system of signalling. What we are doing now is only a commencement. I believe before we are much older we shall see all our intermediate signal boxes worked automatically.'[30] The trial took place on 31 July 1901 at Grately, Hampshire, with six sections of pneumatic signals between that station and Andover. The work was undertaken by the newly formed British Pneumatic Railway Signal Company, of which the Outdoor Assistant was Arthur Frank Bound (1878–1957), of whom more later.

The enormous station at Waterloo had been enlarged haphazardly, but Fay, not long before he left, recommended to the directors its rebuilding and enlargement. It was finally opened in its new form in 1922, and remained largely unaltered until Waterloo International was opened in 1994.[31] According to the L&SWR records, a Board Meeting, held on 21 November 1901, was told that the Superintendent of the Line, Mr S. Fay, had tendered his resignation, as from 31 December next, in consequence of his appointment as General Manager of the Great Central Railway. 'The Directors, while deeply regretting his resignation, desire to place on record their very high appreciation of the valuable services rendered by Mr Fay during the time he has been with the Company.'[32]

30   The Institute of Railway Signal Engineers AGM, 16 March 1917, page 1.
31   William Fay, *Sir Sam Fay – London and South Western Days*, 2008, page 16.
32   National Archives, RAIL 411/28, folio 149.

Fay's Father, Joshua

Fay's Mother, Ann

Fay as a child

Blenheim School, Farnham, Hants

Fay as a teenager

Fay at 21

Fay in shooting gear (1903)

Fay's children:
Samuel Ernest, Annie Clara ('Clarrie'),
Nellie, Frances, Winifred.
Vincent David (1901-1975) was born later.

Pneumatic Signalling – Manchester London Road Station

Arthur Bound

Cover of G.C.R. Timetable, 1903

Great Central Hotel, Marylebone, 1902

Awbridge Danes, as at Fay's retirement

2

Publicity

THE GREAT CENTRAL RAILWAY

A Minute of the Meeting of the Board of Directors of the GCR on 8 November 1901 recorded 'With extreme regret' the retirement as General Manager, Sir William Pollitt on Medical grounds, at an early convenient date in the New Year. A Committee was appointed by the Board to discuss the appointment of a successor – 'Mr Chapman, Lord Cross, Mr Stuart-Wortley, Mr Viccars, and Alexander Henderson, the Chairman. Sir William Pollitt having also afforded them the benefit of his advice.' After considering the applications of several gentlemen, they had come to the conclusion that:

> Mr S.Fay of the London and South Western Railway Company was the most qualified to fill the position of General Manager of this Railway, and they recommended that gentleman's appointment as from 31 March next... the date of Sir William Pollitt's retirement – at a salary of £3,000 per annum, to date from 1 January 1902, when Mr Fay's services with the GC Railway would commence, the engagement to be subject to six month's notice on either side.

The Board approved of the Committee's recommendation, and the terms mentioned.[33]

---

33   National Archives, RAIL 226/5.

At the end of 1901, Sir William Pollitt, General Manager of the GCR, who had been knighted for the sterling way he had managed the development of the MS&LR from its isolation as a cross-country line to its appearance as a mainline company to London, retired. In respect for his sixteen years as General Manager, and a total of forty-five years service, he was appointed to the Board of Directors in March 1902. He died, aged 66, in October 1908, and his funeral in Altrincham was a very impressive affair, the Eulogy being delivered by Sir Alexander Henderson.[34] Pollitt had been influential in the subcommittee appointed to discuss the appointment of his successor, and though there were several applicants for the post, the one supported by Charles Scotter of the L&SWR and former Goods Manager of the MS&LR was chosen. The final decision having rested with Henderson as Chairman; he offered it to Fay, and his offer was accepted.

When Charles Robert Williams, a director of the L&SWR from 1892, learned of Fay's prospective move to the GCR, he tried to dissuade him. He said 'The Great Central will be in receivership before the year is out. I know – I am their banker.'[35] Fay was not at all dismayed, regarding it as another challenge. It is worth noting that Henderson was a well-known and experienced financier of railways internationally, and a major shareholder in the Manchester Ship Canal. He was involved in the development of ports in several countries, and in telephone and electrical systems. He was MP for West Staffordshire from 1898 to 1906, and for St George's Hanover Square from 1913 to his elevation to the peerage as Lord Faringdon in 1916. On 4 June 1917 he was made a Companion of Honour, and his estate formed the asset management company Henderson Global Investments in 1934, to date. He was clearly not lacking in financial acumen, nor the ability to choose his staff with insight.[36]

---

34 National Archives, RAIL 226/529. The file contains seven pages of the names of those present.

35 Williams (1848-1943) an Honorary Colonel of the 4th Battalion, the Dorsetshire Regiment, was a member of the family who founded the Williams Deacons Bank in 1771 (of which he was a director), which became part of the amalgamation of several banks forming the National Westminster Bank in 1970. He was MP for Dorset West from 1895 to 1922: long enough to see his prophecy completely unfulfilled.

36 Sir Alexander (1850-1934) was the Chairman of the GCR from 1899 to 1922, and as Lord Faringdon (from 1916) became Vice Chairman of the LNER from 1923. His youngest son, Eric Brand Butler Henderson (1884-1953) was a director of the GCR from 1918-1922, and on the LNER Board from 1923.

Sam Fay became General Manager of the Great Central on 1 January 1902, at a salary of £3,000 per annum. He was joining a company which, during the previous two years, had assembled a formidable directorial and managerial team. The company solicitor had resigned in 1900, and was replaced by Dixon Henry Davies, who had served his articles in the Great Northern Solicitor's Office, was an accomplished writer and speaker on economics, and was a shrewd man with a sense of humour. He had Parliamentary and general practice, and had piloted the bill to launch the Lancashire, Derbyshire and East Coast Railway in 1890, and his intricate knowledge of that company was invaluable when in 1907 it was absorbed by the Great Central. There were some changes on the Board, including Henry Wilson Worsley-Taylor (1847–1924), who as a barrister had played an important part in the promotion of the London Extension. He was MP for Blackpool from 1900 to 1906, and created Baronet in 1917.[37] Among the officers of the company, William Clow was appointed in 1905 as Assistant Superintendent of the Line. Born in 1863, Clow was a *protégé* of the General Manager. In 1895 he served under Fay on the Midland and South Western Junction, resuming their association in 1903 as his Outdoor Assistant on the Great Central. He became Superintendent of the Line in 1910. With all these changes, and the appointment of Arthur Frank Bound in 1906 in charge of Signalling and Telegraphy, Fay had, inheriting John George Robinson as Locomotive Engineer – Chief Mechanical Engineer from 1902 – a first-class team, most of whom remained with him to the end of the company's existence.

The liaison between the GCR and the Metropolitan Railway, and the common use of the line north of the capital, engineered under Edward Watkin and under his supervision until his retirement in 1900, had become increasingly acrimonious under John Bell, who was both Chairman and Managing Director of the Metropolitan. The latter took 66⅔% of the receipts for the 42 miles from Quainton Road to the Capital, and the GCR 33⅓%. The Great Central therefore had had recourse in 1899 to a new joint operation when the Great Western and Great Central Act was passed, and trains from Marylebone had an alternative main line, less congested,

---

37 He married the daughter of Sir Edward Watkin, and their descendant, Dorothea Margaret Worsley-Taylor (1920-2014) was present with the Queen and President Francois Mitterand at the opening of the Channel Tunnel in 1994.

with fewer tight curves and less heavily graded. With the resignation of John Bell and the relinquishing of the GCR General Managership, due to persistent ill-health, by William Pollitt at the end of July 1901, a more normal relationship began. The new Chairman of the Metropolitan, Colonel John James Mellor,[38] and the new General Manager, A. Charles Ellis, soon formed an amicable relationship with Sam Fay, and the two companies began working more closely together. Goods traffic on the newly formed GW and GC Joint Company began on 20 November 1905, and passenger traffic on 2 April 1906. With its southern and northern links with the Great Central, the Great Western had, by 1906, paid advances to its partner over £1 million, made up as follows: Banbury Branch, £280,360; GW and GC Joint line, £832,295; Ashenden–Grendon Underwood line, £23,452; total, £1,136,107.[39]

An alliance between the North Eastern (NER); and the Lancashire and Yorkshire (L&YR); posed a threat in South Yorkshire, after the GCR had headed off a plan by the North Eastern and the Hull and Barnsley Railway (H&BR); to invade the rich coalfields. The Great Central sought the help of the Midland, which was readily forthcoming. A Sheffield and Midland Committee was formed, and in 1903 common ground was found for a new railway – the South Yorkshire Joint (SYJR); – by the GCR, the Midland, the Great Northern (GNR) and the Lancashire and Yorkshire companies,[40] in which they would all participate equally. It was set up on 14 August 1903. Other joint lines were with the LNWR: the Manchester South Junction and Altrincham Railway (MSJ&AR), the Oldham, Ashton under Lyne and Guide Bridge (OA&GBR), the joint stations at Manchester London Road and Stalybridge, and in 1907 the Macclesfield Committee became the Great Central and North Staffordshire Joint Committee. Most of the developments of note on these lines were on the MSJ&A.[41] The most impressive in its day was the Cheshire Lines Committee: a Great Central, Great Northern, and Midland Joint concern, whose Liverpool to Manchester trains were from 1883 the fastest all-year regular service in the world.

---

38 1830–1916. A brother-in-law of Edward Watkin.

39 Dow, op. cit., pp. 193 and 196.

40 This was the third company bearing the title: the South Yorkshire which was absorbed by the MS&LR in 1874, and the second was the South Yorkshire Junction Railway, worked by the Hull and Barnsley.

41 Dow, op. cit., pp. 206 and 214.

In all his spheres of responsibility, Fay was given free rein to explore his creativity. In George Dow's phrase, he applied himself to 'setting the pace'. Staff Circular No. 5334 notified Alterations to the Working Timetable: 'New Services of Express Passenger Trains for March 1903 between Sheffield, Wakefield, and Leeds (Central), via Rotherham, Dearne Junction, and Moorthorpe Junction'. In addition, the Notice announced speeded-up goods services, listing Deansgate to Retford, departing at 7.35 pm; Stockport to London, 7.20 pm; Lincoln to Manchester, 10.10 pm; Grimsby to Manchester, 8.35 pm, 10.10 pm and 11.15 pm; London to Liverpool, 10.05 pm; Retford to Ashbury's, 6.30 am; among others. The arrival times were not quoted.[42]

Building on Pollitt's inauguration of through passenger services on 1 May 1900 with dining car expresses between Marylebone and Huddersfield, Halifax and Bradford, then summer trains from Leicester and Nottingham to Blackpool and Fleetwood, and Sheffield to Blackpool, Fay followed with through corridor trains between Leicester and Southampton, via Banbury and Oxford, and Marylebone to Scarborough in 1906. He initiated also services of breakfast car trains between Newcastle upon Tyne and Bournemouth in his first year. This last was a particularly ambitious move, traversing the lines of the North Eastern, the Great Central, Great Western, and London and South Western companies. In addition there were express excursions joining Nottingham, Leicester and Bournemouth. On 1 May 1903 he resurrected a Sheffield to Leeds service, formerly run by the MS&L, but taken off in 1893. He put on three trains each way and informed the Great Northern that they would be augmented with four more at the beginning of July. King's Cross opposed the move, citing congestion already at Leeds Central Station, but after Fay and Dixon Davies had visited Leeds to observe the traffic conditions for themselves, the GCR pursued its intentions with the Railway Commissioners, and their case was granted on 1 October 1903. There were several other flurries of new services and accelerations of existing trains, both on the main arterial lines and on the Cheshire lines between Liverpool, Warrington and Stockport, as well as expresses for Lincoln, Yarmouth, and Lowestoft and Cromer; and Reading, Folkestone and Dover.

---

42 National Archives, RAIL 226/644.

Also on 1 October 1903 the timings of non-stop expresses between Marylebone and Sheffield had eight minutes (down trains) and ten minutes (up trains) deducted, at an even three hours each way. This required an average speed of 54.9 miles per hour. On the same date a new through service began between Manchester and Deal. This ran via Sheffield, Nottingham, Leicester, Banbury, Reading, Folkestone and Dover, thus avoiding London. The southbound train left Manchester Central at 9.20 am, and arrived at Deal at 6.30 pm, and the northbound service left at 11 am and arrived in Manchester at 9.40 pm. The summer service in 1904 saw an acceleration of several important trains. The 3.25 pm express from Marylebone to Sheffield took 2 hours 57 minutes, and was extended to Manchester London Road, where it arrived in an overall time of 3 hours 50 minutes. The 5.40 pm express from Marylebone was retimed to 6.20 pm, running non-stop to Nottingham in 2 hours 13 minutes, and reaching Manchester at 10.35 pm. A new express was introduced from Manchester Central at 11.35 am. It called at Sheffield and Nottingham, then at Leicester, where, leaving at 1.45 pm, it ran the remaining 103 miles to Marylebone in 105 minutes. On one occasion in 1903, 4-4-0 Class 11B engine no. 1040 ran the 126½ miles from Marylebone to Nottingham in 123 minutes, and continued to Manchester London Road in 219 minutes, nearly half an hour less than the fastest timing ever scheduled of 245 minutes between these two points.[43] The coastal resorts of Yorkshire and Norfolk had their through trains restored to them, with the addition of two through carriage services: Halifax, Huddersfield, Leeds, Wakefield and Sheffield, via Banbury and the Didcot West Curve to Bath and Bristol, connecting with the down *Cornishman* of the GWR. A reciprocal service connected with the up *Cornishman*. The other through carriage facility ran with the 8.20 am from Leicester to Aberystwyth via Nottingham and Sheffield, with a return service at 12.15 pm. The high point of Fay's vision must have been in his inauguration of a through carriage service between Aberdeen and Penzance, a journey of 742¾ miles. It was re-established after the War in 1919.

Fay was the first to introduce a system of weekly zone season tickets for local journeys. This was to combat competition from electric tramways, and was launched in Manchester on 21 March 1904, and shortly afterwards in Sheffield. Further developments in the timetables took place in the

---

43   Allan Brown, *Locomotives of the LNER*, Part 3B, page 69.

period 1905 to 1907. Another Manchester to Plymouth excursion ran on Thursday, 20 April. It was booked to cover the 373¾ miles from London Road to Millbay in 9 hrs 10 min with thirteen intermediate stops, hauled by 4-4-0 No. 1041 as far as Leicester, where Atlantic No. 265 took over for the remainder of the journey. The train was worked back empty on the following morning. The stimulus given to through working by Great Central initiatives had been reflected in the summer timetables of 1905. In that year, British train services were notable for the number of accelerated through trains and carriages between the North and the Midlands and the South coast. In the summer of 1906, beginning in July, Fay switched three weekday trains each between Marylebone and Manchester and Marylebone and Bradford from the congested route via Harrow, to the GW and GC Joint Line. The steamship services for Hamburg, Rotterdam and Antwerp, from Grimsby, were retimed to combat increasing competition from the Lancashire and Yorkshire and North Eastern for the Continental traffic. Slip carriages were scheduled for Woodford (for Stratford on Avon), from the 6.20 pm from Marylebone (1 July 1907), and the winter service improved the journey to Stratford to 2 hrs 5 mins. A slip carriage appeared in the suburban services, with one attached on Saturdays to the 1.40 pm down express arriving at Amersham at 2.13 pm, and Great Missenden 11 minutes later. On 1 July 1909 an improved service to and from Bradford and Huddersfield included a carriage slipped at Penistone from the 3.15 pm (formerly 3.20 pm) non-stop express from Marylebone to Sheffield and Manchester Central (to connect with the Cheshire Lines Express to Warrington and Liverpool, bringing the latter to five hours from London).

In 1907 a new feature was a daily Tourist Train from Leicester to Cleethorpes at 7.35 pm (except Saturdays), and at 6.30 pm on Saturdays calling at Loughborough, Nottingham Arkwright Street, Worksop, Gainsborough and Brigg. The return train left Cleethorpes at 7.35 pm. A new express from Sheffield at 8.53 am for Grimsby and Cleethorpes connected with the 7.45 am express from Manchester London Road, and a new train returned from Cleethorpes at 5.10 pm for Doncaster, Rotherham, Sheffield and Manchester. Considerable improvement in London suburban services were made by additional trains between Marylebone, Rickmansworth, Chesham, Aylesbury, South Harrow, Gerrards Cross, Beaconsfield and High Wycombe. The fastest start-to-stop run from Leicester to Marylebone, 103 miles, was covered in 110 minutes. The longest run without a stop was still the 3.25 pm Marylebone to Sheffield: the 'Sheffield Special' was altered to leave at 3.20 pm.[44]

Because of Fay's progressive policy of increasing traffic it had become obvious as early as 1903 that Gorton Works, which built 183 new locomotives between 1900 and 1909, in addition to heavy repairs and much rebuilding of old engines, had become inadequate for carriage and wagon work as well. No further expansion at Gorton was possible, so land had to be obtained somewhere else. It was decided to buy 29½ acres half a mile east of Guide Bridge station on the down side of the main line, at Dukinfield. This was effected in 1903, and J.G. Robinson was asked for plans for a new carriage and wagon workshops complex. The unusual step was taken of inviting suitable contractors to submit, instead of simply tenders, their own ideas for the works. On the advice of Robinson, the submission of Craven Brothers Ltd of Manchester and Markham & Co. Ltd of Chesterfield (which had offered a joint scheme) were assigned to the work in 1905. The maximum sum was £165,000, using British-manufactured steel. An electrical substation was ordered from the British Electrical Company in June 1906, and a few months later a subsidiary contract for a down loop line and retaining wall to Evans & Markham. Dukinfield Works came into operation towards the end of 1910, when the stripping of locomotives which were in for repairs was taken over from Gorton, in addition to the carriage and wagon remit.

The years 1903 to 1907 saw some other bold developments towards the up-to-date efficiency of traffic working. The earliest of these was the principle of operating signals and points by compressed air. Fay had been experimenting with the idea during his time on the L&SWR, and the first trial, at Grately, Hampshire (see above) was followed by further installations at Salisbury and Staines, and after the widening of the GC main line between Ardwick and Hyde Junction, on the GCR in October 1903. Fay convinced the Board that it would be good to equip that section with the system. In January 1904, the British Pneumatic Railway Signal Company was awarded a contract for the work, and at the end of the year another low pressure system was authorised for the signalling in the up tunnel at Woodhead. Fay astutely took care to ensure that he

---

44 The Great Central Railway Journal, August 1907, page 36.

was supported expertly in the innovation: in November 1903, before any orders were placed, the British Pneumatic Company's Outdoor Assistant, A.F. Bound, was appointed Assistant Superintendent of Signalling and Telegraphy on the Great Central, and on the retirement at age 65 of the Superintendent, Thomas Wharmby, Bound succeeded him. He was only 28 years old.[45] In the April 1906 issue of the GCR *Journal*, pages 228–231 were devoted to an article by A.F. Bound. It was written in response to many questions about automatic signalling, and it gave a detailed account of how it worked, with an instructive diagram. The final description of the system appeared in the *Journal* of December 1917 (pages 94 and 95), when a relief Signalman who had had considerable experience of it, described the 'mixed feelings with which it was regarded by many signalmen, but gradually its many benefits were appreciated, and few, if any, would like to go back to the old system'.

The *Magazine of Commerce*, in an article of 1905, eulogised the new Great Central Manager of the GCR: 'Mr Fay has done much for the Great Central, and the line has done much for England.' He described Sam Fay as a person:

> smooth and amiable, which though he be a commander-in-chief of thousands, is at the same time characteristic of a generalissimo. But he wears a steel casing to his velvet glove, which is the fine art of railway management, or indeed of any service needing command or authority. It is a phase of strength which behoves the exercise of will, and the general manager of a railway is the eyes and ears of a corporation which owes its success to observation, enterprise, and the moral strength to enforce both.

The editor of the Great Central *Journal* praised the Chairman of the GCR, 'Sir Alexander Henderson, who was in many ways the mainspring of promoting the Great Central, for his choice of General Manager. They are both young, have views in common, and are both a model of sagacious co-operation for the benefit of the shareholders.' He concludes by quoting one newspaper's description of the new manager:

---

45   Dow, Volume III, pages 89 and 90. Further such installations were made at London Road Station, Manchester, and at Wath Concentration Yard towards the end of 1909.

Although short in stature, and slight of build, Mr Fay is man of singularly distinguished appearance. With his pale well-cut features, dark brown eyes, dark hair and beard, small hands and feet, erect carriage and the general air of having just come out of a bandbox. In manner he is quiet and self-contained… which a polished suavity and courtesy masks, but does not entirely conceal, an inner will. One cannot imagine him ever ruffled, but he gives the impression of a man who would be very deadly when roused. Mr Fay is married, and has pronounced literacy tastes.

The Great Central Railway *Journal* had been founded, with the full cooperation of the General Manager, in July 1905. There were to be two editions each month, the ordinary one for a penny, and the other on art paper, supplied to subscribers at twopence. It was most competently produced, and eventually it carried a fair amount of advertising. Articles dealt with personalities, developments on the system, local staff news, locomotive notes, technical explanations of new equipment, and Letters to the Editor were regular features, well illustrated by photographs, diagrams and cartoons. The early issues regularly expressed the impact of the new Manager. Mr Jacob of the Solicitor's Department sent in a limerick: 'Our General Manager, Fay,/ Makes all things hum the right way./ His latest success/ Is the 'Ophir' express./ He'll be made a knight some day.'[46] The *Journal* for January 1906 (page 156) included a cartoon depicting two well-dressed top-hatted gentlemen standing in front of a GCR billboard advertising excursions and services; the first gent is saying, 'Don't you think the GC are becoming quite *au fait*?' A passing young lad, wearing a cloth cap, retorts, 'Owe Fay? – Rather!' A full-page cartoon in the April 1906 issue (page 234), depicted Fay as a barber cutting the hair of a uniformed GC railwayman, with a shower of cut hair marked 'Old Ideas'.

By late 1907, such items had become less frequent as Fay became a normal feature of everyday life. An anonymous correspondent wrote to the Editor to ask, 'Why have we not heard much of Mr Fay lately?' The Editor replied, after deploring the practice of complaining anonymously, that by the same post he had received a cutting from the *Southern Daily*

---

46 Vol. 1, No. 1, page 33. Reference for 'Orphir' not traced. Perhaps in the literal sense of 'Orphic' meaning 'pertaining to mysteriousness'.

Echo, quoting Lord Robert Bruce who criticised the Midland and South Western Railway. Bruce said: 'The excursion traffic... is most inadequately advertised, as will be recognised if a comparison be made with the system which prevailed under the able management of Mr Sam Fay.'[47] The correspondent was also confounded by an item in the *Journal* for December 1907[48] which reproduced an article appearing in the magazine *Vanity Fair*[49] showing a cartoon of Fay, with his customary cigar, and giving an account of his career:

> His ideas are not only advanced but democratic, and they have made for smoothness of working by introducing a strong sense of solidarity between managers and men. His schemes for the improvement of their position have been uniformly successful. He is still a true child of the New Forest, burly, brisk, and outspoken. The father of a large family [and] as an Englishman should be he shoots, plays golf, and is uncommonly quick on his feet and an excellent walker. He lives in a house once dwelt in by [Judge] 'Bloody Jeffries.'... You are face to face with a true out-of-doors Englishman.

About this time, a Commission on the Railways of South Africa was held, in 1907,[50] during which was raised the question of decentralisation in management. 'How far can departmental managers make their own policy and practical decisions, if necessary disregarding rulings made by a General Manager?' The Commissioners' Report stated unequivocally that:

> If departmental officers are permitted to oppose the authority of the General Manager, the example may work mischief throughout the entire staff... The chief executive head should be slow to interfere, and guard against doing his under-managers' work as well as his own. But the idea that he should leave them alone to do their best is an ideal, but quite impractical.

---

47 *Journal*, October 1907, page 83.
48 Page 131.
49 Mentioned above.
50 Reported in the *Journal* of 1908, page 284 and 285.

It is not clear why the Editor of the *Journal* should make a point of quoting this part of the South Africa Report, but it could have been a reflection of a discussion in the company's supporting of the new manager's style, or questioning it. Finally on this point, a quotation from the magazine *Truth*:

> Like many other prosperous commercial undertakings, [the GCR] has grown from small beginnings... Originally formed to supply a connection between Manchester and Sheffield, it has grown into one of the principal trunk railways of the country... Today, that the 'Forward' policy which animated Sir Edward Watkin, inspires the present general manager, Mr Sam Fay will be obvious to anyone who makes use of the great system under his control.[51]

While the technical advances were being introduced, Fay did not lose sight of his concern for staff benefits. His keen interest in the welfare of widows and orphans of the L&SW Railway has been noted, and on the GCR he continued with innovations which had been introduced by Sir Edward Watkin, in particular his Special Award Fund, awarded annually to about 100 employees for rendering service of exceptionally meritorious character, and the Great Central Mutual Providence Society and Joint Lines Friendly Society, both founded on 18 July 1866. At a meeting held on 9 April 1908, these two were brought together as one, the Patrons being the Chairman and Directors, and the Trustees numbering three, of whom Fay was one. The joint office was at London Road Station, Manchester.[52] Under the heading of 'Labouring Class Housing at Loughborough', a rehousing scheme was launched in 1909: 26 new houses were built to replace 43 which were built in 1893. The cost was £6,051 10s 3d.[53] Further new developments in the company and major expansions began with the establishment of a Publicity Department.

---

51 The Magazine '*Truth*, 3 July 1907', Travel Supplement; quoted in *GCR Journal*, August 1907, page 38.
52 National Archives, RAIL 226/530.
53 National Archives, RAIL 226/178.

Fay 1904

Poster – 'Live in the Country'

Poster – Cup Final 1904

Poster – 'Great Central Railway'

Poster – Manchester Weekly Zone Tickets

ADMIRABLE SITES FOR WORKS, FACTORIES, &c.

THE GREAT CENTRAL RAILWAY passes from the Metropolis Northwards through the centre of industrial England, throwing out its branches Eastward and Westward to the Coast.

¶ ITS LINES RUN OVER THE GREAT MIDLAND COALFIELD (of over 4,000 square miles area) which extends into the counties of York, Nottingham, Derby and Lincoln. THIS COALFIELD IS THE LARGEST IN THE BRITISH ISLES, and is estimated to contain not less than forty-nine thousand million (49,000,000,000) tons of coal.

¶ THE IMPORTANT COALFIELDS OF LANCASHIRE AND NORTH WALES are also traversed by the Company's lines.

¶ THERE IS THUS AFFORDED AN EASILY ACCESSIBLE SOURCE OF FUEL SUPPLY.

¶ THE NEW EASTERN PORT OF IMMINGHAM should particularly attract traders, as its modern equipment and accessibility at any time of the day or night, irrespective of tides, are important time and labour saving factors.

¶ ADJOINING THE GREAT CENTRAL RAILROAD at various parts of the system are situated VALUABLE SITES FOR WORKS, where, by the introduction of siding accommodation, goods can pass right into and directly out of the works, which GREATLY ASSISTS THE MANUFACTURER to attain his desired position in the World's Markets.

¶ For information please communicate with the G.C.R. Publicity Office, 216, Marylebone Road, London, N.W.

¶ **Owners and Agents of LAND AND BUILDINGS FOR SALE OR TO BE LET near the Great Central Railway are requested to send particulars to the Company's Estate Agent, Mr. J. Oldham, 12 Paton Street, Piccadilly, Manchester.**
                                             SAM FAY *General Manager.*

Poster – 'Site for Workshops'

3

Wath-On-Dearne Marshalling Yard,
And Other Developments

Sam Fay was the first main line General Manager to grasp fully the potential of public relations and pictorial publicity. Posters and virile imaginative slogans combined to set in the public eye the details of the latest developments on the Great Central. An innovation, advertised immediately by handbill, was the introduction in March 1904 of weekly Zone Season Tickets for local journeys, designed to combat electric tramway competition. The tickets were introduced in Manchester, and not long afterwards in Sheffield. The system of handbills, brochures, and posters also included advertisements in newspapers.

Fay appointed as his manager for his new department W.J. Stuart, an author and artist with a flair for advertising. By the end of 1904 almost every available medium had been exploited to publicize Great Central services and facilities. Vacant window spaces in the telephone kiosks of inner London were taken for the display of notices; pocket match-cases had inside details of train services; notepaper, envelopes and picture postcards were supplied in corridor trains, and the folder *Great Central Holiday and Health Resorts* included colour illustrations for the rural and coastal scenes.[54] The Great Central Journal for October 1905 (pages 109 and 110), carried an illustrated article from the magazine *Advertising* under the title of 'The Art of Advertising of a Railway', devoted to a study of W.J. Stuart. It said:

---

54   George Dow, op cit, Volume III, pages 32 and 35

The only railway running into London that makes any pretence of using advertisements in the press as will compare with contemporary trade efforts is that Company which has made its slogan the words 'Rapid Travel in Luxury' – a neat phrase expressing so much in its four words. It is practically only since the Great Central Railway pushed its way into London that railway advertising has been worthy of notice as advertising, and its influence may be seen upon all the other companies.

The article continued:

Probably the name best-known to the public in connection with this well-appointed system is that of the General Manager, Mr Sam Fay, and it is a noteworthy tribute to the loyalty and esteem of the staff for their chief that they all insist that [he] is primarily responsible for the policy and progress of the Company, and any good work that may be done.

Mr W.J. Stuart was questioned on the effectiveness of railway advertising, and what was the form – press advertising, posters and handbills – and why. Finally, he was asked if the phrase 'Rapid Transport in Luxury' justified its use as advertisement. Mr Stuart replied that it had most decidedly done so: the phrase had been very much appreciated by the public for the point it made instantly. 'And by the way,' he added, 'It was composed by my General Manager and chief, Mr Sam Fay.'

Publicity for the widespread passenger services of the Great Central Railway (GCR) was well sustained by poster and press advertising as the policy developed. Novelties were the not-so-good idea of circular-shaped pocket timetables for the suburban services over the GC and GW Joint Line, and the much better one of packs of playing cards, 1 shilling each, bearing views of London, Sheffield, Manchester, Liverpool and Stratford-on- Avon on the backs.[55]

Some rivalry in publication had to be overcome in the early days. A dispute arose regarding advertising displays at Wakefield Westgate station, and a meeting took place of representatives of the Midland, the Great Northern

---

55 Dow, Volume III, page 102.

and the GCR (represented by William Clow), to discuss the lettering of advertising boards on the upside north end platform, the upside south end, the down side south end, and the lettering of the boards – 4 feet high in black and gold – on 5 August 1903. Their decision as to the size and positioning for the three companies was found unsatisfactory by the GCR, which wanted equal exposure, and registered a further complaint against an 'Unfair and disadvantaged allotment of space for Timetable Sheets in the booking hall of companies which had a competitive route to the South – the Midland, the GNR, and the Midland and South Western Junction' (!). A memo from William Stuart to Sam Fay said that the representatives of the Publicity Department Managers of the Midland and the GNR asked Fay to meet their two General Managers to resolve the disparity. A meeting of Midland, GNR and GCR (with William Clow as the GC representative) took place on 22 October 1903, and all seemed to have been be amicably settled.[56]

The *Southern Daily Echo* published in 1907 a long letter from Lord Robert Bruce, in which he said 'The Excursion Traffic [of the Midland and South Western Junction Railway] is most inadequately advertised, as will be recognised if a comparison be made with the system which prevailed under the able management of Mr Sam Fay.'

One of the most audacious railway posters ever produced was a depiction of the winning goal being scored in the forthcoming FA Cup Final at Crystal Palace in 1904. Measuring an impressive 7 feet by 8 feet, it was exhibited for a fortnight outside the company's offices in Piccadilly, Manchester. It showed Billy Meredith of Manchester City scoring the winning goal in exactly the way it happened on the day, for Manchester City against Bolton Wanderers. It successfully predicted the result, the score, the scorer and the method of its execution.[57] When the magazine *Household Words* ran a competition in 1904 asking its readers to name which six railways of twenty English, Scottish and Irish lines were the best and most progressive, the Great Central came out on top.[58]

Changes in 1903 came in the Hotels and Catering Department. The GCR

---

56   National Archives, RAIL 226/682.

57   City's home ground in those days was at Hyde Road; it was owned by the GCR.

58   Fay's pioneering work was followed after the1914-1918 War by all four of the grouping companies, and the example they set was continued by British Railways in 1948 (Andrew Dow, *Steam World*, January 2010, page 54).

had, in total, five hotels and three first class dining rooms.[59] The flagship hotel was that at Marylebone. The Assistant Manager there became the Manager of the Royal Victoria in Sheffield on 8 May, and on 12 June, W. Ingram was appointed as Supervisory Manager of the company's hotels and refreshment rooms, excepting those at Sheffield. A move by the London County Council in 1903 to force the Great Central to demolish the gates and the covered way to the hotel from Marylebone Station to the hotel was defeated.[60]

On 28–30 October 1904 the GCR achieved the then longest runs ever made by one engine without coming off its train: an excursion from Manchester to Plymouth and back. The locomotive was a new 8B Class 4-4-2, no. 267. Leaving Manchester London Road at 11.30 pm, it reached Plymouth at 9.50 am the following day, 15 minutes before time, having covered the distance of 374 miles in 10 hours 20 minutes, including station stops and signal checks. The train was made up of five GC coaches, weighing 142 tons as far as Exeter, where two GWR coaches were attached, bringing up the total weight to 184 tons. The same loads from Plymouth were returned at 12.03 am on 30 October, arriving in Manchester at 9.50 am.

The travel firm of Dean & Dawson was adept at gathering business for its railway company, and it deserves some of the credit for building up the much-needed passenger traffic on the new line. Fay disliked travel agencies: the terms for their commission must have seemed like lost revenue. A severe *contretemps* over the non-appearance of GCR posters at Southport Lord Street station lasted longer than Fay's patience, and the firm received notice of termination of contract. Passenger receipts began at once to drop ominously. The decision was made to buy out Dean & Dawson's and constitute it as a limited company, with its three partners and four Great Central representatives as directors. Dow argues that Fay had been unfair in the matter, and as a consequence was later more cautious in his dealings with commercial contracts.[61]

Fay's audacity in the advertising of the company was illustrated again in the 1908 *Great Central Railway Illustrated Guide*, a book of 'London Retreats and

---

59 New Holland, 1844; Victoria, Sheffield, 1883; Royal Dock, Grimsby, 1890; Yarborough Hotel, Grimsby, 1890; Great Central, Marylebone, 1899. There were first class dining rooms at Manchester London Road, Manchester Central and Liverpool Central. All were to be closed or sold off, or converted to buffets from 1950.

60 Dow, op. cit., page 39.

61 Dow, op. cit., pages 44 and 45.

Holiday Resorts Served by the Great Central Railway', with a list of 'Seaside Farmhouses and Country Lodgings, Hotels and Boarding Houses and other useful information'. It included Chester, Knutsford, Blackpool and Church Stretton, and does not in fact seem to exclude anywhere in England as being served by the GCR.[62] This was a characteristic to an even greater extent of the 1914 edition, by then entitled *The ABC Guide to Health and Holiday Resorts Served by the Great Central Railway*, which advertised services to Penzance, Edinburgh, the whole Eastern side of England, Lancashire and the Isle of Man, and all of Wales, plus steamer services to Ireland and Europe.[63]

Fay's policy of progressive improvement and development was continued with the construction of the marshalling yard at Wath. The amount of coal originating in the South Yorkshire coalfield was increasing at a great rate, and the loaded wagons were taking coal destined for different parts of the country, but mainly over the Woodhead route over the Pennines to Lancashire, which became more and more congested. By the turn of the century getting coal over the line became a matter of concern, and Fay made it one of his personal priorities: he instituted a system of single or double loads – trains of either thirty or sixty loaded wagons – with allocation of appropriate banking locomotive arrangements. At the same time, Robinson was designing locomotives of sufficient flexibility and power to deal with the operating requirements. A traffic survey in 1900 showed the scale of these problems: the two tracks handled 252 eastbound trains and 265 westbound every twenty-four hours. Sorting sidings to separate private-owner from company-owned wagons were built at Dunford Bridge, then passing loops were put in, making a route of three or four tracks for most of the way.

An amendment to the 'permissive block' signalling methods allowed the improved occupation of passing loops. The next great advance in the speeding up of train marshalling was the planning of a huge 'marshalling yard' at Wath. This was the quickest method, via a 'hump yard', to facilitate the sorting of miscellaneous wagons to their efficient destinations. The most appropriate 'marshalling yard' was one in which the wagons were pushed over a 'hump', descending by gravity to their allocated siding, to

---

62 National Archives, 226/236. That copy had belonged to S.W.A. Newton, the photographer who had chronicled the building of the London Extension.

63 Ibid., 226/237.

be hauled away by another locomotive. The first example of the world's logically designed yard, with arrival, sorting and departure tracks, was that in St Etienne, France, built in 1863. In 1873, the LNWR built a yard at Edge Hill, Liverpool, but although it was 'gravity-assisted' that was achieved by using the lie of the land, and not by a specially built 'hump'. The world's first strict definition of a 'marshalling yard' was that which opened in 1876 at Mulheim-Speldorf, and the second, with the refinement of twin hump yards with east- and westbound traffic, was at Oberhausen Osterfeld Sud, and this was the first to use mechanical retarders.

The first of many examples in the USA was built in 1890, and one at Oak Island, New Jersey was visited in 1903 by officers of the British North Eastern Railway, while officers of the Great Central Railway (GCR) visited the Altoona Yard of the Pennsylvania Railroad at about the same time. This led four years later to the UK's first purpose-built yard at Wath. It lay at the heart of the South Yorkshire coalfields, surrounded by forty-five collieries. On 7 April 1905 the Directors committed themselves to a works programme designed by Sam Fay, at a cost of £350,000, £191,000 of which was for Wath, and the rest for a smaller yard at Worksop to relieve congestion on the lines between Woodhouse and Retford for eastbound traffic. Wath had thirty tracks in each of the twin yards, and had a wagon capacity of 5,000 wagons per twenty-four hours. It was built by Logan & Hemingway of Manchester (which had been one of the contractors for the GC Extension), to a contract signed in October 1905. After a partial opening in 1907, it opened completely in November of that year. Unusually, access to the sorting sidings was controlled by two signal boxes, controlled by pneumatically operated points, the first automated hump yard in Britain. Such a vast operation required much more powerful locomotives, and J.G. Robinson produced a three-cylinder 0-8-4Tank, Class 8H, of which four were built by Beyer, Peacock in 1907–1908, and two more were added by the London and North Eastern Railway (LNER) (as Class S1) in 1932.[64]

---

64 When fitted with a booster on the rear four wheels, these became the third most-powerful engines in the British Isles, on a tractive effort basis of 46,896 lb. (The second most-powerful were the booster-fitted LNER P1 class 2-8-2s, at 47,000 lb.)

THE LANCASHIRE, DERBYSHIRE AND EAST COAST RAILWAY

This company was promoted in 1891 by Derbyshire and Nottinghamshire coalfield owners, to create new outlets both to the west and to the east, and it was supported by landowners and every town along its proposed route. It claimed for itself the distinction of being the most important railway scheme, in capital and in mileage, ever to be sanctioned by Parliament in a single bill.[65] It obtained its Act of Incorporation on 5 August 1891, despite being opposed by the Manchester, Sheffield and Lincolnshire Railway, the Midland, and the LNWR, though it was supported by the Great Eastern.[66] The main line was to run from a deep water dock on the Manchester Ship Canal at Warrington to new docks at Sutton-on-Sea, 2 miles south of Mablethorpe, with connections along the way with the Cheshire Lines Committee, the North Staffordshire Railway, the Midland, the LNWR, the Great Northern, and the MS&LR. Its 170 miles included deep cuttings, high embankments, and a mile-and-a-half long tunnel, and highly impressive viaducts, but it achieved only the 56 miles between Chesterfield and Lincoln. A Sheffield branch from Langwith Junction to Beighton, and connections with the GN and GC lines proved useful, but by mid-1905 it became clear that the aims of the company were never going to be fulfilled, and the Board resolved on 7 November of that year to offer the whole concern to the Great Northern Railway. However, the General Manager of the GN, Oliver Bury, replied that none of the three proposed alternative methods of such a purchase was acceptable, and the LD&ECR Directors invited three representatives of the Great Central – Sam Fay, Dixon Davies (Solicitor) and Frank Williams (Chief Accountant) – to discussions. The outcome was agreement to the sale of the company to the GCR as a going concern, on 27 March 1906.[67]

KEADBY LIFT BRIDGE

A further facilitation of traffic movements was provided with a completely

---

65 George Dow, op cit, Volume III, page 153.
66 The Chairman of the GER, Claude Hamilton, went onto the Board of the LD&ECR.
67 Dow, op. cit., page 184.

new bridge in North Lincolnshire. In 1910, the 46-year-old Swing Bridge at Keadby, carrying the line over the River Trent between Keadby and Frodingham, proved to be completely out of date, and in need of renewal. The company authorized the building of a deviation line in that year, which included the provision of a new bridge in the form of a Scherzer rolling lift type, combining the railway and a roadway. Work started in 1912, with Fay laying the foundation stone, and it was opened in May 1916, at a cost of nearly £250,000.

The Scherzer Bridge was a development of the drawbridge type which allowed shipping to pass underneath a road or a railway. The first large-scale example was opened in 1850 in St Petersburg, Russia, and Tower Bridge in London is of the double pattern. After some improved versions, the American engineer William Scherzer (1858–1893) produced a rolling version, running backwards on rails, as distinct from one having a fixed trunnion. It was installed in Chicago in 1909, and has proved to be the most widely used. According to his son Edgar, Fay was closely interest in all developments in the USA, and this was a further example.

The company's Signal Engineer, Arthur Bound, 'blazed a new trail at Keadby with a pneumatic and electrical signal system, using three-aspect upper-quadrant signals'.[68]

CORPORATE SPIRIT, DISCIPLINE,[69] TRAINING.

Remember, my friends, you are part of a great system – a railroad system that is as near perfection as human ingenuity can make it. But any system can be defeated by one single man who places himself out of harmony with it. The perfect success of a perfect system depends upon your loyalty and individual co-operation. And yet no man can defeat a Great System excepting for a single instant; yet in that instant he may hurl scores to their death, and if he himself does not go down to destruction he will live only in pitiable disgrace.

---

68 Dow, op. cit., pages 288 and 290.
69 George H. Daniel, in an address to some of his employees of the New York Central Railway, February 1902. Quoted in the *Great Central Journal*, July 1905, page 12.

Your success and mine hinges on our perfect sympathy, undivided service, unalloyed devotion. By working for the good of all we work for the good of ourselves – we only succeed if we work for the good of the whole. Keep in harmony with the system.

One of Fay's great achievements was to reinforce the corporate spirit which the GCR had inherited from the Manchester, Sheffield and Lincolnshire Railway: the common commitment to the good of the company, and its service of the public. All railways are dependent on the loyalty of their staff, from the lowest ranks to the topmost, but not all companies had the insight as to how this was to be achieved and maintained. The Great Central Journal, from July 1905, had the full support of the General Manager. He appointed F.H. Hart as Editor, who was the Chief Goods Accounts Clerk at Leicester, and founder of the Great Central (Southern Division) Debating Society. The *Journal* of January 1908[70] returned to the subject of corporate efficiency, or *esprit de corps*: the question of 'fitness of purpose' and corporate loyalty, rather than nepotism or favouritism, was emphasised in an article by W. Wardle of the District Engineer's Office at Leicester, being a paper read at a meeting of the GCR Debating Society on Saturday 23 November 1907, in Sheffield. It was entitled 'Efficient Discipline', and the speaker evidently knew his Alexander Pope, his opening words being 'Order is Heaven's First Law': permanence and stability depend upon law, and every government or state has a code of laws or rules for the guidance of its people; every phase of life is governed by rules, immutable or otherwise. 'Law and authority', he argued, 'in homes, schools, colleges, armies, navies, states and business are essential; efficient discipline spells success, and violation and anarchy spells ruin'. He applied this principle to the running of a railway, which required that individual units work together with one common purpose. As trains are guided by the rails of the 'Permanent Way', so do rules and regulations guide the actions of employees within certain bounds, for the success and prosperity of the undertaking.

Wardle disarmed misunderstanding of the word 'discipline', as implying some sort of punishment for offences, or a Sword of Damocles hanging over the men to enforce the rules of their duty. The dictionary definition was rather 'correction, teaching, instruction, cultivation of the

70   Pages 152–156.

mind, special training to act in accordance with rules'. Of these words he selected 'instruction and education'. In his opinion, not enough attention had been paid to the training of railway employees: the teaching of the larger responsibility which goes with the simplest work. He admitted that punishment and correction were part of the learning process, but it should be characterized by justice and mercy; encouragement rather than the opposite. Mistakes were more often from misunderstandings than from fatal shortcomings, and correction is aimed at bringing out of a man the best he is capable of doing, and fitting him for advancement. He ended by urging a more acceptable understanding between employer and employee, between the idea of 'master' and 'man', and the instilling of a realization on both sides that they have a common desire: the well-being of the organization in cooperation: that the existence of labour is dependent on capital, and capital is dependent on labour.[71]

The principle of systematic staff training had been a feature on the MS&LR and the GCR for many years, and it was firmly emphasized under Fay's management. The March 1906 issue of the *Journal*[72] recognized as 'a sign of the times' that railway companies saw the benefits of educating their employees in the science of railway working. A number of leading companies gave financial support to various educational institutions, among them the School of Economics of London University, the Victorian University of Manchester, and the City of Liverpool School of Commerce. Lectures had been given, with undeniable success, on railway economics and transport at these institutions.[73] The company paid half of the fees for such courses for the employees who attended them. Fay detested the insular departmental outlook prevalent on railways at the time, and in 1907 initiated examinations designed to create opportunities for promising young members of the staff to equip themselves for more responsible posts right across the company. Successful examinees were given a four-year tour of nearly every department: Civil Engineers, Locomotive and Rolling Stock,

---

71   In this he seemed to echo the words of the former Chairman of the company, in the aftermath of the Hexthorpe disaster in 1887. (See J.N. Greaves, *Sir Edward Watkin Bt, 1819–1901*, 2005, pp. 229 and 230 The Book Guild Ltd, 2005).

72   Page 212.

73   For some time, in fact, Sir Sam was a Director, in his retirement, of the London School of Economics, though he did not like the attitude of some of the academics towards 'the real world'.

Stores and Marine, as well as those concerned directly with traffic matters. With it went a prized First Class All-Line Pass. The first of the Company's staff to benefit from this higher grade scheme of training was H.S. Owen, whose Matriculation Certificate was accepted in lieu of examination. He was made Examination Secretary, and subsequently he assisted in the training programme. The first examinations were held in January 1908, and to D.R. Lamb went the distinction of being the first to attain the pass standard in all subjects. Lamb ended his career as the Editor of *Modern Transport*, having played a part in founding the Institute of Transport in 1919.[74]

In the July 1905 issue of the Journal appeared also an article on 'Promotion in Railway Service', in which the author, E.B. Watts, a Goods Manager for over twenty years, found an outlet for what was an apparent long-standing grievance. He advocated 'More efficiency and merit to be a qualification for advancement in pay or position', as opposed to the present system of 'Patronage and Favouritism and Length of Service'. He had no objection at all to the latter, but he strongly objected to the presence of the former in considerations for promotion, which he had seen 'too often'. He deplored considerations of 'manner, appearance, dress, or address'.

In the case of the last collection of conditions, however, an unconnected letter appeared in the December issue of 1907 from a passenger, G.R. Sims, describing a journey he had made to Sheffield, in which he noted, 'the smart uniform and the military appearance of the young Great Central guards'.[75] The travelling public admires smartness in appearance, and the analogy with the Army is one often made between the railways and military discipline.

STAFF CONCILIATION SCHEME

Trade union pressure led in 1907 to the formation of a Staff Conciliation Scheme, in which employers and trade union representatives could discuss mutual problems without the antagonism of disagreements and strikes. It was put across as the answer by Lloyd George, the then President of the

---

74 Dow, op. cit., page 82
75 Page 132. He complimented also 'the Great Central corridor trains', which he thought to be 'in every way equal to the best in *De Luxe* that the Continent can show, and in many ways superior'.

Board of Trade, but it was largely the work of Sam Fay, who submitted it to Lloyd George on 6 November. Sir Hubert Llewellyn-Smith, Permanent Secretary to the Board of Trade, added the finishing touches. George Dow commented, somewhat acidly, that had its drafters or sponsors been known to railwaymen, it would have been found unacceptable.[76] However, on the Great Central, six Sectional Boards, labelled A to F, were established in 1908. They covered drivers, signalmen, guards, carriage and wagon examiners, porters, and permanent way gangers, respectively. On each Board, management and staff were equally represented usually by six on each side, the management side almost invariably a Director, a departmental officer, an inspector, and a clerical supervisor. Above these was a central Board. This was made up of two Directors, the General Manager, a district officer, and a staff clerk on the management side; and one representative of each of the Sectional Boards on the employees' side. Fay made F.H. Hart the Secretary of the Sectional and Central Boards, and in this new sphere he was as successful as he was as Editor of the GCR *Journal*.

In the development of the Staff Conciliation Scheme, and in the other events of the years 1905–1909, Fay reached full maturity. By his brother officers and his immediate subordinates he came to be regarded as a thoroughly practical railwayman without idiosyncrasies. By the rank and file he was considered to be rather autocratic, but astute and fair in his dealings with them. To the public at large, he was enterprising and adventurous, with less of the complacency which characterized some of his peers.[77] In 1911, a revision of the Conciliation Scheme was instituted.

76 Dow, op cit., page 85.
77 Ibid., page 86.

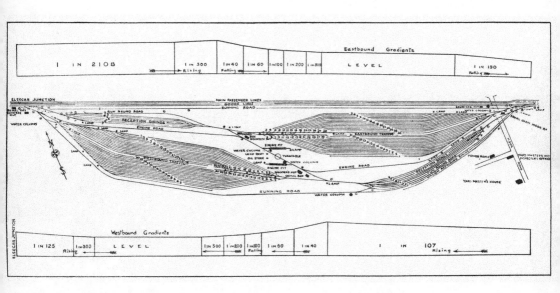

Yard Plan, Wath

Keadby Lift Bridge

Keadby Lift bridge Trowel , Laying of Foundation

4

The GCR-GNR Working Arrangement

Late in the year 1907, something more momentous was afoot: the Joint GN and GC proposed Agreement. At an Extraordinary Meeting of the shareholders held in Manchester on 20 December 1907, set up to explain a proposition for a form of alliance with the Great Northern Company, the Chairman, Sir Alexander Henderson, made some revelatory statements. He pointed out that almost to the day seventeen years before (19 December 1890) a meeting was held in this room to approve a bill to extend the Manchester Sheffield and Lincolnshire Railway to London. He said:

> the gauntlet may then be said to have been thrown down to the Great Northern Company, and today we are to ask your permission to pick it up again. To renew a treaty of peace that existed between our companies prior to 1890, a proposal too important to postpone until the Ordinary Meeting in February.

He could readily understand the existence of a bitter feeling of disappointment in the minds of those who listened to the arguments put before them in 1890 and 1891, when the question of extension from Annesley to the South was being discussed. He went on:

> The dreams of those who contemplated a through route from Manchester... to London, then, via the Metropolitan, on to the

South Eastern system to Dover, from Dover to Calais via the Channel Tunnel… to Paris and the East of Europe will be shattered, and not unnaturally the question may be asked whether the Extension to London was not altogether a fatal mistake. Although I had nothing to do with the inception of the London Extension Scheme,[78] I am not at all disposed to think that a mistake was made.

He believed that the agreement now submitted would bring benefits to the proprietors and the public, south of Nottingham to London, which is not a competitive area. The hauling of cross-town merchandise, Marylebone to King's Cross through worsening congestion, causes great problems, and forms one of the largest items of expenditure. A West End and a City depot would ease the situation regarding merchandise and minerals, and enable passenger services to be increased. He pointed out that the two systems were intertwined in the northern part of their territories; running powers had been granted by Parliament to the Great Northern Company over 326 miles of the Great Central system, and similarly the Great Central Company have Parliamentary running powers over 169 miles of the Great Northern system. Taking the mileage of the two systems at 1,332, it will be seen that the two companies already have running powers over nearly forty per cent of this length… Including Joint lines, there are 713 miles common to both Companies. Referring to an Act of 1858 concerning the relations of interassociation and mutual co-operation of the two companies, he said, 'These powers are still in force as part of the law of the land… and they provide among other things for the management and conduct of both the undertakings or any part thereof exactly as is provided by the Agreement we are about to submit to you.'

Henderson then went on to an analysis of the financial proposals: 'Taking 1906 as a basis year… the Great Northern net receipts were £2,151,518; the Great Central published accounts show a receipt of £1,630,129… including provisions for Compensation for Accidents [£16,785 and £5,000 respectively], the total is £3,803,332, and the proportions respectively 57 and 43 per cent.' He went further into financial detail to demonstrate a gross revenue fast approaching £10

---

78   Though he was its committed financier by May 1894 (Dow, op. cit. Volume II, page 250).

million sterling, and the combination of the companies would result in an increase in net revenue of £300,000. He added that the lines recently acquired and known as the Lancashire, Derbyshire and East Coast Railway, and the Sheffield District Railway, were excluded from the arrangements, in accordance with the terms under which Parliament permitted the purchase of undertakings. Referring to the question of leadership of the proposed arrangement, the Chairman revealed that:

> the first Chairman of the Joint Committee would be Lord Allerton[79] with himself as the Deputy. Should Lord Allerton cease to be the Chairman of the Great Northern, I, if still the Chairman of the Great Central, to become Chairman of the Joint Committee. If either of these were to fail, the post will be decided by the Committee themselves.

'The success of the scheme,' he explained:

> must depend on the ability of the General Manager who is appointed to look after the affairs of the joint concern, and I have pleasure in informing you that Mr Fay has been selected for that position. Mr Fay, as I know, has the complete confidence of our employees, and with him at the helm they will find that their welfare is assured. Traders have ever found him ready to do his utmost to meet their reasonable requirements, and the public recognize that a service under his control will not be lacking in facilities.

Henderson concluded by expressing a hope that 'the principle of co-operation we endorse, by commending your acceptance of the agreement, will be the forerunner of other arrangements that may result in providing increased reserve to meet the ever-increasing expenses of the railways of our country'.[80] The meeting was attended by 170 shareholders.

It would seem that the Great Central General Manager was the source

---

79 Chairman of the Great Northern Railway, 1895–1908. William Lawies Jackson (1840–1917), Privy Councillor, Yorkshire businessman and politician, created Baron Allerton of Chapel Allerton in 1902.

80 GCR *Journal*, February 1908, pages 185–189; and March 1908, pages 208–209.

of this revolutionary proposal. During the course of the negotiations over
the Lancashire, Derbyshire and East Coast Railway, Fay had got on well
with Oliver Bury, his opposite number on the Great Northern. They met
in the Victoria Hotel in Sheffield in 1907 to settle outstanding claims
between the two companies. There were counter-claims of roughly equal
magnitude – about £80,000 – and they soon reached agreement. However,
their conversation continued, and they went on to discuss the idea of the
amalgamation of their two companies: the Working Agreement of 1858 was
soon to expire. They decided to take their views to the respective Boards, and
after a lukewarm reception the Directors of both decided to take the next
step. Before the end of 1907 the Heads of Agreement had been approved,
and led to the formation of a Joint Committee, the final aim being complete
unification.

The chief appointments, beside those of Chairman and General
Manager, were to be Richard Dawe (GNR) as Solicitor, and C.L. Edwards
(GNR) as Accountant to the Joint Committee. Suitably adequate
compensation, paid for out of their respective company funds, to be
paid to the men displaced by these appointments.[81] Fay commented, 'We
adapted a system of inter-working, one arrangement of rates and fares,
equal to, if not quite, out-and-out amalgamation. Barristers and lawyers
earned enough to keep them in champagne for the rest of their lives.'

On 6 February 1908, Sir Charles Scotter, Chairman of the London
and South Western Company, at its half-yearly meeting, said that they
were watching with interest the result of the application to the Railway
Commissioners for the proposed working agreement between the Great
Central and the Great Northern Railway. He spoke warmly of cooperation
rather than competition in the railway service of the country. He raised the
prospect that it might presage a grand scheme for railway companies uniting
to save enormous expense and fruitless competition.[82] The magazine *Punch*,
in a sketch entitled 'Railway Combinations', emphasized the advantages of
'Reducing the Waste and Reducing the Figure'. Many sections of the press
applauded the scheme as set out: 'Any impartial mind, examining both sides
of the question, will be justified in concluding that the change will be on

---

81   Dow, op cit., Volume III, pp. 116 and 117.
82   *Journal*, March 1908, page 209.

the whole as beneficial as sweeping.'[83] A cartoon in the GCR *Journal* for March 1908, page 208, depicted the GN and GC Chairmen rowing a boat named '*Great Central and Great Northern Railways*' along a sizeable river towards 'Prosperity'. It is captioned 'Pulling Together', but unfortunately and prophetically it is veering towards the bank of the river.

But it could hardly be expected that the companies neighbouring the GCR and the GNR would be happy with this proposed agreement. There was a perceived threat to the locomotive, carriage and wagon business; there were objections from a few civic corporations and county councils. Twenty-seven objections had been lodged when the Railway and Canal Commissioners, on 2 March 1908, declared the agreement of the Act of 1858 *ultra vires*, and their views were upheld by the Court of Appeal eight days later. The two General Managers were asked to look into a new arrangement for achieving economies. After a meeting shortly afterwards, the General Manager of the Great Eastern Railway, one of the chief objectors to the original scheme, accused Fay of joining forces with its greatest competitor; whereupon Sam asked, 'Then why not come into the amalgamation also?' The offer was accepted, and after the Midland had been given the same opportunity and declined, but saying that it had no objection to the revised plan, negotiations for a tripartite working union were begun, in preparation for submission to Parliament. However, as Fay reported to the Board at its meeting on bills in Parliament on 29 January 1909, the proposed working union was defeated.[84] George Dow, in his account of these proceedings,[85] concludes:

> The lack of any coherent transport policy since the advent of canals in the eighteenth century, parliamentary rulings had been totally inconsistent. Because the previous such railway scheme – that of the South Eastern Railway with the London Chatham and Dover Working Union – was authorized (on 1 January 1899), the present attempt to do so would not succeed.

---

83 *Daily Telegraph.*

84 National Archives, RAIL 226/537. Other bills were 'passed practically intact, including Junctions with the LYR at Ashton Moss and at Wigan, and the closing of the level crossing on Welsh Road at Hawarden'.

85 Dow, op cit, Volume III, pages 120 and 121.

And so, with, in Dow's words, 'the sublime ineptitude of politicians in transport affairs', it did not. There were 52 objections to the Second Reading in Parliament in 1909, though it was passed, but the President of the Board of Trade (Winston Churchill) recommended that it be rejected at the Third Reading. 'Thus ended a noteworthy effort to simplify working, reduce operating and other costs and some future capital expenditure. Yet within twelve years, under the Railway Act of 1921, Parliament forcibly combined the same three railways, with others, to form the London and North Eastern Railway.'[86]

Two points emerged from the Great Central President's Address at the Extraordinary General Meeting of the proprietors. First, that as early as December 1907, doubts had arisen at the highest level of the viability of the Great Central Main Line Extension, and that the reason for such doubts stemmed directly from the non-success of Sir Edward Watkin's Herculean attempts to achieve his scheme for a Channel Tunnel.[87] The two ventures had been interdependent parts of a whole, and the failure of the one had been the Achilles heel of the other. Watkin's visionary idea of connecting the world's first Industrial City with European and Indian markets (much of Manchester's output of cotton garments were sold in the Subcontinent) was foiled by the politico-military lobby. But admittedly it was well before its time. Railway historians have been sceptical, not to say contemptuous, of Watkin, always accusing him of venturing into vanity projects, and mentioning his few disappointments (the Tunnel, the Wembley Tower), myopically ignoring his great achievements and his magnanimous nature.[88]

Secondly, the fact that the GCR Main Line was so successful an enterprise highlighted Sir Sam Fay's management genius, and this was recognized as early as 1907 in the confidence invested in him by an almost uniquely qualified Board of Directors, and by those of three major companies hoping to work together. A development of the inter-company discussions was that from Monday 15 December 1915, the Directors of the GCR, the GNR and

---

86 Dow, op. cit..

87 Up to the year 1895, he had brought the Channel Tunnel Scheme to Parliament no fewer than eleven times.

88 For a full account of his life, see John Neville Greaves, *Sir Edward Watkin, 1819–1901: The Last of the Railway Kings*, Book Guild Ltd, 2005; Revised Paperback, Melrose Press Ltd, 2014.

the GER issued a notice that 'Open goods wagons, having sides of three or more planks, and also wagon sheets, must be dealt with as common stock, for the purposes of the three companies.' This was also a contextual spin-off from the appointment by the Railway Clearing House of Sir Sam Fay, with W. Bailey, the Accountant of the Midland Railway, as a small committee to report on both the common use of merchandise wagons and the pooling of coal wagons. Within a week, Fay had written to the General Manager of the L&NWR proposing that representatives of the leading companies meet to consider the more economical use of rolling stock. On 7 December 1915, as a result, six men formed a Common User Committee of the RCH, and passed a resolution that such a measure would be a distinct advantage, and result in a large saving.[89]

---

89 *The Railway Clearing House in the British Economy*, 1812-1924, Philip Bagwell, George Allen & Unwin, 1968, quoted, William Charlton Fay, op cit.

Horse cart, GCR, GNR, GER

5

Post Office Pay

One of the consequences of Sam Fay's growing reputation was seen from time to time in requests for his engagement in other matters requiring sound business and financial judgement. An example of this occurred in 1904, when an issue arose concerning overwork in the General Post Office at the beginning of the twentieth century. Post Office employees of nearly all grades were working in excess of the eight-hour day rule, the cause being inconsiderate alterations of duties by heads of departments. An official enquiry into the scales of pay of Post Office servants was held; the Committee was presided over by Sir Edward Bradford,[90] and it included Sam Fay, Charles Booth the eminent sociologist, the Managing Director of the Co-operative Wholesale Society and the General Manager of Harrod's Stores.

The terms of reference were to enquire into the wages of the Post Office staff, with power to compare with rates current in other occupations. Evidence was given by London and Provincial sorters, telegraphists and postmen, and the Committee's findings were, in due time, placed on the table of the House of Commons. The Committee's Report, in 1906, was 'pithy and businesslike', as any Great Central employee might proudly have expected. It witnessed that on the evidence and arguments put forward, the minimum wage was not a living wage, and that the scale of sorters was

---

90   Sir Edward Ridley Colborne Bradford (1836–1911). After a distinguished military career, he was appointed Head of the London Metropolitan Police Force, 1890–1903.

not sufficient to support a wife and family; remuneration for counter clerks was inadequate for the irregular hours and uncertain duties, compared with employees of other services, and avenues for promotion were fewer. Women who performed much the same kind of work were unable to support themselves on their earnings.

The Controller of the London Postal Service admitted that the evidence was accurate. Sweeping changes were recommended, but these were so modified by the then Postmaster-General and the Treasury that the concessions granted were of a very trifling nature. The continuing debate spread over into broader controversial issues behind the problem: that 'the Post Office was a huge monopoly, worked by the hide-bound rules of State, held up by such an arrangement as a pattern of good management', a judgement which was contested by those who criticize the 'imposition of limitations on freedom of action'. The Committee of Enquiry put the whole matter in a nutshell, the kernel being 'Competition versus Monopoly: Competition brings out the motive to excel. Monopoly stifles all such desire, and minimizes progress.'

This led to a comparative assessment of the management of railways. Nationalisation was a recurrent theme at the beginning of the twentieth century. The reporter in the GCR *Journal* of these proceedings[91] went on to record that:

> At the recent Dinner of the London GC Staff, Lord Robert Cecil proposed 'Success to the Great Central Railway', adding that we had great reason to be satisfied with our railway system... The managements are principally concerned in the comfort and well-being of the passengers, and they recognise that hard and fast regulations rigidly enforced do not conduce to the convenience of the travelling public... English railways are renowned for the civility and courtesy of the officials. Attention, alacrity and courtesy are part of their nature... It is not any sort of man that can come to the top in the railway service. It is a combination of qualities not common to everyday man to fill a leading position in the railway world. On our own line, promotion to the highest office in the service has invariably emanated from the iron school of experience;

91   May 1906, pages 253–257.

there is not a chief officer who has not risen from the ranks... and we can with justifiable pride claim to have in Mr Fay the most enterprising and democratic manager of the day... Towards the construction of our railways, the State has furnished no funds, but individuals... have executed the works. The lines are managed not for their common interests alone, but also for the public good.

Can it be seriously suggested that State management would be able to work the railways equal to the efficient commercial management of today? Latest Board of Trade returns show that net earnings on the Capital invested in the railway companies of the United Kingdom are only 3¼%. No one can say, therefore, that railways are being exploited for the purpose of big dividends at the expense of public interest. 'It is not the business of a Government to trade, but to govern': That is the dictum of an illustrious statesman, and it is to be desired that the voice of this meeting, will – in the words of our late great Chairman, Sir Edward Watkin – be given against 'the intrusion of Government in the action of our railways, and that transit, like our own liberties, will remain unfettered by Government and State control'.[92],[93]

In 1911, possibly as a result of the enquiry into Post Office rates of pay, Fay ordered a survey of the income and expenditure of clerks employed at various stations of the GCR. The report was entitled 'Analysis of the Weekly Household Budgets of Forty-One Average Senior Clerks Employed by the Great Central Railway at Various Stations and Depots in London, and at Barnsley, Birkenhead, Brymbo, Grimsby, Guide Bridge, Hull, Leeds, Leicester, Liverpool, Loughboro [sic], Manchester, Newton, Plas Power, Rotherham, Rugby, St Helens, Sheffield, Tinsley, Wath, Wigan, Woodley, Wrexham, in 1911.' The number of persons in each family, the salary, and exact details of expenditure, are listed on a closely written sheet of foolscap, and it is accompanied by a summary of the findings. The total salaries,

---

92 Lord Edgar Algernon Robert Gascoigne-Cecil (1864–1958) could speak from some knowledge of railway management. His father, the Marquess of Salisbury, one of the greatest of Britain's Prime Ministers, had been, at one period of his life (1868–1872) the Chairman, at Edward Watkin's behest, of the Great Eastern Railway. It was near bankruptcy, and by astute management he restored its fortunes handsomely.

93 Quoted from full report in the *Journal* for May 1906, pp. 256 and 257.

including supplementary earnings of a child over 15, amounted to £71 7s 8d, an average weekly income of £1 14s 10d; and the total expenditure was £71 11s 11½d, with an average of £1 14s 11d, 1d more than income. It is a study of senior clerks, and even they were finding it difficult to make ends meet, and it is noticeable that only 18 of the 41 paid anything for holidays; such payment averaged only 1 shilling per week. The incomes of the far greater number of waged employees must have caused some hardship. These documents included also a 'Statement re Increased Cost of Living', a study based on figures published by the Board of Trade and the Wholesale Prices Index over the years 1896 to 1910, showing the rise of the cost of essential foods between those years.[94] It also included a report from Birmingham University which showed that the cost of clothing and fuel had also risen proportionately.[95] The record does not seem to include a report of any action taken on these findings, but it is obvious that Fay took seriously the welfare of the Great Central staff.[96]

There was interesting event in the history of the Manchester, Sheffield and Lincolnshire Railway of Edward Watkin's attitude to justice in the treatment of the employees. In a meeting held in the boardroom of the company at Manchester London Road Station on 4 October 1887, he said that in the relationship between capital and labour:

> We have always desired that it should be a partnership on just and equal terms; the shareholders on one side and those who work for pay are very much an equality… The total net profit earned last year was £770,056; we paid in regular wages and salaries… £685,609. There are 11,396 shareholders, and their share of net profit was £67 11s 0d per head. The Company employed 9,935 persons, and their share came to £69 0s 2d per head… there is not so much a difference between the man who finds the capital and the man who works.[97]

---

94   With a base figure of 100 for 1900, 62 was the figure for 1895, that for 1909 was 74.
95   National Archives, RAIL 226/573.
96   See Appendix 2 for details of Fay's findings.
97   *Sir Edward Watkin, 1819–1901, the Last of the Railway Kings*, Revised Paperback Edition, 2014, page 226. John Neville Greaves.

6

Immingham Dock

The year 1907 marked the beginning of another development of the company's facilities, with a serious discussion of the building of a new harbour to relieve pressure on Grimsby. The genesis of such an idea can be traced back to the early 1870s, when Charles Liddell,[98] later one of the engineers of the GCR main line, was asked by the Manchester, Sheffield and Lincolnshire Railway to undertake borings along the Humber estuary north-west of Grimsby. He reported at the Company's Board Meeting of April 1874 in favour of a new dock at Killingholme, near the village of Immingham. The Chairman, Edward Watkin, decided, uncharacteristically, against attempting anything at that time.[99] By 1900, the still-growing pressure on the port of Grimsby was addressed again. Negotiations began when the Great Central and certain interests in Grimsby met to discuss creating a new dock close to the existing installations. On 7 July of that year, Henderson reported to the Board that a company called Commercial Dock Company Ltd, with a nominal capital of £15,000, had been registered to initiate the project. The GCR promised to facilitate the enterprise in every way, subject to the support of the people and officials of the town. On 9

---

98 1813–1894, son of the Rector of Easington, Co. Durham, and a pupil of George Stephenson.

99 The most likely explanation of his reluctance is that the year 1874 was the one in which Watkin decided to throw his weight publicly behind the French idea of a Channel Tunnel, a project which was to occupy much of his time and energy thereafter.

August 1901 Parliamentary authority was secured with the passing of the first Humber Commercial and Railway Dock Act. Before finally committing itself to the scheme, the Great Central sought the advice of Sir John Wolfe Barry,[100] an eminent engineer, who had a special knowledge of the Humber, and of the docks at Hull. After making several investigations, he arrived at Liddell's conclusions of 1874.

The bill had been passed by the House of Commons, but it introduced a clause which held the Great Central responsible for making good any defect which might subsequently occur in the channels of the Humber as a consequence of the new dock. The GCR whereupon withdrew the bill and, despite great pressure, refused to support it in a future session if a similar qualification was likely to be attached. A deputation, which included Sir George Doughty,[101] the Earl of Yarborough (who was selling the necessary land for the project) and Sir Alexander Henderson, made a representation to the Board of Trade. Their plea that the failure of the bill would plunge the shipping industry on the south side of the Humber into a disastrous uncertainty was followed by a special inspection by the Board of Trade, which revealed that no serious injury to the river, or interference with navigation, were to be feared.

After several objections had been met, the work was sanctioned on 22 July 1904, with the declared support of everyone of importance on the south side of the Humber. The traditional sod-cutting ceremony took place on 12 July 1906. Near to the venue, on a field to the south of a flat bank of the river, a huge marquee was erected, accommodating 682 luncheon covers, arrangements being in the hands of W. Ingram, Manager of the GCR Hotels and Refreshment Rooms Department. Four special trains – one each from Marylebone, Manchester London Road, Chesterfield and Cleethorpes – brought the guests.

The proceedings began with a short religious service conducted by the Bishop of Lincoln, the Right Reverend Edward King,[102] with choristers from St James's Church, Grimsby. Then J. Price, for the contractors,

---

100 1836–1918, the architect of London's Tower Bridge, and son of Sir Charles Barry, who designed the Houses of Parliament.

101 1854–1914, Grimsby ship owner; MP for Great Grimsby, 1895–1914.

102 A great supporter of the Guild of Railwaymen, a former Army Chaplain in the Boer War, and later revered for his saintliness by the Church of England.

presented Lady Henderson with a splendid spade and barrow to carry out the cutting of the first sod, and the ceremony concluded with the hymn 'O God our help in ages past, our hope for years to come' and a presentation of a bouquet of flowers to Lady Henderson by Edward Chapman, the Deputy Chairman of the GCR. After the meal and loyal toasts, a huge steam navvy and a steam crane moved in to continue the digging operation.

The formal opening of the Immingham Dock took place on Monday 22 July 1912, King George the Fifth having consented to open the ceremony. The total water area of the dock was 45 acres, and along the length of the 2,350 feet of South Quay were placed seven hydraulic coaling hoists which could handle 700 tons each an hour. Each hoist was fed by eighty gravity sidings, accommodating 350 16-ton wagons, a total of 2,560 for the whole group. Reception and storage sidings held a further 9,120 wagons. The rapid handling of empties ensured that there was no danger, even at the busiest of times, of congestion. The total mileage at Immingham of sidings and other lines amounted to 170 miles of track, affording an overall capacity of 16,850 wagons. Electric arc lamps, 350 in all, illuminated night operations. It was altogether a gigantic achievement.

The scope of the arrangements and the thoroughness and precision of their planning and execution exceeded any previous ceremonies staged by the company. As George Dow observed, 'That is saying something', in view of Edward Watkin's appreciation of public relations on the grand scale. Some 4,000 people were invited to be present, and 1,418 covers were laid for the celebration banquet, 104 at the top table and the remainder on 18 sprigs. Two 2-4-0 locomotives on the duplicate list were connected to the water mains, supplying boiling water to the proceedings. Purdon Viccars, of the Board of Directors, took the chair at the luncheon in the absence of Henderson and Fay, who were at Grimsby Town station to receive the King and Queen. Afterwards the royal train, hauled by the suitably bedecked compound Atlantic locomotive Class 8E no. 364, *Lady Henderson*, reached the special platform opposite the dock. After the dedication of the New Dock, the King declared that he had much pleasure in declaring open the Immingham Dock, which in future would be known as 'The King's Dock'. This was greeted by loud cheers, and the playing of 'Rule Britannia' by the band of the 1st Life Guards, bringing the formal arrangements to an end.

But to the surprise and utmost delight of those present, Sam Fay was conducted to the dais and presented again to the King by Henderson. Borrowing the sword of his equerry, Colonel the Hon. Sir Harry Charles Legge,[103] the King asked Fay to kneel, bestowed the Accolade, and bade 'Sir Sam' to rise. Only Henderson had prior knowledge of this, but it was so loudly acclaimed that the cheers were heard in Grimsby.[104] At a Board meeting held on 26 July at Marylebone Station, the Chairman submitted a communication from the King's Secretary, who said he:

> had been directed by His Majesty to acquaint the Chairman and the Directors of the Great Central Railway with his satisfaction at all the arrangements made on the occasion of His Majesty's opening a new dock at Immingham. He greatly appreciated the cordiality of the reception he had received from the inhabitants of the neighbouring districts and from the staff and the employees of the Great Central Railway on that occasion. He was deeply interested in the important development which the new dock promises to trade and industries of the Humber and of the counties adjacent to it. He trusts that the enterprise, courage, and skill of the Chairman and Directors will meet with a fitting reward through the speedy expansion of the commerce of the new port, admirably equipped as it is by the latest appliances of science to handle the ever growing trade of the country.

At the same time Sir Alexander was prompt to express on behalf of the Directors to acknowledge the admirable manner in which all the arrangements in connection with ceremony had been conducted, and the meeting 'Resolved That Sir Sam Fay be congratulated on the honour of Knighthood publicly conferred upon him, and that he and Lady Fay may long be spared to enjoy this well-deserved appreciation of his unremitting energy in the development of Railway enterprise.'[105]

The *Financial Standard* of four days later made Sir Sam the subject of

---

103 1852–1924, KCVO; second son of the Earl of Dartmouth, Equerry to the Royal Household, 1893–1915; Coldstream Guards from 1872.

104 The knighthood was Gazetted as 22 July *London Gazette*, 2 August 1912, 28632, page 5722.

105 National Archives, RAIL 226/575.

that week's issue, with a full-page photograph of him on the cover. It said of him that 'there was none so popular a personage as the General Manager of that huge undertaking, the Great Central Railway'. After an account of his career up to 1902, it continued:

> So brilliant were his services on the L&SWR, and so impressed were the Directors of other railways with his marvellous abilities, that he succeeded the late Sir William Pollitt as General Manager of the GCR... No one could be more popular with those above or under him. He is always cheerful, gives a willing ear and every consideration to any grievance brought to his notice; hence the high regard the men have for him... Last year he was unanimously elected as Chairman of the General Managers' Conference; he is also a valued member of the Advisory Committee on Railway Subjects at the London School of Economics and he is a Lieutenant Colonel in the Engineer and Railway Staff Corps... Immingham stands out as the most complete and remarkable enterprise in which a British railway has, in recent years, been associated.

An article in the GCR *Journal* of November 1913[106] contained a testimony to the contribution of the GCR management team to the success of the organisation at Immingham, particularly that of William Lee Howard, who was Private Clerk to the General Manager. Because of his 'back room' function, according to the article, Howard had not attracted the credit due to him in the prior organisation of the opening event. He entered the service of the Great Central in May 1887, at a little over seventeen years of age, in the Superintendent's Department, where, among other things, he had charge of new works. In 1907, he became Private Clerk to the General Manager. He had an omnivorous appetite for work, and his extraordinary capacity for taking pains and attention to detail found ample scope; an example of these qualities was shown in 1912 when he arranged the proceedings for 22 July for the opening of the Immingham Dock. He had been appointed in March 1911 as Assistant Traffic Manager, Manchester, but in the May of that year he had been recalled by Fay to London as his Assistant. 'It is certain that no general manager had a more devoted and loyal assistant.

---

106 Page 149.

His loyalty and determination to be of help to his chief were touching to witness', continued the writer. 'His transparent honesty and devotion to duty were an example to others.'

There were many men on the Great Central Railway who owed a debt impossible to repay for the kindness, help and unfailing courtesy shown to them by William Howard. He was the embodiment of George Herbert's 'Do all things like a man, not sneakingly. Think the King doth see thee still; for his King does.'[107] There are many men on the Great Central Railway who owe a debt impossible to repay for the kindness, assistance, and unfailing courtesy shown to them by William Howard. Happy in his home life, happy in his work, trusted implicitly by his General Manager, there was no position in the railway world to which he could not legitimately aspire; but at forty-four years of age he was dead. He lived in Stalybridge, until the transfer to London of the General Manager's Department, and for several years he was member of Holy Trinity Church there, which accounted for the presence of the Revd Charles Sutcliffe, the Vicar,[108] and Mr Mills of the Holy Trinity Mission (St Matthew's), at his funeral in Bradford in October 1913. 'Those who knew would be the first to acknowledge that the credit and the honour for the smoothness which characterised the proceedings of 22 July in Immingham belonged to W.L. Howard.' The recognition and appointment of men like William Howard was a key factor in Sam Fay's skill in management, a perspicacity borne out by his team's consistent performance.

The completion of the new dock facility at Immingham marked a happy ending to a superbly organized day, and the establishment of what was to become one of the Great Central's most enduring and valuable contributions to the economy of the country.

INSHORE FISHING

Whether or not arising from Sir Sam's high-profile publicity over the opening of the Immingham Docks, or his long connection with Grimsby's

---

107 The quotation is from Herbert's poem "The Church Porch", lines 121 and 122. "The King" to Herbert and to Howard, was of course God.

108 He was the Vicar there from 1881–1917, having been Vicar of Dinting Vale from 1875 to 1881.

fishing businesses,[109] he was asked to sit on a committee of ten members appointed by the President of the Board of Agriculture and Fisheries to advise on the development and preservation of inshore fishing, under the Chairmanship of Sir E.S. Howard, Chairman of the Wye Board of Conservators.[110] Known as the 'Howard Committee', its brief was to enquire into inshore fishing in Devon and Cornwall, but with a broader concern for the sustainability of stocks. There was a wide-ranging discussion of the business, and the long-term effect on many aspects of the local economy and environment. It began in 1912, and the report was delivered in 1914.

---

109 Sam was, in fact, a keen fisherman for his relaxation.
110 It followed a Committee on Deep Sea Fisheries of 1894.

Sod-cutting ceremony, cutting the first Sod of Immingham Dock, 12 July 1906.
The Lord Bishop of Lincoln is conducting the service. To the right is Lady
Henderson and Sir Alexander sharing the sheet. The lady with the large hat is Mrs
Harry Pollitt, Sam Fay is in front of her, with his wife, then Lady Pollitt
and Fay's two eldest daughters.

Sam Fay, Henderson, meet the King & Queen

Accolade, Sir Sam, King George V
(Hulton Archive/Getty Images)

Immingham Dock

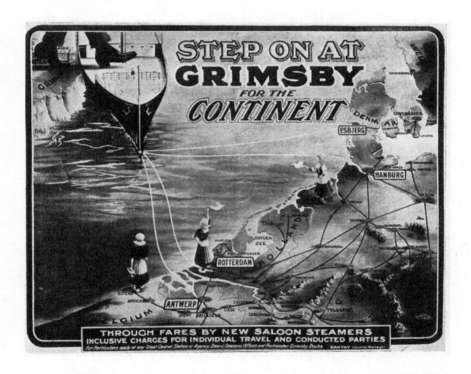

Poster – 'Grimsby for the Continent'

Fay, 'Caught off Guard'
(Hulton Archive/Getty Images)

7

Assessment, 1910-1914

Steady growth in the passenger train services and facilities gave impetus, in the Summer Timetable of 1910, to combined rail and sea trips to the Isle of Man and coastal places in North Wales: Bangor and the Menai Straits in association with the Isle of Man Steam Packet Company and the Liverpool and North Wales Steamship Company. These ran from Sheffield to Liverpool, with free conveyance to the ships. In the following summer, a new breakfast car was put on from Sheffield (7.20 am), calling at Chesterfield, Nottingham and Leicester, and scheduled to run the 103 miles from there, via Aylesbury, to Marylebone in 110 minutes. The Leeds to Bristol breakfast car express was extended to Taunton and Ifracombe. The Manchester–Grimsby–Cleethorpes service was accelerated, the 10 am from London Road being booked to leave Sheffield at 11.15 am, and to run non-stop to Grimsby Town in an hour and twenty minutes, and a similar express in the reverse direction.

The summer season of 1913 introduced a night service by extending the Bristol to Leicester train to York, running via Sheffield and arriving at York at 2.45 am. This effected a connection with the East Coast trains to Newcastle, Edinburgh and Aberdeen, and in the reverse direction the arrival in Bristol connected with GWR expresses to South Wales and to the South West of England. Clearly, Fay had by no means exhausted his creativity. Sheffield had become the hub of the country's through services, practically all of them passing through it. The GCR, by 1914, could boast of seven non-stop runs (including one with a slip-coach) of 100 miles or more. The Great Central attained the peak of its development during these years. *The Financial Times* of 29 September 1913 carried an article dealing favourably with the financial position and prospects of the company, which concluded with a personal note:

> The Great Central has the exceptional advantage of an able Chairman and General Manager who are firm believers in the future of the undertaking for which they are responsible. We would further point out that the General Manager, Sir Sam Fay, has all the exceptional qualities necessary for the successful handling of a large body of men, an aspect of great value in these times. [He] has the popularity with the men, the tact, and we will even add the sense of humour which will go a great deal further in settling labour troubles than fifty million syndicates.

The *Railway Magazine* for April 1914 reported that 'increases in nearly all branches of traffic were recorded by the Central Railway Company'. By that time Fay had achieved several major works: the absorption of the Lancashire, Derbyshire and East Coast Railway; the massive new rail and road bridge at Keadby; Wath Marshalling Yard; and Immingham Docks – the crowning achievement of the company – had been completed. Also established were the Grimsby and District and the Barton and Immingham Light Railways; the opening-out of Darnall tunnel in Sheffield; and track widening between Darnall and Woodhouse, and between Wrawby Junction and Brocklesby near Grimsby. Most of John Robinson's best designs for locomotives and rolling stock were in service by 1915,[111] and by that time the company was running no fewer than twenty restaurant cars, all except two of which were made up of its own coaching stock. The odd ones were the Great Western train on the Barry to Newcastle upon Tyne service, and the London and South Western train on the Bournemouth to Newcastle service, which operated alternately with a Great Central train. Many of these services started and terminated far beyond the confines of the system.[112]

The one great blemish on the period was the first national rail strike in

111 Exceptions being the 8N, 9P and 9Q 4-6-0s.
112 Dow, Volume III, page 223.

August 1911. It was common to most railway companies that the waged staff were dissatisfied with the working of the Conciliation Scheme of 1907. There had been an unsatisfactory delay between the lodging of a grievance or a claim, and the appropriate response of the Conciliation Board, when as last constructed it was too often met by obstructionist tactics on the employers' side. Above all, the long-standing complaint was that the railway companies were adamant in their refusal to negotiate with the trade unions: practically nothing had been conceded by the companies. On the contrary, there were 1,000 fewer men employed on the railways in 1910 than in 1907, and the Board of Trade revealed that there had been a drop in the average wages earned by railwaymen. Yet the LNWR paid a 6% dividend, and placed £100,000 in its Reserve Fund in addition to carrying forward a balance of £141,000. Proportionately, other companies were doing the same, and most of the huge sums amassed were the result of economies effected by fewer staff doing more work.[113]

On the Great Central, while trade unions were regarded with suspicion, the tradition of staff management was much more enlightened.[114] The company had paid nothing to the shareholders of its Ordinary Stocks since 1898, and had only once carried forward as much as £10,000. But the conditions of the wages staff compared favourably with those of other companies. This was openly recognised by a deputation of drivers and firemen and cleaners received by the Directors on 22 April 1910, when no promise of further concessions could be made by the company.

Nationally, a representation from four railway trade unions[115] was sent to meet the President of the Board of Trade[116] to demand that the Government compel the railway managements to meet the accredited Trade Union representatives. This was refused. On 12 August 1911, the (Liberal) Prime Minister, H.H. Asquith, met the trade union leaders. He told them bluntly that the Government would use all civil and military forces at its disposal

---

113 Norman McKillop, *The Lighted Flame*, 1950, Thomas Nelson & Sons Ltd, London, 1950.

114 Vide *Sir Edward Watkin, Last of the Railway Kings*, Revised Paperback Edition, 2014, pages 225 to 234.

115 The Associated Society of Locomotive Engineers and Firemen, the Amalgamated Society of Railway Servants, the United Pointsmen and Signals Society and the General Railway Workers' Union.

116 Sydney Charles Buxton. He was MP for Poplar, London, from 1886 to 1914.

to prevent interference with the commerce of the country. Instructions were sent out that evening, and on Friday 18 August the railway was partly paralysed. The Great Central, through its wide connections, was particularly afflicted.

However, within days it was all over. Representatives of the Cabinet gave way, and instructed, peremptorily, the railway companies to hold a meeting at once, and unconditionally, with the trade unions. After a short space of time the representatives of the four unions, helped by Ramsey MacDonald and Arthur Henderson had, in an 11½-hour meeting, hammered out a settlement with the railway managers. It seemed to have been realised that otherwise the Government would fall if the policy of bayonets and bullets continued.[117] But the doors had been opened to collective bargaining.

The immediate effect on the Great Central was that of improvement of conditions of service by Sir Edward Fraser, the Director who had the Sectional Conciliation Boards under his guidance. Sam Fay took part in the national settlement. At the last moment he was called upon to be one of the representatives of the railways on a Government Committee of Enquiry, and a meeting of the GC Board on 15 December 1911 paid special tribute to his efforts. Called to give evidence, Fay demonstrated his impish sense of humour. When one of the Committee members suggested that he had some ill-feeling against labour leaders, he repudiated the accusation, adding (with the only joke that emerged from this fraught business) that he was 'Just as ready to shake hands with a labour leader as with a duke, but he preferred not to live with either.'[118]

One of the GCR's rare accidents took place at Marylebone on 28 March 1913, when incoming and outgoing trains collided. One passenger was killed and about 32 injured. At the Board of Trade enquiry the jury returned a verdict of accidental death, and the driver of the Princes Risborough train was found to be 'negligent' but not guilty of 'culpable negligence'. £10,830 2s 10d was paid out in compensation.[119]

---

117 George Dow, op cit., Volume III, pp. 224–226. Dow comments that 'the whole matter had sealed the fate of the Liberal Party, as it could no longer count on the support of the working-class vote'.

118 The magazine *Punch* commented that 'It was now time for someone to say a good word for the Dukes'.

119 National Archives, RAIL, 226/589.

A change in the Board of Directors took place in 1914, when Viscount Cross, the longest-serving member, died on 8 January in his ninety-first year and Gerard Powys Dewhurst, Chairman of a Manchester cotton business and later of Williams Deacons Bank and a Director of the Royal Bank of Scotland, was elected in his stead on 6 February.[120]

In August 1914 the beginning of the European War raised problems issuing from staff volunteering for service in the Armed Forces,[121] and the railway companies had to start assessing the effect on manpower available for maintaining services. Fay wrote to O.S. Holt, the Great Central General Secretary, on 8 August: 'Please let me know the number of men of all grades who have left your department to join the Naval and Military Services. The number should be given as existing today, at the end of Tuesday next, and again on Saturday next.' Two days later he wrote again: 'Please do not, without my authority, fill up the positions of any of your staff who have joined the Colours.' On the same day, marked 'URGENT', he wrote again: 'Please let me know whether there will be any difficulty in keeping any of your men fully occupied, and if not, what measures should be taken to deal with the matter.' He asked if any men had been placed on short time, or if he considered such a course may be necessary in the near future, and how many men had been called up as Reservists or Territorials, showing what percentage their number represented of the total number employed, Clerical and Wages staff to be shown separately.' He ended, 'I require this information by 9 o'clock Wednesday morning at the latest.' Holt replied on the Tuesday: 'Have no difficulty in keeping my staff fully occupied or placed on short time. Three clerks have joined the Territorials, being 6% of the total number of this department.' On the 14th he wrote to add that all three had volunteered for full service.

On this latter date Fay received a letter from Colonel J.C. Chriterson, the Secretary of the Territorial Force Association of the County of London, asking whether the same leave of absence would be given to members of the Voluntary Aid Detachments, employed by the GCR, as that given to

---

120 Born in 1872 in Lymm, Cheshire, and died in 1956, educated at Repton School and Cambridge, Dewhurst was a prominent amateur footballer. He played for Corinthians, and the (professional) Liverpool side against Crewe Alexandra in 1894, and for England against Wales in 1895.

121 Full conscription was not brought in until 27 January 1916.

members of the Territorial Force. Sam's reply, dated 17 August, was that he was sorry, but the men could not be spared: 'They are doing far better work on the Railways than they would be in the Ambulance and Red Cross Detachments... We have no more men for the working of traffic than are needed.' There was evidently much concern about how what became known as the category of 'Reserved Occupation' was to be applied, and obviously no one could at that stage foretell how the demands for front-line troops and for a basic minimum of railway staff were going to be balanced.

On 24 March 1915 it was recorded that Lord Kitchener desired a scheme for determining the lowest number of men required for the efficient working of the railways, and to consider how many men between the ages of 18 and 45 may be replaced by youths under 18, men over 45 (or retired), or by women.[122]

122 National Archives, RAIL 226/596.

Sir Sam, signed photo of 1913

Fay, 1910

8

Female Clerks

The GCR *Journal* for May 1916 (on page 3) carried a summary of a recent High Court case of 'An action for libel brought by Mr Albert Leigh the Assistant Audit Accountant, of the Great Central Audit Office, Manchester, against the Editor, Publishers and Printers of *The Railway Clerk*, official organ of the Railway Clerk's Association.'[123] In the edition of 15 December 1915 there had appeared an article headed 'Great Central Clerks Victimised', which contained an account of a report to the General Secretary of the RCA, that four girls in the office of the Great Central Audit Officer had heard of an advanced War Bonus. They decided to ask for it, but Mr Leigh called the girl responsible before him, and:

> after bullying her said he had a good mind to give them all a week's notice and get a fresh lot of girls at half their wages, as he had a 150 on his books waiting for positions. The girl in question was in tears when he had finished with her.

The same issue of the RCA Journal carried a further reference to the matter, reporting a mass meeting of the RCA in Manchester, in which 'Mr A.G. Walkden,[124] the General Secretary of the RCA, said "the Great Central official ought to be horsewhipped," and was loudly applauded.'

---

123 Renamed the Transport Salaried Staffs Association in 1951.
124 Alexander George Walkden (1873–1951), General Secretary of the RCA, 1906–1936; MP for Bristol South, 1929–1945. Created Baron Walkden of Great Bookham, Surrey, in 1945.

The lady clerks referred to wrote at once to the editor of the *Railway Clerk*, denying emphatically that there was a word of truth in the paragraph, but although they requested him to give their letter the same prominence as the article, he did not see fit to comply.

Sir Sam, having heard of the circumstances, and the fact that the whole matter was to be raised in Parliament, wrote on 13 December 1915 to every member of the House of Commons to complain about the waste of Parliamentary time in a period 'of the greatest struggle in our national history, when the energy of every man and woman should be devoted to the art or practice of killing Germans'. He described the four female typists, who were taking the places of clerks now at the Front, as having declined to subscribe to the office rules under which male clerks worked. They had been moved to another office in the same building, and were no worse off in a pecuniary sense than before, and no objection had been, nor was being, raised to membership of the Clerks' Society, excepting only in the administrative offices where the work was confidential. Surely this was not the season to raise new points of domestic controversy, he wrote. He added a final sentence advocating an 'overdue protest against the advertising methods of the Railway Clerks' Association', and signed himself 'Sam Fay'.[125] The same issue of the Great Central *Journal*[126] carried a comprehensive account of the Parliamentary Debate of 16 December 1915, which had included multiloquence and outright misstatement, and a harsh criticism of 'the gentleman who signed himself "Sam Fay."' It might be admitted that Fay's letter could be seen as 'vulgar and in bad taste',[127] but the President of the Board of Trade,[128] after referring to a similar case that had arisen on the North Eastern Railway in 1909,[129] summed up the Debate in these words:

It is only to say, however much my honourable Friends might dislike the circular sent round by Sir Sam Fay, that everyone who

---

125 Great Central *Journal*, January 1916, page 7.

126 Page 3.

127 Words used in the Debate by George James Wardle (1865–1947), MP for Stockport (1906–1920), Editor of the *Railway Review*.

128 Walter Runciman, 1914–1915.

129 Where the compromise was to admit staff to membership of the RCA, but that the definition of 'confidential matters' should be made not by an under-official of the railway, but by the General Manager.

knows [him] knows the way with which he deals with some of these matters in a drastic manner, and with a great deal of good feeling. It is only just to say that there are few general managers in England who are on better terms with their servants than he. I should like to add, as my honourable Friend has cast some aspersions on Sir Sam Fay, I know of no one outside the Government service who has given more generously of his time to the service of his country since the War broke out. He is a member of the Railway Executive Committee, and has served us in dozen ways, and I cannot believe, knowing him as I do, that he would do what is unfair or unjust in this case.

The President of the Board of Trade took the view that if the Great Central policy was as stated had existed prior to the War, the matter should be held in abeyance until its conclusion; but if the policy had been instituted since the beginning of the War, he would ask the company to revert to the status quo.

The trial for Mr Leigh's libel case began on 28 March 1916, but as no witnesses were called to defend the charge, the court was adjourned. It was resumed by Mr Justice Darling with a special jury on 4 and 5 April as a High Court Libel case, when the judge gave the jury a definition of libel:

Anything which is printed or written or published about another which holds him up to dislike. Which is derogatory to him, which makes those with whom he has relations think worse of him and especially anything which would be calculated to injure him with his employers would be liable if written and published about him.

During the trial, Leigh denied bullying his staff: there had been no tears, and it had in fact been a 'friendly and jocular interview'. The jury accepted that William Stott, of the RCA, and Gray's Inn Press, were in the wrong, and the defendants were found guilty. The judge returned a verdict in favour of Mr Leigh for £600 damages and costs. The case had been taken to court by Sir Sam, and Leigh's expenses were paid by the GCR. The *Railway Clerk* of 16 March 1916 (page 7) reported that Mr Bowden, the Audit Accountant of the GCR in Manchester, arranged for a number of his clerks to 'sign a testimonial or letter commendatory of Mr Albert Leigh'. The article commented that the RCA believed this 'To be the first occasion in the history of a leading railway that any office staff have been asked to give testimonial and commendatory letters to their "chief," and we congratulate the GCR Company on this further evidence of their "Forward" policy.'

In what was really a separate case, but of similar principle, Alexander Walkden heard that in the Marylebone office of the Chief Goods Manager, female staff had been warned of the consequences of their being members of the RCA and attending its meetings. They refused the advice, and so were transferred to another department, at lower wages. He took up the matter with the General Manager, to tell him that the managers were exceeding their duties. He expected a positive response, knowing that Fay was a strong Liberal,[130] and such an earnest upholder of the working class. But his letters were ignored, and he took up the matter with the President of the Board of Trade, whose Parliamentary Secretary replied that the railway company had no objection to their clerks joining a trade union except those employed in confidential positions at their head office. Walkden persisted, however, believing the question to be one of principle: that is, the right of all staff to have membership of a trade union as a precaution against mismanagement. He succeeded in having the withdrawal of the rule denying RCA membership in any office at all.[131]

A news item in the *Railway Clerk* of 15 December 1915 (page 295) – the same issue carrying the article about 'Great Central Women Clerks Victimised' (page 307) – stated that:

the railway company that probably employs the largest number of female labour is the Great Central, which has nearly 1,300 women on the staff, an increase of 1,000 since the War began… One of the most interesting points about the Great Central's plans is that they

---

130 He was President of the Liberal Association of South Buckinghamshire, Beaconsfield Liberal Party (86 Fulmer Drive, Gerrards Cross), in 1906, and in that year there was a landslide victory for the Liberal Party, which laid the original foundation for the welfare state.

131 RCA Official History, Chapter 8, pages 5 and 6. The present author expresses his gratitude for the complete and open cooperation he has received from the Communications Manager of the TSSA, Ben Soffa, on this course of events.

contemplate the promotion of women to important administrative posts, should they prove themselves possessed of the necessary gifts.

There was a history of great opposition to trade union membership during the late nineteenth century, and especially on the railways, where there was already a highly structured discipline of rules to adhere to. The trade unions were regarded as an intrusion between management and staff, giving the latter recourse to legal action against managers. The companies valued loyalty from a railway servant, but human nature being what it is, the managers did not always act as though the loyalty was in fact also due on their side. Edward Watkin did not favour such 'intrusion', but then he had an enviable way of treating staff responsibly, and they responded accordingly. Some companies could be in blatant violation of such humane considerations, and objections to bad attitudes were quite understandable. The other point arising from this whole sequence of events is that the GCR generally, and Sir Sam in particular, was seen to be abreast of, if not ahead of, the sociological changes taking place.

9

Prelude To Fay's War Office Period

At the Annual Shareholders' Meeting in Manchester on Friday 18 February 1916,[132] the Chairman, Lord Faringdon, began by reporting 'the death of our esteemed colleague, Colonel Clement Royds,[133] a man of great personal charm, who assisted us with sound advice during our most troublous years':

> The Government control of railways [has] practically eliminated a statement of revenue from our Accounts, [but] it will be seen that we have a gain of £20,785 over the figures of 1914, though this is a decrease from £24,551 of the figures of 1913. However, this is better than last year... and we will arrive at an improvement of our Revenue of £25,293, and we now have a balance of net Revenue of £2,207,279, which provides for all our Preference Shares in full, down to and including the 1891 Preference Stock, and leaves 1% for 1894 Stock and a balance forward of £7,294.

He continued that the proprietors would understand that the company, having undertaken to do its utmost to manufacture munitions for the

---

132 Report in the GCR *Journal*, March 1916, pages 206–209.
133 Sir Clement Molyneux Royds, 1842–1916; Knight of Justice of the Royal Order of St John of Jerusalem in England, 1908; Chairman of the Williams Deacons Bank; High Sheriff of Lancashire, 1889; MP for Rochdale, 1895–1906; Director the GCR, 1897–1916.

Government, had been obliged to restrict largely its renewal of engines, carriages and wagons. Its track relaying was also in arrear... and when it is possible to do this deferred work, the reserves... would necessarily be used up. 'Our arrangement with the Government', he explained, 'gives us nothing in respect of the Capital spent during the year 1913, which amounted to £50,000, during 1914 to £386,000, and during 1915 to £266,000. [With] interest on these three sums, [it] comes to £1,152,000. Our case is in the hands of the Railway Executive Committee.' He announced:

> With the view of facilitating economical working of our line and the two Companies closely associated with us, the Great Northern and the Great Eastern, we have pooled practically all our open wagons for goods and coal. We believe this will lead us to an economy of working, and will make up to some extent the shortage in wagon stock that is now being felt throughout the country. The Proprietors will be glad to hear that the ventilating shaft in the Woodhead tunnel has greatly improved the atmosphere in the tunnel.

The *GCR Journal* for February 1917[134] reported an official announcement: 'With effect from Monday, 15 January 1917, Sir Sam Fay, General Manager of the Great Central Railway, has assumed responsibility in the War Office for the Directory of Movements.' The Editor added:

> Among the many press comments, the *Daily News* has the most interesting: 'There could not have been a better choice than that of Sir Sam Fay for his new post. His experience of railway work is probably unrivalled in its way... Whatever his new trials, they can scarcely be worse than his old; and Sir Sam Fay is warranted to face them with considerable equanimity.'

The same piece in the *Journal* recorded that W.M. Clow, the Superintendent of the Line, had been appointed to the staff of Sir Eric Geddes with the rank of Major in the Royal Engineers, and took up his duties in France at the beginning of January.

---

134 Page 154.

In the July 1917 *Journal* there appeared a lengthy article[135] by Charles Travis, an author of several books on Railway Working and Economics. It was entitled 'Railway Working under War Conditions'. Briefly summarised, it comprised an Introduction, Working Difficulties, Reduction of Passenger Facilities, Goods Trains – Co-ordination with Passenger Trains, Summary. In the Introduction, he says:

If the future should see the compilation of a narrative showing the great part which the world's railways have played in this terrible conflict, it will be hopelessly incomplete if it does not contain extended reference to the effect on a British railway working of the present crisis on our national history... Owing to the almost entire cessation of coastwise services, enormous volumes of traffic previously carried by sea have been thrust upon the railways, which at the same time have had... to grapple with a vastly enhanced military and civil traffic. Working difficulties have been felt in demands on working space for munitions and special trains of coaches for ambulance work; there has been a diminution of staff from enlistment on a significant scale. Before the War, British Passenger Train services were as good as any in the world. They have been reduced to war time essentials, and as a deterrent to travel, a 50% fare increase. Considering the special difficulties, the degree of punctuality has been remarkable. The enormous increase in goods traffic has made the peacetime standards of efficiency unrealisable. Goods depots and terminals have been exceedingly difficult to manage: in some places there has been a 70% increase on pre-war levels. The congestion has made it impossible to avoid the curtailment of passenger services. Considering the difficulties of railway operation, moreover, the degree of punctuality is remarkable. During the course of 50,000 miles of travel in almost every section of the British Isles during 1916, I was astonished to find how creditably the passenger services were maintained. Important long distance connecting trains have made their connections punctually, whilst the slower 'intermediates' have done sound work. To those who are acquainted with the

135 Pages 2, 3, 4 and 5.

tremendous difficulties of the times there is something wonderful in this fact, for the degree of punctuality attained is the surest index to the relative efficiency of railway operation.

'It all speaks volumes', concludes CharlesTravis, 'for the men who have the task of maintaining an efficient operation.'

Sir Sam would have been gladdened to see a set of figures revealed in the *Journal* of February 1917 (page 154), of the comparative amounts contributed in staff collections for the Railwaymen's Convalescent Homes in 1916:

GCR £879	MID £518
L&NW £793	GE £510
GN £662	GW £461
L&Y £654	L&SW £425
NE £538	LB&SC £409
SE&C £529	

10

The Years at The War Office, 1916-1919

It is obvious from his diaries of 1878 to 1881 that Sam took a keen interest in national and international affairs, attending House of Commons debates and writing up his comments on the issues involved, especially on the South African War (8 March 1878), The Russian attitude to the Berlin Conference (22 March), and the War with Afghanistan which started on 5 December. On 22 April 1879 he recorded 'Very bad news from the Cape of Good Hope – [The Zulu War], 580 of the 24th Regiment annihilated and colours captured.'[136] 24 July 1879, 'News of a great victory over the Zulus.'[137] On 17 December he wrote that Charles Farbrother (his fiancee's brother), enlisted in the Army, was on the march to Cabul to relieve General Roberts[138] who was surrounded by 30,000 Afghans. He listened, on 1 January 1881, to the continuing debate in Parliament on Irish Home Rule: 'The Parnellians will get themselves locked up if they are not careful.' On 7 February he observed that 'We are at war again in the Transvaal, with the Boers now.'

Five years later Fay opened his account of his experience at the War Office itself with an explanation of how he came in touch with that esteemed department of government:

---

136 This was the Battle of Islandlwana, 22 January 1879.
137 The Defence of Rorke's Drift, 22–23 January 1879, was followed by final victory on 4 July.
138 Later (1901), Earl Roberts of Kandahar.

On 8 October 1886 the unemployed and others in Trafalgar Square processed to Pall Mall, where they smashed the windows of several clubs. It was this fracas which introduced me to the War Office. The retired army officers in their deep armchairs behind these windows saw the fabric of society cracking as the plate glass starred and crashed. Their dismay was shared by the War Office, at that time also situated in Pall Mall. It speedily communicated itself to the Government.

Railway management found itself involved in this event, as troops were mobilised and special trains requisitioned to carry them from military centres to London. Fay was at that time in the office of the Superintendent of the Line of the L&SWR, and as the line served Aldershot, he was thus principally affected by the events. Among other instructions, there were orders to provide a train to carry a certain regiment from Portsmouth to London. The train was duly provided, but soon afterwards the Portsmouth Stationmaster sent an urgent telegram to say that not only had the regiment failed to entrain, but, as Fay put it, 'Local enquiries had failed to discover its whereabouts or even its existence.'

E.W. Verrinder, Fay's chief, sent him to the War Office to pursue enquiries. It was then, he said, that he became acquainted with the military face of those days, and found it anything but helpful. He was passed on from one office to another, and in each office were medicine bottles on the mantelpiece, causing him to wonder about the state of health of the Army's administration. Becoming tired of the uninterested attitude of the staff, he rapped the table of one individual who didn't bother to look up when he explained his errand, and demanded to see the Quartermaster General. After a while he met that gentleman, in a cold, comfortless building with badly furnished rooms and a general air of poverty. Troop records were defective, and Sam came away with instructions to cancel the train until further orders. 'The army may have found the regiment, but the railway never did,' he concluded.

That was his experience of the old War Office, and he quoted a military writer of a former epoch who stated that 'The officers of the War Department led an administrative life of exquisite confusion', and Lord Wolseley, who as Adjutant General spoke in the House of Lords in 1888 to say: 'The forces are not organised as they should be to guarantee even the safety of the Capital.'

Fay's next encounter with the War Office was at the outbreak of the South African War, though he had worked with the Quartermaster General's department on the occasion of Reviews at Aldershot and Windsor, and Manoeuvres on Salisbury Plain. He was L&SWR Superintendent of the Line when he received a telegram at Waterloo requesting to see him on a matter of urgency. This was, under the strictest secrecy, that it was intended to embark an Army corps at Southampton within six days, involving personnel, artillery, horses and all the necessary equipment for field service. The officer doubted if it could be done, but Fay assured him that there would be no insuperable difficulty for the railway and dock facilities, provided always that ships were berthed and ready before the trains arrived. At first, slow ships were chartered for reasons of economy, but later 'as depression seized the political powers, following a series of military defeats, the fastest ships were employed'. 21 October 1909 saw a movement of 20 troop trains to Southampton, and the embarkation of 4,847 officers and men, 103 horses, 19 guns, and 73 vehicles of equipment; but in the first seven months of the war there passed through Southampton 5,872 officers, 206,500 men, 27,000 horses, 286 wagons for field guns and maxims, and 900 equipment vehicles. All this, though thought remarkable at the time, became normal during the Great War, and the experience proved valuable in many directions.[139] Fay recollected that the officer concerned in troop transport was Lieutenant Colonel Cowans, Deputy-Assistant Quartermaster General, who he was to meet again later. He wrote that:

As practically the whole of the arrangements were dealt with through the South-Western Railway via Southampton, my intercourse with Cowans was continuous throughout the war. He was as able as he was courteous, a pleasure to work with him, and our friendship, begun in 1899, stood the test in later years of a situation that might have been anything but comfortable.

Sam's next experience of the War Office was in 1911, when Richard

---

139 There were 1,800 troop trains to Southampton in August 1914 alone.

Haldane[140] set up a committee of six railway managers, of whom Fay was one, to study and report on the possibility of feeding London from Western ports in the event of the North Sea becoming sterilised by enemy action. The Under Secretary of State, Colonel Seely (later Lord Mottistone), explained that they were to assume that ports from Hull to Portsmouth were closed, but not Southampton. After dealing with other issues, the committee concluded their report by a recommendation that:

> the railway general managers who had been consulted be formed into a permanent committee with the power to add to their number... and be nominated by the Secretary of State immediately an emergency is declared, to carry out the powers set forth in the Regulation of Forces Act of 1871

This sounds suspiciously as though it were formulated by Fay, because he records that the general managers did not regard their duties so seriously, even though they gave their earnest attention to the issues involved. He remembered one of them saying, 'It's damned nonsense wasting time over something that will never happen.' 'He lived', wrote Fay, 'long enough to revise his opinion.'

Sam had been admitted to the Army ranks in his own right as early as June 1902, shortly after the end of the Boer War. He was Gazetted as Lieutenant Colonel in the Engineers and Volunteer Staff Corps, which was set up in 1865.[141] When the E&VSC became the Engineer and Railway Staff Corps of the Royal Engineers in April 1908, he was re-Gazetted at the same rank.[142]

An Army Railway Council had been formed in 1896[143] following concern by the Duke of Wellington, with representation from the railway companies, charged with the preparation of mobilisation timetables. In 1905 the War Office and the railway companies examined the possibility of setting up plans for the use of locomotives and rolling stock for use overseas. In 1911, with the increasing likelihood of a war, these plans

---

140 Richard Burdon Haldane (1856–1928), First Viscount Haldane, Liberal imperialist and later Labour politician; Secretary of State for War, 1905–1912; Lord Chancellor, 1912–1915. Influential writer on philosophy.
141 *London Gazette* No. 27439, page 3612, 3 June 1902.
142 Ibid., No. 28207, page 9758, 22 December 1908.
143 Renamed 'War Council' in 1903.

were revised and several managers made specific recommendations on the management of railways during wartime. These proposals led to the creation in November 1912 of the Railway Executive Committee, which became the instrument of the Government's control in August 1914. The Executive Committee assembled in the London and North Western Railway offices at 35 Parliament Street, and the official Chairman was the President of the Board of Trade, but the Committee selected its own Chairman, Sir Frank Ree, Chairman of the LNWR. Upon his death in 1914, Sir Herbert Walker of the LSWR was elected unanimously by his colleagues. The welding together of the railway systems into a common organisation was not an easy task. Sir Sam reported:

> To a chairman of less tact, the leadership of such a committee, composed as it was of men wholly by nature or training possessed of strong argumentative powers, and to whom independence of thought and the 'lure of competition,' were the essence of their official careers, would have proved a task full of difficulty, not to say exasperation.

He commented that the committee was equally fortunate in the selection, as Secretary, of Gilbert Szumpler, a civil engineer, also of the South Western Railway.

In 1915, Fay was appointed a member of a committee under the Chairmanship of Lord Inchcape[144] to solve the problem of acute congestion at the ports. Sam 'had a struggle to avoid being given a military rank, preferring the freedom of civilian status'. There was consternation among the military at finding a civilian-suited figure with an un-military beard sitting among the generals.[145]

1916

Fay remained a member of the Railway Executive when he was appointed to the War Office in December 1916. Responsibility for military transport

---

144 James Lyle MacKay (1852–1932), created Baron Inchcape of Strathnaver, Sutherland in 1911, and Earl of Inchcape in 1929.
145 Edgar Stewart Fay, *Memoirs* (unpublished), page 41.

at the outbreak of war and for two years rested with the Quartermaster General, who from 1912 to 1919 was Lieutenant-Colonel (acting Brigadier General) Sir John Cowans.[146] The part of his organisation dealing with the movement of troops, guns, ammunition and supplies was the Movements Directorate under Major General Richard Stuart-Wortley, a member of the branch of a highly distinguished family. Fay knew one of them, Charles Beilby Stuart Wortley (1851–1926), who was a Director of the Manchester, Sheffield and Lincolnshire Railway and the Great Central from 1893 to 1922.[147]

In August 1916, in consequence of transport services failing to give satisfaction, particularly on the Western Front, Eric Geddes[148] was entrusted with an investigation into transport arrangements in connection with the British Expeditionary Forces, both at home and abroad. Shortly afterwards he was detailed to act as deputy to the Quartermaster General in matters of transport, with the title of Director General of Railways. Later in 1916, having been knighted, Sir Eric ceased to be deputy to the QMG, and authorised to report directly to the Secretary of State, and to attend meetings of the Army Council when matters pertaining to his department were under discussion. Sir Douglas Haig explained that 'The principle underlying the appointment was to employ individuals in wartime on work which they have been accustomed to doing in peace.' Sir Guy Granet,[149] General Manager of the Midland Railway, and a member of the Railway Executive Committee, agreed to act as deputy to Geddes in London, the situation in France demanding the latter's presence there.

In December 1916, Sir Guy asked Sir Sam to help, which he 'very willingly did', and attended at Granet's offices in the Hotel Cecil. His first

---

146 John Steven Cowans (1862–1921), who had been befriended by Sam at the time of the Boer War.

147 In 1917 he was created the first (and last) Baron Stuart-Wortley of the City of Sheffield.

148 Eric Campbell Geddes (1867–1943), son of a Scottish civil engineer involved in building railways in India. After a rebellious youth in Britain he went to the USA, working on railways. After many different jobs he was involved in India on railways there, impressing Lord Kitchener with his capacity for organisation. Returning to England in 1904 he worked for the North Eastern Railway and by 1911 had become its General Manager. It became the most financially strong company in Britain.

149 William Guy Granet (1867–1943), General Manager of the Midland Railway; Director General of Military Railways, 1915, and later Chairman of the London Midland and Scottish Railway, 1924–1927.

job was in connection with the supply of wagons for French railways, a growing demand throughout the war.

1917

On 6 January 1917 Granet asked Fay if he was prepared to take over the Directorate of Movements at the War Office, explain that the existing arrangements were anything but satisfactory. Sam replied that he knew something about the Movements Directorate, but he knew also that there were many military duties attached to it, of which he was ignorant, being, however, willing to do his best if requested to take the post. On the next day, 7 January, he received a phone call from Lord Derby, Secretary of State for War, asking him to call upon him at 11 am. He found Geddes and Granet already there. Lord Derby explained that he was very glad that Fay had agreed to take the position of Director of Movements, and that the position would be independent of the Quartermaster General. The change would take place at the end of a week when Major General Richard Stuart Wortley, Director of Movements, would take three weeks' holiday. A military deputy to Fay would be Ryley of the Adjutant General's Department, recommended by General Cowans.

Geddes told Sir Sam later that Lord Derby said if any difficulty was met with military officers, Fay should be made a full General. But Sam replied that he desired no military rank. The next morning, Cowans said he was a fool for refusing, arguing that the job was a military post. Sam replied that he was there to try to be helpful, and with goodwill hoped to pull through. Sam must have been weary of this particular exchange of views: his mind was set on not becoming part of the Army hierarchy. After a long discussion, Cowans promised to help him all he could, and Fay commented in his diary that he was as good as his word, right up to demobilisation. From that encounter he went to see Major General Stuart-Wortley, who was more upset and angry at his being deposed, however 'temporarily', than the QMG had been. Subsequently, Fay 'gave Messrs Geddes and Granet an account of his reception'. On 12 January 1917, Sir Sam had a long talk with these two, to decide a line of action at military meetings to follow, and on the 16th the Master General of Ordnance, Major-General Furse (Sir

William Furse, KCB), 'sent for me, or rather asked if he were to come to him, or he to me,[150] to discuss ammunition for Salonica'.

On the 19th, the Prime Minister, now Lloyd George, sent for him, and he went over to Downing Street. He met coming out Field Marshall Sir William Robertson, Chief of the Imperial General Staff, and had a word or two with him. It appeared that Lloyd George had instructed him what to tell me. He wanted 'a first-class railwayman to go to Russia in three or four days' time with a Military and Diplomatic mission to study Russian railways and advise'. Fay replied, 'Rather a tall order to give at a minute's notice.' After consideration he advised that George Bury,[151] the Vice President of the Canadian Pacific Company, was the best man; failing him, Thornton, General Manager of the Great Eastern Railway; and failing him, Aldington, Superintendent of the Great Western, was a good railwayman. But neither of the last two were equal to Bury for such a job. In making this recommendation Fay had in mind the long stretches of single line in Russia for which there was no counterpart in these islands. The Canadian Pacific, on the other hand, was mainly single line, reaching 3,000 miles from seaboard to seaboard. Bury would therefore be more able to appreciate the position than an English railway manager. Fay knew him, having seen him at work in Winnipeg, and his cheery optimism had impressed him. Bury had just left England for Canada, but Sam found him in Montreal. He returned to Downing Street and reported this, and the Prime Minister cabled Bury to return, next ship.

Also in January, Sam had to face some complaints of misdeeds of the Director of Movements staff. The most furious on paper was that a Roman Catholic priest had got drunk the night before embarkation of the troops to which he was attached. There were demands that orders be sent forthwith to all transport officers that for purpose of discipline they are under commands ('OC Commands say it ought to be dealt with by Court Marshall'). Sir Sam replied 'Sorry', and felt he might have added, 'What has this to do with the War, and why take up time of overworked men about a parson on the drunk?' The question of padres brought him later into conflict with Lord Salisbury, Chairman of the Advisory Committee on Church of England Chaplains:

---

150 Sam added here in parenthesis: 'This was a trifle sarcastic.'
151 George Joseph Aloysius Bury (1866–1958), Vice President of the CPR, 1914. Knighted 1917. Retired 1918.

He accused me of giving berths to Holy Roman priests while refusing them to Church of England parsons. I told him that every berth on long-distance transports was precious and needed for combatants; that clergymen of all sects had been refused permission to accompany troops... It might be that instances had occurred of berths being wangled by Roman priests, but it was contrary to instructions. He was none too pleasant and... looked upon me as a Jesuit. No compliment to my Huguenot ancestors!

On 2 February he lunched with George Bury, the day before he was to leave for Russia, commenting that 'He was in good form, ready for anything.' Luncheon on 10 February was at the Carlton Club with Granet, Eric Geddes and his brother Auckland,[152] Director of Recruiting, who said he had heard they were trying to swamp Fay with files at the War Office. This was a reference to papers forwarded to Fay 'upon subjects of no interest to Movements Directorate'. On returning to his office he took the files as they came in and minuted them all over the various branches: 'This for you', or 'You should see this'. The next day personal protests from the recipients were many. He told them the medicine was of their own prescription. 'This stopped the game.'

After a month, Sir Sam had 'become fairly well acquainted with the War Office and its peculiarities'. Before the War the staff there numbered less than 2,000, and within three years it had grown to nearly 15,000. The greatest increase was in connection with Military Intelligence and Censorship, which totalled upwards of 4,000, including counter-espionage, cipher examination and all the detail work and intelligence regarding the doings of allies, as well as enemy agents. Lloyd George called the War Office 'that tranquil sanctuary of the God of War'. Sir Sam commented on this that:

His experience of its tranquillity must surely have been limited to the regulation salute of the janitor at the main entrance prior to the

---

152 Auckland Campbell-Geddes (1879–1954), Acting Brigadier in France, then at the War Office, 1916–1917. Before 1914 he was Professor of Anatomy at McGill University, Montreal. MP for Basingstoke, 1917–1920. President of the Board of Trade, 1919–1920. Created Baron Geddes in 1942.

stately march up the marble stairway, to his reception by secretaries endowed with perfect bedside manners, followed by departmental chiefs who modulated their voice customary when conversing with ministers of the Crown.

He continued:

Had he explored adjacent rooms of that huge building, had he probed the heights above and the depths below, he would have discovered... an energetic and busy mass of officers and civil servants (men and women, thousands of them), intent on schemes for defeating the enemy, in organising instructing and providing the hundred and one requisites for our army in the several battle areas.

His battles for more accommodation were successful, but he had other fences to get over before settling down to a regular routine of work. One was a (continuing) fight by the Army to get him into uniform. The arguments were that he occupied a military post, and that under the King's Regulations no soldier need obey any order that he, as a civilian, might issue. It was settled eventually at an Army Council meeting, with Sir Willam Robertson in the chair. Fay had mentioned the question with him beforehand, and after hearing the pros and cons he said, 'I think you had better remain as you are.' It may seem strange that Fay refused the rank of General, only two or three steps above the one he already held, but he explained to his diary that he had no objection at all to the King's uniform:

But to walk down Whitehall in a general's dress, and be there saluted by real soldiers was repugnant to me. Further, if I had taken military rank, there were others of higher rank, to whom I might have to kow-tow. As an independent of a rather unknown quantity, I felt on safer ground.

He admitted 'to the book', that he held a commission as a Lieutenant Colonel in the Engineers and Railway Staff Corps, signed 'Edward R&I' and dated 1902. This recited, as do all Commissions:

You are at all times to exercise and well discipline both the inferior officers and men serving under you and use your best endeavour to keep them in good Order and Discipline. And we herby command them to obey you as their superior Officer; and you to observe and follow such Orders and Directions as from time to time receive from Us or any superior officer according to the Rules and Discipline of War in pursuance of the Trust hereby reposed in you.

If the generals had known of this Commission, he reflected, he might have had more trouble. The Engineer and Railway Staff Corps was a curious combination of prominent engineers and railway officials. It possessed a Colonel and a number of Lieutenant Colonels and Majors, but no rank-and-file. It was established for the purpose of rendering expert assistance in time of war, and 'singularly enough was the only military or semi-military force not mobilised as such during the Great War', though all its members, in one form or another, rendered service to the state throughout the great struggle.

Sometimes his visible rank proved awkward. He recalled that on one occasion a dug-out Colonel in charge of some transport arrangements on the Thames, who evidently had the King's Regulations in mind, argued at length upon his telling him exactly how he wished the work to be carried out. After a moment or two of hesitation however the Colonel came to attention when Fay said, 'Look here, Colonel, I'm not ASKING you to do anything, I'm giving you an ORDER.' Another problem was that among the War Office staff generally there existed a sympathy for Stuart Wortley (whose job Sir Sam had taken over), together with a resentment at the surrender to a civilian of a recognised military position. He felt there was nothing personal in it, but for a short time he had to bear the brunt of an unpleasant atmosphere and unhelpfulness. He discovered that rumours had been circulating to the effect that he was being paid an enormous salary, and that his motive in entering the War Office was to collect honours. He explained to the principal officers of the directorate that his salary was being paid by the Great Central Railway Company, and that whatever honours came to the department they were welcome to. He would take none from the War Office. He felt it was fortunate that he had known General Robertson, now Chief of the Imperial General Staff, during the South African War: he welcomed Fay straight away. They had a close and confidential relationship, and it was due to him and General Cowans that, after a time, a cordial relationship became established between Sir Sam and the War Office.

On 28 February he attended the meeting of the Military Members of the Army Council, having been asked to attend by General Robertson because of transport matters being involved in many of the subjects under discussion. Later in the day, he saw the Quartermaster General (Cowans) in the afternoon. He said, 'the duty of the general staff was "to think" not act, and that it was improper to deal with his supply officers and Director of Munitions in administrative matters'. Fay's distance from that assumption is not recorded by him.

One of Sam's difficulties in the work was communications with ports of daily embarkation: the need to know of their efficiency and daily problems. Use of the telephone and telegraph was barred on grounds of secrecy. He asked for messengers to bring a record from London termini of the day's transactions at the ports, but was told that there were no messengers available. He had to 'borrow' porters from Marylebone Station for the job. In February 1917 the Movements Directorate was reorganised, and Sir Sam took over as Director of Movements with, as deputy, a Lieutenant Colonel (acting Brigadier General), plus a Lieutenant Colonel as Deputy Assistant and a host of Majors and Captains in a list of detailed responsibilities. It is easy to see why the authorities wanted Sam to assume the rank of General, but also to understand why he wanted to be a free spirit in the exercise of the responsibility in which he had proven expertise.

On 9 March he recorded that Granet had been appointed Director General of Movements and Railways, to include the supervision of the three Directorates – Movements; Railways and Roads; and Inland Waterways and Docks – with Geddes as Director General of Transportation (France) and Inspector General of Transport, All Theatres. These complicated switches of duties and appointments were very necessary in the direction of quick decisions, explained Sir Sam, adding that they did not alter to any extent the relationship between him and Guy Granet. On 6 March he saw Granet about engines and wagons for France, which were badly needed. On 14 March, General Furse, Master General of Ordnance, just back from France, raised the question of railway wagons there. Fay said: 'Delay in getting his ammunition over to France was due to... the shortage of ships. He replied

"Then stop some ammunition and put ships on wagon supply." I agreed.'
Five days later: 'the French have given up repairs to 600 miles of lines,
and say we must do it. Haig asks for a hundred miles of line to be sent
out at once.' He attended a meeting at the Admiralty with Geddes and
Granet on 13 March, regarding a general shortage of ships: too many were
being lost to submarine attacks. Later the Shipping Controller calculated
that if the present rate of loss were to continue, 'There was a definite and
not-long-ahead date upon which the country would starve.' On 22 March,
Fay remarked that, 'Among the officers suggested as Inspector-General of
Communications is one who is a thick-head. If he is appointed and anything
happens in the shape of invasion, God help us.'

Not in his diary, but very much to the point at this time, the magazine
Truth stated that: 'Sir Sam Fay, who had been Director of Movements for
the past fifteen months, was taking over from Sir Guy Granet as Director-
Central General of Movements and Railways. As General Manager of the
Great Central Railway since 1902, he had acquired a reputation for railway
organisation second to none in England.'

On 29 May he was considering dock arrangements in France which had
been discussed with Ralph Wedgwood, Director of Ports.[153] On 6 April,
Good Friday, he registered a terse statement – 'America came into the War' –
and went on to say that he left home at 9 am in a snowstorm in the Daimler
car he had possessed since the war began. It had been sent from Coventry to
Grimsby just before the war, *en route* to Leipzig for the owners of the Sedan
Hotel at that place. It was held up by the outbreak of hostilities:

> a 25/40 hp open car, holding seven; goes well, beautifully appointed.
> I ought to have handed it over to Controller of Enemy Effects, but
> didn't, and kept it for the duration. It was better than the ordinary
> car allotted to principal officials of the War Office – I made good use

---

153 Ralph Lewis Wedgwood (1874–1956). His elder brother was Josiah Wedgwood (1st
Baron). Knighted 1924, created Baronet 1942. Educated at Clifton College and
Cambridge, where he met and befriended his second cousin, Ralph Vaughan Williams,
who later dedicated to him two of his compositions: 'In the Fen Country' and 'Sea
Symphony'. He became the Chief General Manager of the LNER, 1923–1939, and the
day after he retired (13 March 1939) an A4 Class locomotive 4469 was named after him
at Marylebone Station. Later he was Chairman of the Railway Executive Committee
from 1939 to 1941.

of it, and it saved time. It was sold after the war by the Committee for £1,000.

At the military meeting on 11 April, Fay reported: 'Good news from the Front: Our artillery splendid – 1,250 self-propelled bombs in a row, a yard apart, all fired electronically at once at 1,200 yards range.' On the same day, 'a meeting was finally set up organisation for emergency, i.e. invasion. Got it right', he thought. On 16 April, Clow[154] came back from France, 'telling a poor tale of disorganisation of staff arrangements there... The old gang, who were there before Geddes took over, fight with new crowd and prevent improvement'.

On 16 April, Fay met again Sir William Robertson, Chief of the Imperial General Staff, going out to lunch. He asked Sam how he was getting on and he replied that he had the hang of things. The CIGS then said, 'There's plenty of trouble about, isn't there?' Fay replied, 'Yes, we don't have to look for it, it comes.' Sir William said he would like to talk about it one of these days. The talk came about the following week. Robertson was very much concerned at the situation which had developed between the War Cabinet and the Army Council including Haig, as a result of putting the latter under Nivelle.[155] It was not only the placing of the Army under a foreign officer that gave offence, it was the manner in which it was done by the War Cabinet that astonished the British General Staff. No previous notification had been given to Robertson or Haig, or even to the Secretary of State for War. They pointed out that the composition of the War Cabinet was singular in that the Secretary of State for War was not a member of it, notwithstanding Privy Council Orders, repeated from Buckingham Palace on 20 April 1917, which clearly stated that 'the Secretary of State is to be responsible to His Majesty and Parliament for all business of the Army Council'.

---

154 William Clow, a protégé of the General Manager, Superintendent of the Line, GCR, also called up for National Service.

155 Robert George Nivelle (1856–1924), who succeeded General Joseph Joffre as Commander-in-Chief of the Armies of the North and North East in December 1916. In conjunction with the British armies he prepared the great offensive of the 16 April 1917, near Soissons, but after this near defeat he was replaced by General Henri Pétain in the command of the French armies. Nivelle was the originator of the order '*Ils ne passeront pas*' (They shall not pass'), though sometimes attributed to Pétain.

The first either of them had heard of French control was at an allied conference, supported by Lloyd George, who stated that the War Cabinet had decided upon it in the previous week at a meeting which Robertson was told he need not attend unless he had any special question to bring forward. Sam commented:

> The annals of the British army could have been sufficient indication to politicians that army chiefs merited confidence and consideration, or at any rate equality with foreign generals, allied as they were. The handing over to Nivelle – a General limited in experience – of the British Army – including its war material, without consultation with the army and without the knowledge of the Secretary of State for War or Parliament – filled Robertson with apprehension and alarm. On the one hand the safety of the British army was at stake; on the other it showed clearly a lack of confidence in his and Haig's ability, whilst the secrecy with which the agreement had been arrived at, shocked him. At a blow, all confidence in the War Cabinet ceased, never to be regained. Thereforward the War Office was at war on a new front – at home.

The CIGS stated that it was the first time that differences of opinion had arisen between the General Staff and the Prime Minister, particularly regarding the relative importance of Turkey in the war, and the suggestion of a large force in Italy. We had not the means either in men or transport capable of carrying on a really big offensive apart from the Western Front… France and Germany had been preparing for the conflict over many years… The Cabinet, when discussing Eastern movements, talked as if troops and ships were inexhaustible… It was a comparatively simple operation to convey and keep going large numbers of troops with ammunition and equipment across the English Channel, quite another to find big ships and continual supplies for armies in the east.

In his extended comment on this disagreement between the Government and the head of the armed forces, Sir Sam admitted that there was every sympathy with the Government at their difficulties – the Prime Minister's orations, which aroused the patriotism of the people, and the full value of the energy displayed in the social services, but what they expected was open confidence and helpful co-operation not hostility – an exhibition to our French ally of want of confidence in British Military leaders. 'Robertson expressed fear of an inconclusive peace, having regard to the position of Russia, the German victories, and the submarine menace... with the known views of influential politicians here and in France. Altogether, the CIGS was none too happy over the outlook.'

It is impressive to see the confidence existing between Sir Sam, a civilian, and the Chief of Staff of all the Armed Forces. Robertson was clearly a man of sufficient wisdom to be aware of whom he could trust with confidentiality in such sensitive matters.

On 21 April 1917, 'At Club had a long "jaw" with Cecil Harmsworth[156] on things in general, including sea fishing.' Fishing was one of Sam's outdoors activities, on which he was something of a well-known authority. Two days later he was asked to attend a meeting of the War Cabinet on the question of the closing of a store at Avonmouth Dock. He had to air a serious shipping question, but was asked to wait; which he did, all day. He deplored the bogging down of the Cabinet in such minor issues. He recalled later that General Smuts referred to this in August 1917, when he said: 'The War Cabinet is snowed under by papers and details. Ministers have no time to think out the really great problems of the war. At the end of the week the mind is in a haze owing to the number and complexity of the problems which have arisen.' About this time, Sam noted that the winter had lasted seven months: 'April the hardest on record.' Shipping losses were serious, in St George's Channel as well as in the Atlantic. Thousands upon thousands of horses were dying from lack of food.

However, on 1 May, at a Ministry of Movements meeting, attended by Fay, Geddes and Granet, Robertson asked how many ships would be required to bring 500,000 men from America to France and to maintain them on the same basis as English troops. Fay calculated 90 ships for three divisions a month, six weeks turn-round, six months to complete; to maintain with 5,000-ton ships, about double.

On 2 May there was a discussion as to the retention of 2,000 buses at 1

---

156 Cecil Harmsworth (1869–1948), MP, 1st Baron Harmsworth of Egham, 1939. Member of Prime Minister's Secretariat, 1917–1919. Chairman of Associated Newspapers, founded by his brother, Lord Northcliffe. In 1942 he published *A Little Fishing Book*. Published by Frederick Muller, 1944.

shilling each a day for use in case of invasion. Later that month Fay was at a luncheon for US railway officers, chaplains and others, who were *en route* to France. Fay sat next to the US Military Attaché. He noted also that Geddes had been appointed as Third Sea Lord as Controller at the Admiralty. Sir Philip Nash[157] was to be Geddes's successor as Director General of Transportation (France). Fay also met, on 9 June, General Pershing of the US Army, who had arrived in Britain the previous day.

As a further item of disenchantment with the War Office, he recorded on 11 June that:

The Chinese labourers we have been bringing through Liverpool and Folkestone have caught the mumps to the tune of 700 of them, and have had to be put in separate camps. There was a fiasco with them over their food. Some genius or other reported that a special food, in the shape of cuttle-fish and old-time eggs would be necessary to keep them healthy. Three shiploads appeared off Liverpool with the idea of landing the stuff for transit by rail to a southern port, and thence to France. The olfactory nerves of Liverpool's sanitary officials being duly assailed, a permit to land was refused. The ships were ordered to Dieppe, where a considerable number of Chinese worked in the army bakery. They laughed when presented with their "native food." They were grain-eaters from Northern China, despising Southern China's specialities.

The load was quickly dumped into the Channel after a voyage of over 10,000 miles.

On the same day he met Lord Derby with Granet to meet two USA officials awaiting information on transport questions. He saw Brigadier General Bernard Hitchcock,[158] Director of Demobilisation. He proposed setting up a little War Office especially for demobilisation. Fay thought he was going too far and that the existing arrangements could deal with it: 'It meant a new establishment, with all the attendant lavish expenses.'

---

157 Philip Arthur Manley Nash (1875–1936), Major General. Later (1922), Chairman of Metropolitan Vickers, Trafford Park, Manchester.
158 1877–1938. Played cricket for Hampshire, 1896; this qualification was evidently not enough to endear him to Sir Sam.

18 June 1917: Lieutenant Colonel Francis Woodbine Parish,[159] Director of several South American railways, was appointed Deputy Assistant Director Movements. On the next day, following Nivelle's failure, 'whispers had been going round the War Office of mutiny amongst French troops, and threats of marching on Paris'. The General Staff were distressed, fearing that unless Haig could obtain a success, the French would seek an armistice. 'If the Germans got to know about it and attacked, the position of the army would be very serious.' A long discussion was held at a meeting of the Railway Executive Committee as to sending 600 locomotives to France for the Cherbourg–Taranto service, which opened that this month for personnel.

Also on 19 June, he recorded a dinner at the Savoy given by Dicky Jowett, a bachelor, and leader in the Sheffield spring steel industry, 'rich and generous to a degree – giving frequent dinners to his friends and helping many a lame dog over a stile'. Iron and steel men were generally present as Fay's natural allies, but he was never happier than when he was entertaining a circle of men engaged in various industries, and the opportunity of meeting together outside strict business association. Fay records as present Sir Vincent Raven of the North Eastern Railway, now with Geddes at the Admiralty; F.C. Goodenough, of Barclay's Bank; Weir and McLennen, Glasgow; Charlie Clark and F. Mills, South Wales; Gordon Selfridge[160] was always welcome; Manville of Coventry Motors; and there was a sprinkling of railway managers, but no politicians: Jowett had no use for the 'Talkies'. Sam had sympathy for this view on the part of a man who much preferred action to talking about it. These meetings were especially appreciated at a time when the guests were all, variously, engaged in war work.

28 June: 'Unrest and slack working on the part of dock workers at Cardiff and other South Wales ports, threatening serious delay to the loading of military stores.' Fay went down to Cardiff to see a committee

---

159 MC, DSO, CMG, CBE, born in 1884, in St Petersburg, Russia. He married Dorothy Mary Catherine Drew (1847–1927), daughter of the Revd Henry Drew and Mary Gladstone. Drew was Curate of Hawarden, then in 1904 became Rector of Buckley, Flint. Parish died in 1922 from wounds received in action.

160 Harry Gordon Selfridge (1858–1947), the Minnesota-born proprietor of the departmental store in Oxford Street, London. A man like Fay, in dynamism, efficiency, and in providing staff training and customer service, and also in susceptibility to feminine charms.

of the men, and meet Ernest Bevin, Organiser of the Transport Workers' Union; Ben Tillett; and others:

> They talked from 10 am to 1.30 pm, in the style of two labour leaders. They were acquainted with me to know well enough to know that I could discount three parts of their verbiage, aware that it was not for my benefit as much as to impress the committee accompanying them. I said very little beyond reference to Mary Atkins at eighteen pence a day, and that if there was serious trouble in loading ships, the dockers might experience unpleasant results. They argued for workers' participation, particularly in arrangements for working ships, and gave numerous instances of bad arrangements, and made a good case.

Fay promised he would recommend to Lord Derby a greater representation on Transit and Port Committees.

On 30 June the Military Movements Committee studied maps in relation to the battles of Ypres and Passchendale:

> The telephone of the Quartermaster-General [Cowans] rang while he was out of the room. The Adjutant-General[161] said to me 'Answer it, Sam. Tell her, 'Yes Dear, I will be with you for lunch.' At that moment Cowans returned, answering the phone in the A-G's exact words. Then we laughed!'

Fay reflected that Cowans 'was a great lover – rather too great! In some ways he was a youngster of twenty, and I well believe that any pretty woman with design could twist him round her little finger!' No wonder he and Sam enjoyed a close friendship. He went on to say that Cowans possessed another outstanding qualification: 'he had a nose for finding the best possible assistants. Generals Crofton Atkins, Birkbeck, Percival, Torver,[162] and others on his staff could not be surpassed for knowledge and

---

161 Sir Cecil Frederick Nevil Mcready (1862–1946). Adjutant General, 1916–1918.
162 Brigadier General Cyril Scheister Crofton Atkins; Major General Sir William Birkbeck; Colonel Sir Harold Percival; Major General Torver, Colonel Commandant, RASC.

adaptability.' On 11 July, 'Thomas[163] came to lunch at Marylebone, and discussed things in general, including the railway position after the war, and train stop signalling'.[164]

Fay recorded further air raids during this period. He was awakened one night at 4 am in the Savoy Hotel, and by 5 am, guns were blazing all around:

> Everybody coming out of rooms with hair off and teeth out, where the natural wasn't fixed on. Funny crowd, including self. Stayed on first floor in waiters' room. Safe there as anywhere... Official announcement was twenty-five raiders over, but only six got through the barrage. A few killed, some injured, two enemy planes brought down.'

On 28 January 1918, things came a bit closer: at the Savoy Court flat again, Guns began to go at dinner time, and by midnight the bombardment was heavier than ever. Bombs fell, shaking the hotel, and when he got to his room, he found that Savoy Mansions, about 50 feet from him, had been struck, with much damage. On 17 December, he had recorded that:

> last night's raid on London had been pretty bad. St Pancras Hotel had been hit, and one guest who had half his ceiling down and his room demolished. He tried the electric light and also his bell without effect then found his door had jammed. He lit a candle and waved it up and down at the window: the police came up and took him in charge for signalling to the enemy.

By 17 August 1917 there was agitation among railway men. The position with the Drivers and Firemens Union was acute. There was talk of striking at weekend on an eight-hour day. Fay held a meeting with Great Central drivers on general conciliation questions, hoping that they would not come out at this time of crisis. 'But if their Executive so decided', he

---

163 David Alfred Thomas (1856–1918), MP for Merthyr Tydfil, 1st Viscount Rhondda, 1916–1918. Minister of Food Control, 1917–1918.

164 Presumably A.F. Bound's 'Reliostop' Mechanical Brake Control system of locomotive cab warning, which if a signal were passed at danger would cause an irrevocable full brake application.

wrote, 'no doubt they will obey.' Two days later he told Lord Derby the position:

> We could stand a fourteen-day strike. He met the enginemen again on 24 August... they asked for an increase from 7 shillings to fourteen shillings a day for drivers and ten shillings for firemen. Fay said there could be no discussion for wages post-war, but would consider a war-wage if they asked for it. They denied the existence of any truce, and said we had broken our promise made in 1915 not to settle with one Union without the other. Thomas, for the National Union of Railwaymen, said that if we increase what we have settled with them, they will demand another sovereign, and strike within a week to get it... Truly a nice mess!

He confided to his diary a lengthy comment that:

> arrangements with Labour during the War could certainly have been better managed. Increases in price of food and the discomforts of war-time fell upon all alike, and should have been met upon a common basis. Instead of any settled plan for dealing with the various sections of the community, the new State Departments, set up for the purpose of meeting an abnormal situation, were left to make separate arrangements with employees, without reference to the effect upon other people equally entitled to consideration. The result was a constant series of threats and strikes. In some instances the excuse for unrest was profiteering by manufacturers and traders. That profiteering and unduly high prices were demanded in the earlier stages of the war was undoubtedly true, but when the Government took over control and adopted rationing, that ceased. If at any time in the future a national emergency demands control and rationing, the first thing a government should do is stop profiteering in all directions, and thus avoid complaint from those who have perforce to buy the necessaries of life at whatever price traders may demand... The arrangement by which a 12½% increase of pay was given by Mr Churchill to munition workers upset the scales of pay in other industries from one end of the country to the other, and

for a time seriously prejudiced the national effort. A full blast of it fell upon the Railway Executive Committee. The most serious result of political ineptitude in this direction – the Metropolitan Police Strike – stands out as a glaring case of the absence of that vision... Every day of their lives political chiefs saw the police preserving law and order amongst men and women and boys and girls [working on buses and trams] who were in receipt of wages higher than their own... General Macready, in his *Annals of an Active Life* [page 310], said 'During my enquiries I came across cases of men with families who before the pay was [finally] increased were in a pitiable condition.'[165]

On 30 August, at the Port and Transit Committee, Sir Norman Hill, Bt, said he had asked the Prime Minister for 5,000 more men for a Transport Workers' Battalion. Fay 'doubted its wisdom, having regard to Labour suspicion of the use of military labour'.

Sir Sam visited the Front on 22 and 23 October, motoring to Monthuit, General Headquarters of Transport. He was 'quartered in a charming old French chateau in the middle of a park. Very comfortable; the half-dozen generals who run Transport living there in every comfort as to attendance and food.' On the 25th he went with Wedgwood, Director of Docks at Dunkirk, passing through English, Portugese, French and Belgian lines, and found not being in uniform a nuisance, having to show his passport, photograph and permit to cross lines. The 26th found him inspecting docks with Wedgwood at Calais and Vendreau: 'German prisoners and Chinese at work doing very well. Chinese at docks are excellent when properly used. They cannot stand extreme bombing. We have about 60,000 of them in France altogether.' He got back to Monhuit late, after calling on Cecil Paget,[166] in charge of the Railway Operating Division (ROD). He cooks his own food, having had a course of cooking in Midland Hotels:

---

165 Fay, *The War Office at War*, pages 83–85.
166 Sir Cecil Paget (1874–1936), Bt, Lieutenant Colonel, Royal Engineers, formerly Superintendent of the Midland Railway, and son of the Midland Railway Chairman, 1890–1911. Mentioned in Despatches, and awarded French and Belgian honours.

A 'very clever man,' he acted as the equivalent of the Superintendent of the Line, in conjunction with the French railway officers, with whom he was always on the best terms. His administration was a subject of admiration. He could have been graded as a general if he had so wished: he was more intent upon his duties than upon advance in military rank.

The following day he visited Arras, Vimy Ridge and Lens, then on to Bethune and Lillers, seeing much desolation and death. On 28th they motored to Boesinghe, Pilkem Ridge and Holthurst Wood: 'heavy fighting and terrific gunfire – told to keep fingers in ears. We took out our helmets, and had a bag with our gas-masks, but we did not have to use the latter. The scene on the road was marvellous – they were kept clear.' He commented that the Roads Directorate under General Maybury, and the Light Railways with General Harrison[167] at the head, interested and impressed him, as it did everyone:

But for their efforts the advance of the army to the front line, together with the transport of their supplies, could not have been so rapid, or so admirable as it was. Much of the construction and repair was carried out under shellfire. They deserved the encomium passed upon them by the Commander-in-Chief.

He returned to Boesinghe by rail motor to Paget's train, had tea with him, and went back to Hazebrouk for the night, dining with Barrington-Ward (later Superintendent of the Line, LNER). 'Travelled to St Vallery to look at our shipping arrangements, and later inspected Docks and new engine repair depot at St Etienne.' He returned to GHQ via Neufchatel and Abbeville, commenting in his entry for 31 October 1917 that the organisation in the offices there was good. Eric Geddes had done a good job; elaborate, but not more than prospects demanded. 'His drive and the enthusiasm he inspired saved the transport situation.' On 14 November he 'met Wordley, Army Medical Corps… Talked of operations at Great Central Hotel hospital.'

At this time he wrote that:

---

167 A railway engineer, later Chairman of Brazil Great Western and a Director of other South American railways.

Home Front Warfare was boiling up fiercely. Sir John French and General Wilson had... produced critical papers upon the conduct of the war, together with proposals for future management, and engaged with Lloyd George in formulating an attack on Robertson and Haig... A section of the House of Commons who looked upon Wilson as their military leader... was plotting in his interest, and all the elements were present for an open clash between politicians and the army.

The main results of the efforts of French and Wilson, commented Sir Sam, was a recommendation that a Supreme War Council should not only coordinate policy, but be advised on military operations independent of the Chiefs of Staff of each of the Allies. The Army Council was in favour of agreement to secure cooperation in policy, but not on an independent authority of technical advisers upon whom no such responsibility rested. The Prime Minister had indicated that Henry Wilson was to be the British Technical Adviser, a selection objectionable to Robertson and Haig for a variety of reasons, and Kitchener objected to his employment in any leading position. It was considered that his political activities were detrimental to army command. His frequent meetings with certain Ulster politicians at home and in France gave him opportunity for criticism of all and sundry.

All this personal intrigue was at a critical period of the war, when the Army was wasting away and the enemy rapidly increasing his forces for a final throw. Fay discussed with the American Army their move to France on 23 November and 3 December. He told them that the best thing would be for us to take over feeding and equipment (there were 250,000 tons to go across to France within six months) and for them to pour in troops as fast as their shipping would allow. They had plans for 500,000 to 1 million men, which Sam thought 'would produce the goods'.

On 28 November he recorded that 'Robinson, Great Central Engineer, came up last night about a threat of shopmen at Manchester GCR to strike on Friday over the 12½% increase given time workers by munitions people.' Meanwhile, negotiations were going on with the National Union of Railwaymen for an increase of ten per cent (10 shillings) in the war wage: 'Altogether it is an awful muddle and there is likely to be serious trouble all over the country in a week or two.'

On the same day he attended a Railway Executive meeting. The War Cabinet had met at 9.30 pm the previous evening, and decided that the Executive should settle with the NUR for a 6 shillings increase. 'This will probably be accepted because it will enable the Union to score off the Enginemen's Union who have got only five shillings on an award by the Committee on Production. Another muddle!' The 'muddle' developed, as Sam had predicted.

1918

On 1 January 1918 there was an incident in Lord Derby's room:

> Churchill got up in the middle of the meeting, saying that the Prime Minister wanted to see him. Lord Curzon remarked 'That is about the twelve and a half per cent, Churchill.' No reply. As he was going through the door, Curzon called out again 'It's about the 12½% that he wants to see you, Churchill.' Still no reply. Everybody laughed. The arrangement made by the Ministry of Munitions to pay 12½% on the wages of time workers in certain trades has upset the labour world all round, and by the time it finds a level, if it ever does, it is estimated to cost £120,000,000. Our men at Gorton (about whom he had attended a War Cabinet Labour Committee on 31 December) who had been out for a week, went back yesterday, the 12½% having been conceded by order of the War Cabinet Labour Committee.

He noted on 26 January that he had met Charnley, the Manager of the Cheshire Lines Committee, and discussed with him questions regarding a strike of men at Warrington on the 12.5% increase. There was trouble on other subjects, too: at a Railway Executive Meeting, the National Service Minister wanted to take over railway men, for 'combing out'. 'He can't comb out much from the Great Central Railway', remarked Sam. He recalled that at one station in Derbyshire only eight men out of a staff of thirty-eight reported for duty following Lord Kitchener's appeal.

There was a great onslaught by the sensational press on Lord Derby and

Robertson, practically calling for their retirement (21 January). 'The charges made are quite untrue,' recorded Fay. 'War hysteria flapped its wings up against the War Office. The defenders carried on with the work in hand and kept cool heads.'

Also on 21 January he saw four of the Great Central men who had been interred in Germany since they were taken off GCR ships at the beginning of the war.[168] They were placed in Ruhleben Camp, near Berlin, formed on a former race track north of the Berlin–Hamburg railway line. In addition to men on foreign ships in the ports from Grimsby, Hull and Boston at the outbreak of hostilities, there were those living, working and studying in Germany at the time, between 4,000 and 5,500 prisoners, most of them British. The authorities adhered to the Geneva Convention, and the camp evolved its own mini-society, with educational classes, a printing press, drama and music groups, an impressive orchestra, and a sports section. Prominent in the latter was Steve Bloomer (1874–1938), of Derby County, Middlesbrough, and England, who had been coach to the Brittania Berlin 92 Association Football team from 1914 when arrested.[169] Great Central ships seized were *Bury*, *City of Bradford* and *City of Leeds*, and the crews totalled 89.[170]

At a Railway Executive meeting on 23 January, Fay put a question on the agenda of drivers, firemen and guards who were refusing to lodge, or be away from home at night, because of being unable to obtain food. He offered to try to get the QMG War Office to give the companies rations for their men in those circumstances. Later, he had a meeting at Marylebone with traffic and loco inspectors from all over the line on the situation. It was generally agreed that if Army rations could be supplied, the problem would be met. On return to the War Office, Fay saw Crofton Atkins, the Director of Stores Transport, who readily adopted the suggestion and put up a minute to the QMG, who would have to go to the Secretary of State, but Fay hoped that red tape would not intervene.

On 5 February he noted that there were:

---

168 They reported that Germany had called up boys of sixteen for the Army, and was in pretty bad straits.

169 The Internees acquired celebrity status in Britain, and a Ruhleben Exhibition was held in Westminster Hall in 1919.

170 George Dow, op,cit. page 280.

All sorts of rumours as to Lord Derby's leaving the War Office. The wolves are on his track [but] he's too much of an Englishman and a gentleman for the political crowd of 'Do something, no matter what, but do something and drive blindly on, trusting to luck for it to come right.'

He feared the coming spring, with the Germans stronger on the Western Front, and unrest at home over food shortages.

On 8 February 1918 Fay had William Clow to dinner. They discussed a report he had made on camp railways: 106 miles, in various places, worked through Longmoor Instruction Camp at great cost, and very inefficient. 'Must put it on a better footing', he resolved. Three days later he brought up the subject at a War Cabinet meeting, and offered to take over the camp railways himself, with the help of Clow (Superintendent, GCR) and Randall (late Superintendent, GER), who had reported upon them, as he considered the arrangement through Longmoor unsafe and uneconomical. Lord Derby agreed.

Four days later he reported that the rumours about Lord Derby and Robertson being 'superseded by somebody' were still around. 'It's really deplorable', he commented, 'that these personal squabbles should go on and take up the energy of the people upon whom we rely to win the war.' He lunched at Marylebone with Thomas,[171] for the second time.[172]

At a QMG's meeting on 16 February, the Deputy Chairman of the Wheat Commission[173] said about the supply of oats for France that in nine months' time unless we import more freely from Argentina, as well as from the US, we should be seriously short. The Food Controller had fixed the meat ration without reference to him, and that in place of meat the population would certainly eat more bread. He reported attempts to get rice from Rangoon and maize from the Cape to help out.

The next day the papers announced the resignation of Robertson as Chief of the Imperial General Staff, and Wilson to take his place. 'A nice

---

171 John Henry Thomas (1874–1949). MP for Derby and General Secretary of the NUR. Ex-GWR footplateman.

172 The first time was recorded as on 11 July 1917.

173 Sir John Beale (1874–1935), a Director of the Midland Bank and later of the LMS Railway, and of Guest, Keen & Nettlefold in the iron and steel industry

state of affairs at the supreme crisis of the war!' regretted Fay. Parliamentary reports announced that Robertson had accepted the Eastern Command.

> I met Lord Rhondda, Food Controller, and reminded him that he had not replied to my offer of a deputy to Gibson, District Superintendent, Manchester Great Central, his food transporter, who had had an operation for appendicitis. He replied he had never heard of it, and thought Gibson was still at work.

From time to time Sam had reported on the severity of air raids on London. This day he wrote: 'Last night's raid pretty bad. St Pancras Hotel hit again.'[174] At this point, Sir Sam left his diary to devote a chapter of his book to an appreciation of Sir William Robertson, which is worthy of a lengthy quotation:

> Field Marshall Sir William Robertson, a Goodbye Letter dated 22 February:
> 'My Dear Sir Sam, I left the War Office in a bit of a hurry and had not time to come round to you and say adieu. Let me thank you for all the splendid and willing help you have given me and all the General Staff during the time we have been working together. You railway people are giving great service to the State, and it is a real pleasure to work with you. I shall always have the most pleasant recollections of our acquaintance, and I hope my departure may not entirely sever our connection. Yours very truly, W. Robertson.'

Robertson, referring in his book *From Private to Field Marshall* to the transport side of the War Office, wrote:

> I relied in a special measure upon the advice of Sir Sam Fay and Sir Guy Granet, of the Great Central and Midland Railways respectively, who placed their services at the disposal of the War Office during the war. They were in charge of the arrangements for the conveyance by rail, river and sea, of all men, supplies, stores, etc, for all theatres.

---

174 18 February 1918.

Sam remarked that Sir William Robertson had been referred to by writers on the war as 'Dour':

> This he certainly was not when free from all official duties. He had a keen sense of humour and entertained his friends with many stories grave and [light-hearted] gathered during his exceptional career from a trooper in the cavalry to Chief of the Imperial General Staff. Lord Riddell[175] refers to this in his *War Diary* and it was confirmed by Lloyd George. As an indication of contemporary opinion, Riddell records that before the war, when Robertson was at the Staff College, Winston Churchill said 'I should like to meet an extraordinary fellow named Robertson. From the lowest beginning, with acclamation he has risen to be the head of the Staff College – perhaps the most exclusive institution in the Empire.'

Colonel J.E.B. Seely[176] Secretary of State for War, 1912–1914, who led one of the last great cavalry charges in history, in March 1918, referred to Robertson as 'the greatest man in the British Army. He has educated himself in a marvellous way. He will probably become Commander-in-Chief. He has had a wonderful career. He knows several languages, and is a great authority on military matters. He holds the position with much dignity.'

Sam continued that in 1914, when Sir Charles Douglas, the Chief of the Imperial Staff died:

> Riddell said to Lloyd George 'Why don't they appoint Robertson? He is the cleverest man in the army and has done marvels with the Expeditionary Force. No army has been so well fed.' To which Lloyd George replied 'I agree. He is a fine fellow. Just the man we want.'

William Robertson (1860–1933) was, in Sam's opinion, a sturdy, far-seeing Englishman, who, by unremitting study and without advantage

---

175 Sir George Allardice Riddell, Bt (1865–1934). First Baron Liddell, 1920, Newspaper proprietor and Press Liaison Officer with Lloyd George's Government.
176 1868–1947. Later Baron Mottistone, and many honours.

other than the simple teaching of a village school, had risen to the head of a profession in which birth, education and wealth were deemed to be the basis of success. Fay had a very high opinion of Robertson, the first and only British Army soldier to rise from Private to Field Marshal. Educated in his local church school in Welbourne, Lincolnshire, he joined the Army in 1877 and was noted for his athletic prowess and for sword, lance and shooting. He was promoted to Sergeant Major in 1885, and with the testimony of his officers and the priest of his old parish, he was Commissioned to the Third Dragoon Guards in 1888. He was promoted to Captain in 1895, and attended the Staff College, Camberley, Surrey, despite his being opposed by his 'lacking in breed', in 1897. In spite also of his impecunity, he was saved by his posting to India, and received grants for qualifying as an interpreter, and in 1910 was promoted to Major-General Director of Military Training. He became Lieutenant General in 1915, and in December of that year, Chief of the Imperial General Staff. He was created a Baronet in 1919 and a Field Marshal in 1922. He wrote two books of *Memoirs*, in 1921 and 1926. Sam could write of him that:

> His upright and high-minded integrity and strength of purpose had as much to do with his career in the army as the outstanding ability and calm judgement which pointed him out as a successor to Kitchener, whose long residence in the East had given him very little knowledge of War Office routine or the peculiarities of party politicians. Robertson had joined the army when the acceptance of the Queen's Shilling was regarded, especially in country districts, as equivalent to going to the devil, and when among certain classes and sects, the officer was no other than 'a Gilded Popinjay' – a proud and swaggering fool.

This may have been true', wrote Sam:

> to some extent during the period of 'Commissions to Purchase,' a relic of the days when country gentlemen raised a troop for the King, and recouped themselves for a portion of their expenses by attaching fees to posts of officers of the troop. Still, the Gilded

Popinjay did not fail to shine in the building up of the British Empire, swagger as he might.

It says much for Fay that his observations on the sometimes ludicrous assumptions of the English class system were tempered by his acknowledgement of its successes. 'Robertson served through these changes of public opinion, but it is doubtful if early impressions of the gilded popinjay had been altogether eliminated from the minds of some prominent politicians even in the late stages of the Great War. Lord Derby was constrained to remark in November 1917: 'Some of the War Council think all soldiers fools, and they show it.' But Fay could insist that 'the intelligence, the training, and the general knowledge, not only of their profession but of business principles expressed by the great majority of British officers, was abundantly evident to those who worked closely with them during the war'. Haldane said he found them 'skilled experts, men with trained and reflective minds'. Fay observed that:

the face of the military man had changed with the years. Control of a rank and file, uneducated and wild, needed unbending discipline, accompanied by a stern countenance. Today, Thomas Atkins responds to a fair and kindly treatment, needing little of the rough court martial sentences of former years. The regimental officer's stiff upper lip has given place to the type met with every day in the City amongst leaders of finance, captains of industry and commerce in the Mart and on the Exchange.

That there were mediocrities in the army as in every other walk of life was apparent; but not in greater proportion than elsewhere. That there were a few – very few – whose ambition or jealousy came before duty to the country's cause was unfortunately in evidence. To the others, self-interest came a long way behind their duty to their chiefs and the nation's needs. The war would never have ended in England's favour had it been otherwise. The army overcame all the discouragements, all the carking[177] criticism, all the impatience of politicians craving for some dramatic stroke to strengthen their party,

---

177 'Carking': to be fretful, anxious. 'Carping': to find fault unfairly or frivolously. Probably in the New Forest vernacular they could be interchangeable!

by a stubborn adherence a to organisation and trained leadership, planned by Robertson, Haldane, and their contemporaries, and calculated to extend with the army's growth from thousands to millions.

Referring again to William Robertson's personal qualities, as he observed them at meetings, and recognised them in friendship, Fay recorded that:

In the chair at a conference, Robertson's bearing and manner kept discussion well within the limits of essential points. No searching for epithets or frothy expressions, beloved of certain politicians, emanated from him when on duty. Business to him was business, not an opportunity to shine in clever or sarcastic verbiage. He hated dubiety in regulation or order which might in any way tend to mislead officers or men, and looked for the same consideration at the hands of politicians, but he was no match for people trained in battles of words, and although he could speak and lecture very well, he did not consider it part of a soldier's duty to study the orations of past rhetoricians. He was not prepared to give an [impromptu] opinion on a serious situation, although often pressed to do so. After gathering together, in concert with all his colleagues, all the threads of a situation he held fearlessly on his course with the unconquerable stubbornness of the British soldier.

In January 1914 the Prime Minister had derided the idea of the possibility of a war, and argued that it was the most favourable moment for cutting down on expenditure on armaments; the Chancellor of the Exchequer constantly urged so, being intent only on producing a popular budget. The War Minister, being part of the government, was not to be blamed for the scarcity of funds, and the necessity for keeping the army up to date in its armaments and sufficient reserves, had to be ignored. Robertson asked, in 1913, for hand grenades to be supplied, but they were practically non-existing when the war started, and had to be improvised by filling jam tins with explosives. So, the 'Contemptible Little Army' was hurried across the Channel at a fortnight's notice to fight an enemy equipped with the most up-to-date weapons. They gave such a good account of themselves with their light field-guns, rifles and some tins of jam, that the enemy was convinced that the rapid and deadly rifle-fire could only have emanated from stacks of machine-guns. Their re-action to the jam tins is not on record.

In his *Memoirs*, Lloyd George wrote that it was the politicians who were the first to seize upon the real character of the problem, and to insist on the necessary measure to be taken to equip the army, in the face of prejudices, practices, and rooted traditions of military staffs: a statement which elicited from Fay the comment that this was an illustration of the 'wonderful prescience of politicians – after the event – and no less wonderful the elasticity of the English language when used for the dual purpose of lashing the Old Contemptibles and justifying political whifflers in Downing Street!':

Robertson was always against the political direction of six separate wars in addition to that on the Western Front – Mesopotamia, Egypt, Palestine, Gallipoli, Salonika, and East Africa: the Empire had become as widely engaged as during the long-drawn-out wars of the Napoleonic period. We had committed ourselves to expeditions on vast scale, in remote strategically unsound theatres: the Dardanelles alone had cost us more than a hundred thousand casualties. Haig had told the War Cabinet on 8 October 1917 that success on the Western Front would be decisive, and an indispensable condition of this is that the War Cabinet should have firm faith in its possibility, and concentrate our resources on seeking it and at once. As late as 25 January 1918 Robertson told the War Cabinet the same thing. No action was taken on these representations. Haig was moved to say: 'The unfortunate troops and their Commander are at the mercy of an organiser of defeat.'

Robertson's opposition to the promotion of multiple theatres of war brought him a clash with the Government, and encouraged machinations to have him removed.'

The Official History of the War, pp. 8 and 52, quoted Fay,[178] 'after reviewing the number of troops employed at home and 750,000 in theatres of war other than France, it is declared 'It is obvious that the British Armies in France could have been brought up to full establishment before 21 March 1918 without unduly weakening the forces elsewhere had the Government so willed.' But the Government did not so will. The unfortunate troops had perforce to stand upon the defensive, hammered day after day in an attempt to avert the greatest defeat ever inflicted upon the British Army: from 21 March to the end of May there were casualties of 343,812 officers and men, 70,000 taken prisoner, 750 guns and 4,000 machine guns were lost, together with great stores of material. The truth of Sir William Robertson's warnings had been dreadfully demonstrated.'

'Distorted facts will not survive the test of time', added Fay:

Fifty years hence when all diaries and memoirs will probably have shared in the light of history, when the prejudices have died with those who have specialised in sneers at Robertson's stubbornness and Haig's lack of imagination, intellect, optimism, his supposed thoughts and his religion... the historian of that day, viewing events from the heights, and endowed also with a sense of proportion often lacked by present-day writers, will be impressed by the figures of the world-wide conflict.[179]

He continued:

the historian will be surprised to observe the unfair and often spiteful criticism of military leaders by politicians, coupled with Press self-adulation and complaint that the Army – inadequately munitioned and mainly improvised – failed to achieve what French soldiers did, with all their preparations over a series of

---

178 Sir Sam Fay, *The War Office at War*, Hutchinson, London, 1937, pp. 135 and 136.
179 He gives here the figures for deaths, wounded and prisoners of war for Great Britain and Ireland, Dominions and Colonies, France, Italy, the USA and Germany. *The War Office at War*, op. cit., pp. 137 and 138.

years and failed to do. This coming with bad grace from those who were responsible for the country's unpreparedness upon entry into a war of such magnitude... He will note the politicians' lack of sympathy with the soldiers' aims and difficulties, coupled with support of intrigue within the army itself and unbelief in final victory. The historian may be puzzled in demonstrating the various factors to which victory was due. He will have no difficulty in identifying the people who in the Spring of 1918 all but lost the war.

But Robertson consistently held as a certain belief that whatever befell Germany's allies,[180] she would at the last resort summon all her forces for a mighty effort on the Western Front, at a time and place chosen by herself. But he never once felt or experienced privately or officially any doubt as to our ability to win, provided the Government, supported by the people, put into the what war has always required – adequate men, material and moral resolution – and put them in the right place and at the right time.

The memorial service at Westminster, minus military display or the trappings of war by which his life had been surrounded, served as a fitting farewell by old comrades to the English village lad who became a great soldier and a great administrator, admired for his abilities and beloved for his personal qualities. An example and an inspiration to the young soldier for all time!

Fay's numerous reflections on the conduct of the war give testimony to his admiration of Robertson. It has been remarked that Fay never seems to have aspired to membership of Parliament to inspire in others his balanced views on class, administration of justice and sound values. What emerges from his life, however, is that he had no patience with the party-political system, but a clear-headed and non-politically based belief in sound objective reasoning, cool assessment of expenditure and efficiency and practicality, and at the same time a deep respect for individuals and the problems they may suffer from the system.

---

180 Austro-Hungary, Turkey and Bulgaria.

Returning to his day-to-day diary of events, Sam noted in February 1918 that Henry Wilson had come in place of Robertson. 'The talk now was of moving one division from Basra to Egypt. Cowans said this morning that we all appear to be living in a lunatic asylum.' The food question was at this time at its most anxious. The food controller, Sir Guy Granet, was asked to go to the USA to coordinate and purchase and transport of these vital supplies. He intimated to Sir Sam that he should have to take on the Director Generalship, a thought which made him uneasy. Granet and he had worked together closely and harmoniously, and he disliked the idea of ceasing their active association. The three Directorates: Movements, Military Railways, and Inland Waterways and Docks, were a team in complete unison. Under Granet's supervision, following the Geddes organisation, the two latter directorates had been developed to a degree unforeseen at the beginning of the fight:

> The theatres of war had been supplied with locomotives and wagons, purchased and borrowed, in large numbers through the Railway Executive, one hundred and six miles of military railways in the United Kingdom, engineers had been trained, and been sent overseas to construct railways and roads, accompanied by material... and all other accessories for rapid construction... It was altogether a remarkable achievement within a short time.

'I was as comfortable in the interesting position of Director of Movements as could be expected,' said Fay, 'considering the sudden and often puzzling problems arising out of military operations.' But he knew that someone else who could possibly disrupt the whole department might be appointed, and he therefore assented to the appointment, and that his deputy, Colonel Delano-Osborne,[181] should be the Director of Movements.

On 12 March, at a Railway Executive meeting, there was a further discussion of the reduction of passenger services to 50% of pre-war: 'Seems impossible without failing to carry people on war work', commented

---

181 Osborne Herbert Delano-Osborne (1879–1958). Later, Major General and Governor and Secretary of the Royal Hospital, Chelsea, 1933–1938.

Fay. Three days later he recorded that he had a long talk with Nash.[182] He wanted Thornton, the Great Eastern Railway General Manager and a US citizen not yet naturalised, to be Secretary to the Transportation section of the supreme War Council and to be made Brigadier General in Paris, with an office in London. Fay could not agree, 'because it is likely to cause friction', though twelve days later he made Thornton Director of Movements and Railways in Paris. On 19 March, Fay saw Lord Derby about his position, who said he was glad he 'had agreed to take on Director General of Movements and Railways with a seat on the Army Council'.

Two days later the Germans launched an attack on the Western Front, lasting three days:

Serious – losses heavy – over 40,000; all reserves used up on the first day. The weather is all in favour of the Huns – very dry and fine with ground mists. Really the devil seems to be on the side of the Hun. Last year when we were attacking it rained continuously; now we have the driest and finest March I ever remember.

On 25 March he reported, quoting Haig, that 'the army is fighting magnificently, retreating in good order'. But the situation was very serious:

losses so far about 75,000. The French were moving up 120,000 men, but the Germans are still advancing. Everyone in the War Office is very bitter in condemnation of the War Cabinet, who had been warned again and again by Robertson and the Army Council. If the country only knew the facts they would storm Downing Street.

On 28 March:

[the] QMG, Cowans, wrote a very nasty minute to Osborne because he did not get a lady friend of his out to India, contrary to instructions. This gentleman will get the push one of these days with his women friends if he is not more careful. The

182 J.F. Nash (1875-1965), US citizen.

experience of the Cornwallis-West affair[183] caused no caution to him, apparently.

There was a report that the nurses at Peronna[184] were 'magnificent': 'Although the place was heavily shelled they went about their duties just the same as in peace time. Our evacuation of the wounded was in excellent form throughout the whole front.'

From time to time Fay commented objectively on purely military matters on both sides: in his entry for 31 March 1918 he recorded that south of the Somme, 'The Boche seems as hard up in that sector as ourselves, both sides having fought to a standstill.' By 2 April there was 'Great concern about the transport position in France.' The French were using the line through Beauvais and Ramscamp for moving divisions of their Army, thus cutting off supplies from the north to depots in the area. 'If the enemy advanced beyond Amiens towards Abbeyville it would be very serious – the British army would be penned within a narrow strip with their backs to the sea, and would have to be equipped by sea via Calais and Boulogne, Dunkirk being under severe shellfire and bombing.' The next day's entry included his view that if the Boche advanced much further:

One could see the prospect of the biggest tragedy in history. If our men could not keep the enemy back when they had completed a year's work of wire and trenches, there was great risk that they may not be able to do so in the open country. The poor, silent mass of English men and women know nothing of the prospects, thanks to the camouflage of the Press, printing only stories of heroism. Meanwhile, the enemy is massing… Parliament does not meet, and

---

183 Mary Fitzpatrick (1858–1920), of an aristocratic Irish family, became at the age of 16 the mistress of the Prince of Wales. The affair was discovered, and she was swiftly married to William Cornwallis-West (1835–1917) of Ruthin Castle, and she had three children. She began a relationship with a 23-year-old shell-shocked Sergeant of the Royal Welch Fusiliers, Peter Barrett, and using her influence in society (her first daughter, Constance, married the Duke of Westminster, and her son George became the second husband of Winston Churchill's mother), she contrived to have Barrett promoted in the Army, in which Cowans played a part. The case caused a crisis in the War Office.

184 Péronne – military hospital. A town in Northern France which changed hands regularly during the war.

the War Cabinet talks of calling up men, but does nothing drastic
such as the situation demands.

At the Army Council Meeting on 27 April the President, Lord Derby,
announced that it was his last meeting, 'which was not a surprise, for it had
been expected for some time that he would be "kicked out"'. On the following
day he sent for Sam to say goodbye and to thank him for his help during his
period of office. On the 20th, Sam went to Charing Cross to see him off
on his way to Paris by the 11.50 train. The same day the King appointed
by Letters Patent the composition of His Majesty's Army Council – eleven
members, including the Rt Hon Viscount Alfred Milner, GCB, GCMG, as
President, two Lieutenant Generals, two Major Generals, and Sir Sam Fay.

Returning to matters in hand, Fay records that the situation on the
Western Front was the main thing that mattered, 'But the administration
of an army of five millions wants its head; and questions which are
accumulating will not improve by keeping. The feeling in the War Office
against politicians is bad for the Army, and for the country.' His entry for 2
May 1918 was that 'Churchill is in France with Lloyd George and Milner,
discussing war strategy. They all know, or think they know, more than the
Army Chiefs.' About this time he confided to his diary that 'Because we
have not enough side-shows a new one is being started in Northern Russia.
Troops and transport officers and personnel are to be sent to Murmansk,
together with railway material.'

As the position worsened, Fay asked General Wilson if the rumours were
true that we were to give up the Channel ports. On being asked why he wanted
to know, Sam replied that, if so, the army would be starved and London
too, because the western ports were congested, and railways overstrained,
so that no train ferries could sail from Richborough, the Thames, Dover
or Folkestone, and possibly not from Newhaven either. He had ascertained
that the Admiralty were not prepared to convoy west of the Isle of Wight,
and as Southampton was full up, there was little hope of help. Asked by
Wilson what he proposed to do, Sam replied that he could see no other hope
but Poole, which would require a great deal of alteration to take the traffic.
'Wilson was much perturbed: "You had better start today," he said.'

'To crown it all' continued Fay, 'the Chief of the Imperial General Staff
[Wilson] was pressing upon the French General the necessity of abandoning

the Channel ports over the defence of which war was declared. Foch and Field Marshall Haig refused to agree.' On 7 April, Fay set the Poole scheme going. He recorded that on the 11th, he was looking round for railway sidings, and the harbour alterations, in the event that we lost the Channel ports. On 4 June 1918, there was speculation that Paris was to be evacuated or fall into enemy hands. 'In a country like France it is not the opinion of the wealthy and intelligent that counts. It is the opinion of the masses who do things,' observed Sam.

A shortage of men for the combatant forces was a frequently mentioned problem. Grade 'B' men were being rushed through training and sent into the war area. Their relative unfitness caused a great deal of anxiety to the Commander-in-Chief, and Fay commented that a better example of warrior might be found among those 'sheltering under the umbrella of varying hues of indispensability'. He quoted the Monthuit poet,[185] who wrote:

I know a man who lived in Notts/ His face was one of those with spots;/ He never read, he couldn't think;/ He often nearly died of drink;/ – a man whom you and I could call/ A thorough undesirable./ But he possessed a near relation/ who was a personage of Station/ – a man who wielded an Immense/ and beneficial Influence./ Today I met him over here/ Accoutred as a Brigadier!'

On 6 July 1918 Sam recorded that he and Lady Fay attended the service at St Paul's Cathedral for the Silver Wedding of the King and Queen. 'Our row of seats was allocated to the Army Council and their womenfolk. An impressive service.' The next day, he and two high-ranking officers of his staff visited Keyhaven, a small harbour on the Solent. This was to discuss a new site, perhaps Newhaven, for use in case of the loss of Dover. His son Edgar, who had, with his mother, accompanied Sam on this visit, commented that it was strange to recall that so close to the end of the War, the Allies were so impressed by the enemy's last offensive[186] we contemplated the loss of the Channel Ports.[187]

---

185 A nom-de-plume of Sir Eric Geddes.

186 Ludendorff's final great offensive was on the 15th. It was defeated by 10 August, and the end was in sight.

187 E.S. Fay, *Memoirs*, page 42.

On 11 July he was reminded forcefully of the state of the War Office when he opened the door of a Major General's room and was met by a gust of violent and blasphemous language. For a moment he thought some serious quarrel was going on, but saw there was no one with the General, who, upon Fay's entry 'ceased his imprecations and said "Don't take any notice of me, I'm only having a blow-off. Here I am, sweating blood trying to keep things going, and can get no final decision. The whole ---- place is withering."'

One week later Fay went for a run over the new line from Hesden to Frevent and Candas Cannaile.[188] As an emergency work he thought it was very well done: 'Rough railroading, but good enough.' At a poorly attended meeting of the War Cabinet on 25 July there was a request for a supply of wagons to Italy; it was agreed to send 10,000 English wagons to France, which would supply Italy. He mentioned that the Controller of Mines, Guy Calthrop, was there, the General Manager of the LNWR.[189]

On the Sunday, the 28th, he crossed to Calais, and from there to GHQ, where he received a 'very cordial welcome'. The small dinner party that day included Sir Douglas Haig and his Private Secretary Sir Philip Sassoon,[190] with both of whom Sam went for a pre-breakfast walk around the grounds at 8.20 am on the following morning, and again with Haig alone on the next day. He recorded, not for the first time, being impressed by the calm and confident manner in which Haig discussed the various subjects under review. He complained of the unintelligent interference to which he was subjected, and though he resented it, he spoke without heat. Sam commented:

As a student of military history, he doubtless knew of the difference between Governments and Commanders which often became acute in the stress of our Continental wars... but he contented himself by remarking 'What a lot of weaklings we have in London at the present time, and how ignorant they are of the first principles of

---

188 Near Abbeville, on the Somme.
189 1870–1919. Created Baronet in 1918 for his War service.
190 Philip Albert Gustave David Sassoon (1888–1939), MP; of the Jewish families of Sassoon and Rothschild; Private Secretary to Douglas Haig. Cousin of the poet Siegfried Sassoon.

war.' It is possible that his confidence at this time was strengthened by belief that the enemy had shot his bolt... and the signs of weakening were pronounced.

'Returning to London from GHQ was to exchange the cool breeze from a river bank for the fevered atmosphere of a jungle', he observed.

At this point in his history, Fay records that in his diary for 23 April, an outstanding example of government interference in military affairs was the appointment of Lord Milner[191] as Secretary of State, who from the first day of his appointment interested himself in transport on the Western Front. On the very next day, Milner told Fay that he did not approve of a new Director General of Transportation – a position set up by Eric Geddes in 1916 – to sort out the chaos into which the Army administration had fallen. Milner felt that things had changed, and transport should revert to the Quartermaster General's authority. Such a reversion was against the wishes of the Commander-in-Chief. Sam received a letter on 27 April from General Nash,[192] who argued strongly that 'DGT, as a separate institution is ABSOLUTELY necessary, and the Administrative Services must follow and fit in with the DGT's... policy'. Sam replied that he did not follow the argument that had been set out. The DGT was directly responsible to the Commander-in-Chief, while carrying out the demands of the QMG without being 'subordinate' to him; an arrangement making for delays and inefficiency and additional work.

On 18 May, the Quartermaster General wanted to see Sam at 10.30 am, to get a clear picture of what was happening. He was told that 'We railwaymen are in the army to help, not to obstruct, in this crisis', and he had doubts about the policy of competence of the military man to conduct transportation. However, Milner and the CIGS asked for his view, and he told them that, under the present stress, as everyone else had agreed, he would not object. A week later, Fay suggested at a meeting in the Secretary of State's room that if there were a problem with who should be

---

191 Alfred Milner (1854–1925). Secretary of State for War, 1918–1919, in place of Lord Derby. (See pp. 138, 140, 152, supra.)

192 Major General Sir Philip Arthur Manley Nash (1875–1936), DGT, 1917. He had worked for the GNR, 1897–1899, and then for the East India Railway. Inspector General, Transportation, 1918–1919.

Director General, he recommended Ralph Wedgwood for the post. He saw Wedgwood subsequently, who replied he would have nothing to do with it: 'The army got into a mess before, and were going to get into another now: let them get out of it their own way.' Sam urged him to reconsider, but 'he was deaf to any argument'.

Haig wrote to the Army Council objecting strongly to any change in the Transportation Directorship as being inexpedient, recommending that no change should be enforced, and a decision postponed until the tactical situation was less acute. The Secretary of State, despite the strong urging of the Commander-in-Chief of the armies fighting the War, and their reliance on the maintenance and movement of his troops, urged Haig to carry out their decision 'forthwith'. Milner wanted Fay to tell Haig what the organisation of Transportation should be. Sam objected strongly (exercising his independence of military rank), claiming that the whole responsibility was on the shoulders of the Commander-in-Chief, and he surely should have the organisation he considered suitable. 'To dictate to him was unfair.' At the end of a long argument, Milner wrote to Haig, asking if he would take advantage of Sir Sam's experience in deciding on the organisation, and Sam himself had no objection. Haig replied to the Army Council, saying that he would 'gladly avail myself of Sir Sam Fay's knowledge and experience as soon as I have prepared a general outline of the remodelling that it is considered it can be undertaken'.

On 28 June, Fay wrote to say that letters on the correspondence on transportation questions should be shown to him before dispatch. A Minute to a subsequent meeting of the Army Council by the Secretary of State said: 'It would have been better if all the letters had been shown to Sir Sam Fay.' The Secretary also advised Haig that correspondence on transport questions rested with Sam and not with the Quartermaster General, as he might have been led to suppose. Fay noted that 'this sort of thing would not have happened in the time of Derby and Robertson. The Commander in Chief would have been asked his views BEFORE the Army Council DECIDED.'

The whole episode convinced Fay that open dealings were things of the past, that 'in future I must probe the motives and study the methods of a new politico-military combination at the War Office'. It was to his dismay to learn on 5 July that Marshal Foch was arranging for the Transport Chief to be at his elbow at all times to tell him how the armies could be moved: 'While we are pressing Haig to put transport under the QMG, Foch is working exactly the other way about.'

On the 12th, the Secretary of State urged Fay to go to France and settle questions with Haig and the Quartermaster General. He agreed to go in the next week. On the 18th, Sam met Sir Douglas Haig and gave him his scheme of organisation. 'With Scotch caution,' he reported, 'Haig neither approved nor disapproved, but was very complimentary on what railwaymen had done for him, thinking that the Army Council had not really recognised what we had done.' He invited Sam to dine with him that evening, and he sat between Lawrence[193] and Trenchard.[194] Afterwards, he had an hour with Haig, who agreed with his scheme.

They were in broad agreement about personnel appointments, though as the Army Council decision had to be obeyed, the Director General Transport was to be responsible to the Quartermaster General instead of direct to the Commander-in-Chief.[195] On reporting to Milner what had been arranged, the latter asked Fay who he thought ought to be appointed as DGT. Sam replied that the only competent man on his staff was MacLaren Brown.[196] The next day MacLaren Brown saw the Secretary of State, who approved his appointment. However, at the beginning of September Milner reported to him that statements had been made that MacLaren Brown's experience was not of the character from which General Managers were made (one critic asserted that McLaren Brown was only a ticket agent, and knew nothing about railways). Fay sent to him the man's history, which clearly disproved such a story, and in addition gave him a memorandum, in which he stated:

The selection of a General Manager of a railway is governed not by technical knowledge entirely, but by the administrative ability of the individual, irrespective of the posts he has filled. As examples, on the twelve principal lines in the United Kingdom, the General

193 Sir Herbert Alexander Lawrence (1861–1943), Haig's Chief of Staff.
194 Hugh Montague Trenchard (1873–1956), Head of the Royal Flying Corps in France. Prominent later in the RAF in the Second World War.
195 Later, the Prime Minister himself disagreed with the new arrangement of the status of the DGT.
196 Lieutenant Colonel (later Sir) George Maclaren Brown (1865–1939), Assistant Director of Movements and Railways; former General Manager of the Canadian Pacific Railway.

Managers comprise 6 Operating and Commercial Officers, 2 Civil
Engineers, 2 Mechanical Engineers, 1 Barrister and 1 Solicitor.

In a letter to Douglas Haig on 3 September Milner expressed his satisfaction
with the appointment of MacLaren Brown, having received from
'authoritative quarters' very best reports of him. Before sending off that
letter, Fay had received an invitation to take on the job of Director General
of Transport (France) himself, but answered with a firm refusal, not wanting
to serve such a position under a Quartermaster General.

More urgently, on 18 October, the French railways were on the brink
of breakdown. On 29 October at the Railway Executive Committee, 'the
question was discussed of more railway men to meet the working of lines in
the event of the Boche giving in or being driven back. Not much chance of
getting more men from home.'

The long argument as to whether the DGT was to be subordinate to
the QMG rumbled on into November 1918, with Sam Fay and Douglas
Haig wanting the GDT to be autonomous, and the politicians, with their
sympathisers, and the French Generals, disagreeing. Sam noted in his diary:

If the War was not practically at an end[197] the arrangement for DGT
to be part of QMG establishment would have to be cancelled, and
that quickly. Even now I doubt if we shall end matters without
falling out seriously with the French. The fact is, the British and
French railwaymen understand one another, and are prepared to
give and take, but the French railwaymen do not understand the
British military man.

Agreement between British and French transport officers broke down, and
Sir Sam had to go to Paris. He called on M. Claveille,[198] who had charge of
railway for military as well as civil movements. After his return to England:

Fresh disagreement broke out when the French declared themselves

197 This was on 13 November. The Armistice Agreement of 11 November, not being an
actual Peace Declaration (the peace terms were not agreed until the Paris Conference of
28 June 1919), must have seemed to be inconclusive at the time.
198 An engineer, and former Director, of the State Railway.

unable to provide trains for miners and pivotal men whom we were demobilising for urgent work in England. Questions of demobilisation were insistent [at home], so this problem was settled by correspondence rather than by time wasted in travelling.

At the Armistice, Fay lost the help of MacLaren Brown, who was called back by the Canadian Pacific Railway, but Fay himself was by no means out of the wood. At a meeting on 21 December, he learned from the Secretary of State that General Cowans wanted to take back the transport work (vacated by MacLaren Brown), and Milner asked Sam if he was to remain 'for a considerable time', to which the answer was that:

> he would be glad to get away at once, but there were many things to clear up, and he disliked the idea of handing over his transport team, now working completely in unison, until demobilisation was completely under way. To which the Under-Secretary, MacPherson[199] remarked that to make a change now in organisation would be fatal, looking at what had been the state of affairs before [Sir Sam] came in.

Fay's concern was vindicated when, on 19 January 1919 a telegram came from Haig, expressing his grave anxiety on the transport situation, which had grown steadily worse; not only due to French difficulties in finding men and rolling stock, and for civilians retiring to their homes, but also American demands and our own requirements for demobilisation of troops. Equally serious were the demands of British railway men who, in common with the whole Army, clamoured to be sent home. They were getting out of hand and needed dealing with.

Having seen the country through a particularly important period of the end of the War, Fay reverted in his diary to an account of other events during August 1918 and following. He wrote that on 30 August there was a strike of London policemen: 'the most serious event in this country for very many years'. He had meetings with the Secretary of State to discuss the problems being experienced with the French Director General of Transport,

---

199 Ian Stewart MacPherson (1880–1937), MP for Ross and Cromarty, 1917–1935, created Lord Strathcarron in 1936.

but each time they were interrupted by Milner being called to the War Cabinet on police strike matters. On 1 September, an announcement was made that the Adjutant General, Macready, had been appointed as Chief Commissioner of the London Metropolitan Police Force, having told Fay he had been persuaded by Lloyd George that it was a national necessity that he should go to Scotland Yard. Sam noted that it was a great loss to the War Office, because Macready was very able, and extraordinarily versatile. He also commented that although soldiers were considered (by politicians) to be fools:

> when the Cabinet found themselves up against a really serious situation at home, they discovered at the War Office an Old Contemptible leader who was capable, not only of maintaining discipline, but of commanding the respect of such a force as the London Police, and they could find no one else equally competent.

Fay managed eventually to meet Milner without interruption, to discuss the case for support problems at the Front. He expressed feeling unsafe with having only 400 miles of rails in reserve for the provision of lines to follow up the German retreat. On 3 September he was given a reserve of 500 miles for the end of October, in addition to 25 miles a week new construction from then onward.

The next day he discussed with Sir Alexander Butterworth,[200] head of a committee to settle costs with French authorities on all railway matters, on the question of pulling up lines in France. Five days later Fay went to Richborough Port with General Cooper to meet Lord Milner there. He showed them round the barge quay where were sent off about 6,000 tons a week to France; the train ferry which took on fifty-two wagons of all sorts – ammunition, guns, tanks, pill-boxes, etc – and also the barge-building establishment, and incidentally the building of seaplane carriers for the Navy.

The next day, at Milner's request, he took the Prime Minister of New

---

200 Alexander Kaye Butterworth (1854–1946), General Manager of the North Eastern Railway. Father of George Sainton Kaye Butterworth the composer (1885–1916), dedicatee of Ralph Vaughan Williams's *London Symphony*, but killed at Pozieres, on the Somme, 5 August 1916.

South Wales, William Hughes,[201] to see Geddes, First Lord, to fix up for Australian troops to have leave. He described Hughes as: 'An energetic little man, very direct and incisive in speech and action.' Hughes asked Fay what he was in civilian life, and on telling him, Hughes replied, 'We all get into queer places these days, don't we?'

On 23 September there was a strike of railwaymen in South Wales. 'They asked for ten shillings, got 5 shillings, making total bonus 30 shillings a week.' The next day the strike was spreading. 'Our men on the Cheshire Lines are affected.' On the same day, ammunition was pressed for in France, in preparation for a big push, and the Executive Committee asked him for forty-five trains of sixteen vehicles each, for use by the American army as ambulance trains.[202] On the 25 September, the Board of Trade discussed the Railway Enginemen's strike, and issued a notice that all men who did not return on Friday be relieved of exemption certificates and sent to France.

'Shackleton of Arctic fame came over on 4 October with specimens of equipment for our men who are at Archangel and Murmansk, together with samples of rations.[203] Very interesting,' wrote Sam, 'The clothing is not so heavy as our ordinary winter clothing, although more cold-resisting.'

On 8 October there was a meeting in the room of the Secretary of State with Churchill and Seely,[204] his Secretary, as to locomotive engines versus tanks. 'I had settled a programme with Sir E. Moir (Ministry of Munitions) which included output from the North British Locomotive Company, but Seely had shifted them off onto tanks. It was decided that locomotives held the field.'

The 24th of that month saw Fay engaged with the General Staff:

---

201 William Morris Hughes (1862–1952).

202 The GCR built two, though the second was not completed. The Company had supplied three nine-coach ambulance trains in 1915. (Dow, op. cit., Volume III, pages 280 and 301.)

203 This was the intervention in the Russian civil war, following the Revolution of March 1917, in which the Menshevik Party had promised Russian participation in the war against Germany. However, their Provisional Government was overthrown by the Bolsheviks, determined to take Russia out of the war, in October of that year. The British and American troops withdrew in good order.

204 John Edward Bernard Seely (1868–1947), MP, 1st Baron Mottisden. A former Secretary of State.

fixing up ideas for an Armistice for the Western and other fronts. Very difficult from the transport point of view: while we want the Boche to get out of France and Belgium, the rolling stock is wanted for moving and feeding the French civilian population, apart from the requirements of the British, French and American Armies.

The discussion continued on the next day, and then turned to the difficulty with railway personnel. The French were on the verge of a breakdown. We were asking America to send us 10,000 men for service with our Railway Operating Division in France.

Two days later Tim Harrington[205] gave Fay a copy of a memo prepared after a meeting with the War Cabinet; he was afraid they would give away too much in the Armistice. The French, it was thought, will not trouble about anything else but Alsace Lorraine, whereas we want an all-round settlement to prevent Germany from breaking out anywhere again. 'The fear in some quarters was that if we drove too hard a bargain it may lead to Bolshevism in Germany. Austria had caved in and placed herself at the disposal of the Allies, and by the 31st the enemy on the Western Front appeared to be crumpling.'

At the end of October, Colonel Lawrence of Arabia called at the War Office. He had been helping the Hadjaz Army and apparently was the real commander of those forces. He went three times into Aleppo while it was in Turko-German occupation. He was recommended to the King by the General Staff for a CB and a DSO, but he said he was an Arab soldier, and did not want any decoration.

A meeting of the Ministry of Movements was held on 4 November, and went through the terms of the Armistice which had been settled at Versailles for presentation to the Germans when they gave in. 'The Americans, British and French forged ahead again yesterday, 8 November, and it was decided we should go to France GHQ, and onto Paris on Friday next.'

On the 9th, the German plenipotentiaries had arrived to discuss the terms of the Armistice. 'The only complaint they made was that the butter

---

205 Major-General Sir Charles 'Tim' Harrington Harrington, Deputy CIGS. Later Governor of Gibraltar.

supplied to them was not good.' On the 11th, 'Bells are ringing for the signing of the Armistice.' Fay went with the Army Council to Buckingham Palace to congratulate the King on victory:

> After signing our names in the visitors' book, we went to the King and Queen in the large dining room looking over the balcony at the front of the palace. The King made quite a good speech, thanking all of us for what we had done. He spoke very well, and was evidently moved, as was the Queen.[206] They chatted with us for some time afterwards. The King told us that the massed bands were to come and play national airs at 12.45, and that we ought to stay for it. There was an immense crowd outside, and we went down and stayed in the Courtyard. The King spoke a few words, which carried far, though his voice was husky.

Sam then went to the Carlton Hotel for lunch, through the excited crowds, and a distinguished naval officer came in, with two or three girls. They got a table and were noisy, and called on the 'Admiral' for a speech. When he had stepped down from his chair, Sam went over to him and tapped him on the shoulder. It was Captain Barwick, RM, the GCR Marine Superintendent at Immingham and Grimsby. Fay asked for an introduction to the ladies, but Barwick, who had no business in London, replied that he did not know them; they had collared him and dragged him there for lunch! 'A Great Day!' concluded Sir Sam.

On 12 November it was 'Difficult to give proper attention to work. QMG (France) is objecting to finding men for reconstruction at Ostend and Zeebrugge, although it was arranged by Geddes that this should be done, and that materials were found ready in his time. Could not go to St Paul's for the service, though invited. Too busy.'

'Thanks to Admiral Bacon[207] and the Dover Patrol,' he wrote, 'no troopships had been lost on the passage across the Channel, throughout

---

206 'With his usual exaggeration, General Wilson says in his diary that the Queen cried. There were certainly moist eyes when expressing relief at the terrible anxiety of the past four years.'

207 Sir Reginald Hugh Spencer Bacon (1863–1947), was in command of the Dover Patrol from 1915 to 1917. In September 1918 he was made a full Admiral. A close friend of Admiral Fisher, he became a naval historian.

the War.' 15 November: Discussed affairs generally with Thornton and Nash. Called on Albert Claveille, the Minister for Public Works in France – highly praised for his work by Clemenceau[208] – who had charge of Railways:

A charming, rugged, man, full of jokes, and eminent engineer, self-made; parents peasants. Went to the Embassy, where a French band was playing. Clemenceau and the French Minister were there, and Prince Albert[209] also. Had a chat with Lord Derby and Lady Victoria Stanley. Thornton gave the dinner in the evening at the Ritz. Claveille and the French and Italian Transportation men were present. Claveille very seldom goes out to dinner, and it was an honour to get him. There were no speeches except a toast of Claveille and me. No replies.

On 16 November, Fay dined with some officers of the Supreme War Council at the Versailles International Club: General Hereward Wake,[210] Colonel Lord Bentinck[211] and others present. 17 November:

Lunched at the Villa Romone, HQ of the Supreme War Council, Versailles. General Sackville West[212] and about twenty guests present. Sat next to Mrs Capel, a niece, she said, of Asquith, but not before she asked him what he thought of Asquith's political prospects.

He gave a fairly non-committal answer.

18 November: 'To Amiens, by car… Had lunch there. Evidently France is full of good food. No stint anywhere, except at Hôtel Grillon, where we had no milk or sugar with our morning coffee.' He went from there to

---

208 Georges Clemenceau (1841–1929). Prime Minister of France and Minister of War.
209 Prince Albert of Belgium (1875–1934). King of the Belgians, as Albert I, from 1909 to his death.
210 Major-General Sir Hereward Wake, Bt (1876–1963), of the Allied Supreme War Council, 1917–1919.
211 Lord Henry Cavendish-Bentinck (1863–1931), Derbyshire Imperial Yeomanry.
212 Major-General Charles Sackville West (1870–1962), 4th Baron Sackville. On the War Council, British Military Representative.

Monthuit, where he had arranged to meet Lord Faringdon,[213] and on the 19th they went to Boulogne. Back in England on the 20th for a Ministry of Munitions meeting, and later at a meeting of the Army Council, the main discussion being on demobilisation issues. On the first day of December Fay went with the rest of the Army Council to Charing Cross, to meet Clemenceau and Foch.[214]

At the Railway Executive meeting of 3 December the main subject was Labour Questions, and later that day he met Winston Churchill, at a Ministry of Munitions meeting, who wanted to order 2,000 locomotives and 50,000 wagons to keep labour going. He wanted to be told what class of engines to order: no liability to rest with railway companies. The Railway Executive met on the following day, 'To discuss Churchill's problem. Loco engineers, as usual, all sparring for their own designs without reference to what we were asked to do. The meeting was adjourned until the next day.'[215]

Also on 4 December, Fay asked the GCR agent in Hamburg to come over to tell him what had happened to the three ships on the Grimsby–Hamburg service seized by the Germans at the outbreak of war:

> He sent his son, who had been in the Field Artillery fighting against us nearly the whole period of the war. He could not get into a London hotel, and he came home with me. We sat up until three in the morning discussing his war work. He spoke of his experiences as if he had been playing a game of tennis, hitting balls from one side to the other. He had been at school in England, and showed not the slightest sign of animosity.

He surprised Sam by telling him that: 'The worst time he had as far as food was concerned was at the end of 1916, when, on retiring to rest camps, the

---

213 Alexander Henderson , Chairman of the Great Central Railway, had become Lord Faringdon in 1916.

214 Marshall Ferdinand Foch (1851–1929). Allied Generalissimo during the War.

215 There is no specific reference in the diary to the decision on locomotive type of choice. Apart from the reference on page 131, above, there is no specific guidance as to whether Sir Sam had an influence in the choice of further provision of the GCR 8K 2-8-0s. An oblique reference may be that the engineer in charge of the ROD works at Audruic Works in Northern France had worked at the GCR plant at Gorton, though he would have required higher authority for the choice.

troops were kept in bed most of the time, so that they should not feel their hunger.' The young man would be a Saxon, whose troops were experienced by the largely Anglo-Saxon British Army as far more friendly than Prussians or Bavarians. During the 'Christmas Truce' in 1914 at Houplines, where the trenches of the Royal Welch Fusiliers ran down to the River Lys, the Germans opposite them began calling out in friendly banter. Captain C.I. Stockwell wrote in his diary:

> The Saxons opposite were quite human. One, who spoke excellent English, used to climb up some eyrie in the brewery there and spend his time asking 'How is London getting on? How is Gertie Miller and the Gaiety?' and so on… One night I came out and called 'Who the hell are you?' At once came back the answer 'Ah, the officer – I expect I know you – I used to be the Head Waiter at the Great Central Hotel.'[216]

The lad could not believe that the mud and general conditions at Passchendaele were worse on the British side than they were on the German side.

Fay went over to France on the 5th to try to clear up the trouble with the French over troop trains. He was back in London the 7th, experiencing London packed with people. 'Rush and crush everywhere; a dangerous business.' He was in Southampton on the 14th to see how demobilisation was being organised by the L&SWR, and met Sir Hugh Drummond, the Company's Chairman; Sir Herbert Walker, the General Manager; and Williams, the Marine Superintendent.

On 19 December, Field Marshall Haig and his Generals arrived at Charing Cross Station, and Sam met them as a member of the Army Council. Haig shook hands, with his 'more than glad to see you' style. 'There was a great reception, though there had been some idea of not giving him a public reception at all.' Fay had told General Wilson some

---

216 *Christmas Truce: The Western Front December 1914*, Malcolm Brown and Shirley Seaton (London: Papermac, 1994, page 29). Germans working in England and Wales in 1911 numbered 53,324; they constituted the third-largest of any immigrant group (after Russian Jewish émigrés and the Irish), and 10% of all waiters were German. The Manager of the Great Central Hotel, Marylebone, in 1903 was a 'G. Schmeider'.

days before that 'If we didn't, there would be trouble.' 'No love lost between these two.' The entry for 21 December recorded that he met General Plumer [217] who reminded him that the last time they met was in 1912 in Immingham, when Sam was knighted. 'Bluff old chap', commented the diarist, 'means to keep down Bolshevism in Cologne'. On the same day he had a long interview with Milner, who was evidently tired of the War Office. 'He asked my opinion on General Staff taking over executive work at the War Office, which the Adjutant-General and Quartermaster-General had complained about.' Fay replied that he could not see how in time of war it could be otherwise; the Chief of Staff had to decide quickly on movement of troops, and thought such complaints were unwise. 30 December: 'Dined at United Services Club at Milner's invitation. Haig and his Generals present. Milner and Haig made good speeches.'

1919

There was 'Trouble with men at Richborough'[218] on 7 January 1919. Arrangements had been made by the Director of Demobilisation for men released day by day to be re-engaged as civilians, which would be fatal in view of Army Service Corps men who had asked to be demobilised and paid 6 shillings a day as civilians. Fay had a word with Milner, and it was stopped. The next day, Fay lunched with Sir Francis Dent, General Manager of the South Eastern and Chatham Railway, and asked him if his company would take on Richborough 'in the event of our wishing to do so, and he agreed'. An Army Council meeting took place that afternoon, chaired by Milner. The newspapers said that Churchill was to be War Secretary. Sam commented that he, 'in common with everybody in the War Office, would be glad to see the back of Milner, who has not an idea of the first principles of administration'. He added, 'I am out as soon as I get half a chance for an excuse', but he was anxious to do all he could to keep things straight:

217 Herbert Charles Onslow Plumer (1857–1932), Commander-in-Chief of the British Army of the Rhine. Created Baron Plumer of Messines in October 1919.
218 Richborough, near Sandwich, Kent, was developed as a major port for supplying the British Expeditionary Force in 1916, the first time sea-going train ferries were used in Britain. It functioned also as a port for demobilisation and return of equipment in 1918–1919.

the Army was disgruntled and the transport in France was almost as bad as it could be. 'I have urged time and time again within the last two or three weeks the only remedy is to pay Tommy commercial rates, say 5 shillings or 6 shillings a day, until he is demobilised.' Three days later Churchill came in as War Secretary. 'This may or may not improve matters', Fay said laconically. Later Milner came in to say goodbye. He said it was necessary for someone to come in and look after administration. Fay agreed, and told him that he had taken on too much. He wrote:

I was sorry for Milner. He was so obviously out of place... He would not, or could not, see that the object of Wilson and some others in France was the smash-up of the organisation. He recorded his view that the root of Milner's failure [as Secretary of State], apart from overwork, lay in impressions he brought from the War Cabinet that the Old Contemptible leaders were fools. He paid no attention therefore to their views, seeking instead subordinate opinions, whose purely local experience gave the idea that they knew all about all the branches of Allied administration, forgetting that the Chief receives reports from every quarter, and is, alone, able to decide upon appropriate action. As a literary man, Milner had fixed idea upon the composition of memoranda. He complained that mine were too short and not sufficiently explanatory. In defence, I told him that we railwaymen couched our instruction in as few words as possible, and kept to the point in order to avoid any misunderstanding.

He added:

I tried to amend my style – not always with satisfactory results. Milner's pursuit of General Crookshank, and his objection to Robertson as Commander in Chief Home Forces, gave an impression of vindictiveness. I think the explanation is that he followed the plausible reasoning of Wilson, who could argue with anyone that a horse chestnut must be a chestnut horse, and argue it with apparent conviction.

168

Fay went on to write that 'this whimsical, irrepressible Irishman, with his quips and cranks, his persuasive tongue and gift of expression, held an attraction for many people, inside and outside the Army; people who did not look beneath the surface and see the vanity and vaunting ambition which consumed him. That he was sincere in his love for his native Ulster... is beyond question. He probably gave as much to its fortunes as to the prosecution of the war.'

13 January was Churchill's first day as Secretary of State for War and Air, and he turned up in the afternoon, asking to see Fay. He remarked that they had first met at a Board of Trade meeting when he was there as President. He told Fay that Geddes had recommended that Crookshank or Paget be in charge as Director General of Transport, and did he agree? The reply was 'Yes, provided they were left alone to run the business.' Churchill thought that transport should be parted from the control of the Quartermaster General, and when General Cowans came in on the conversation, he agreed. Afterwards, Sam asked him why he had changed his mind. He replied that it was clear that the QMG and the Director General of Transport combination could not work, and he 'was getting out before the explosion'. And so,' concluded Fay:

> General Crookshank, who was made the centre of a disturbance which never should have arisen, ended his war service as Director-General of Transportation, and on the recommendation of his Commander-in-Chief was made a Knight Commander of the Order of St Michael and St George. 'A great gentleman,' as one of his directors called him.

There was a full meeting on the 14th, where Haig was 'evidently perturbed over the Army, and the impossibility of carrying out the scheme for demobilisation and providing an army of occupation at the same time. He said it was either giving up the scheme or saying to the French that we must retire and leave them to find an army of occupation... ' The Armistice had taken them by surprise. They had set themselves upon a 1919 campaign. He recorded in his diary that Churchill had proposed to take a new scheme to the War Cabinet comprising compulsory service of men recruited in the last twenty-two months, detaining NCOs necessary for each battalion.

Additional pay was to be given. The scheme to be worked out in detail and another meeting was held on Thursday 16 January.

On that day, another large meeting was held with Earl Haig, in the Secretary of State's room, on demobilisation and formation of an Army of Occupation. But the Great Central Railway was asking for Fay to return. He sent a formal letter to Churchill, explaining that:

> The time has come when I must return to my railway business, and the Railway Executive Committee.[219] I have been at the War Office for over two years, and my Company is asking for my return... it would be convenient if I could leave at the end of the present month.

On the following day, Churchill asked to see him, but the Secretary of State was away until evening, and then left for the country until Monday. His Secretary told Fay that he wanted him to stay a month. 'Shall not, if I can help it', confided Sam to his diary. On the 20th, Fay was at a meeting of the Finance Minister's room on pay for the New Army, or rather Army of Occupation. It had been decided, apparently, to give double pay all round, making Tommy's pay 3 shillings instead of 1s 6d. Fay didn't think that would satisfy the men; he thought 5 shillings as a minimum. He noted that the decision on Army pay illustrated democratic Ministers' relative values, as applied to the worker safe at home, his wife going out to market with pounds in her hand, followed by the soldier's wife clutching shillings, whilst her husband faced death overseas 'to make the world safe for democracy'.

He records being invited to dinner at the Savoy, to the American Ambassador, by the American Society in London. 'Sat with seven judges, four opposite and three on my side of the table. Not a very cheerful lot of neighbours.'

---

219 The Railway Executive Committee, 1914-1921, was composed of Herbert Ashcombe Walker, (Chairman), L&SWR; Sir Sam Fay (Deputy Chairman), Great Central Railway; Donald Alexander Matheson, Caledonian Railway; Francis Dent, South Eastern and Chatham Railway; Frank Potter, Great Western Railway; Sir Robert Turnbull, L&NWR; John Audley Frederick Aspinall, Lancashire and Yorkshire Railway ; Sir Guy Granet, Midland Railway; Sir Alexander Kaye Butterworth, North Eastern Railway; Charles Dent, Great Northern Railway; and William Forbes, London Brighton and South Coast Railway.

On 27 January he was setting up terms on which Richborough and the large traffic and train ferries are to be handed over to the South Eastern and Chatham Company. On the same day the War Cabinet agreed, after much discussion, to let the Bolsheviks stew in their own juice, and not attempt to wage war on Russia. The Chief of the Imperial General Staff and the Secretary of State for War were held up at Calais by the strike trouble by the soldiers of all sorts there. The CIGS asked to draft a message to Haig that as the Rhine route to Cologne was being opened up and demobilisation rapid, railway men might be released quickly, and the men so informed. There had been great unrest among them lately on account of overwork and homesickness. On 29 January, Haig replied, objecting. He, or someone in his name, sent a message saying that each individual man wanted to know when he was to be demobilised.

Sam commented that it was not only the railwaymen who were giving trouble. The New Army had enlisted for the duration of the war, and the war was over (although terms of peace had not been signed). The troops had seen enough of the horrors of war; they wanted to secure a place in the new constellation. They wanted to handle some of the war spending that had passed from hand to hand as money had never passed before; they wanted to 'Sport with Amaryllis in the shade.'[220] The Army was beginning to demobilise itself, and the position had assumed a threatening aspect. With Dominion and other overseas troops:

> demobilisation had proceeded quickly and quietly. The Canadian had returned to his farm in the west, the Afrikander to his far-flung veldt, the Australian to his home in the bush, the New Zealander to his flocks and herds, the lad from Malaya to his rubber lands, the tea planter to his Assam valleys, the Princes of Ind to their gorgeous East, with the men who give praise to Allah, or worship the ancient gods, and the flaming British-born youth of the day went back to wherefrom he had wandered. Not so his comrades from the British Isles. They, by ministerial decree, were to be the victims of experiment in the interest of reconstructed commerce...
> Haig, from the first, protested against this idea. He foreshadowed

---

220 Quoted from John Milton (1608–1674), 'Lycidas: Lament for a Friend Drowned in his Passage from Chester on the Irish Sea, 1637', line 68.

unrest and indiscipline among troops if one man was taken and the other left.[221]

Haig considered it unfair to release men without reference to length of service. His objections were overruled:

> When the trouble arose, and men protested... Ministers were peeved, very peeved indeed. But when troops in France actually struck, they bolted under the Cabinet table, after the manner of their kind, and left the War Office to bear the brunt of the soldiers' resentment, public condemnation, and the strictures of the Press.

After an Army Council meeting on 30 January, the CIGS (Field Marshall Sir Henry Wilson) and Fay followed Churchill to his room and tackled him about the unrest among railwaymen in France, and told him that 'it would never do for the authorities there to settle hours of work, as they had done – eight hours a day including meals, and four only for Saturday – without consultation with us here. He agreed, and I left to draft a letter accordingly.' On 1 February, Fay heard that Churchill had held up Fay's letter to Haig on railwaymen's hours. 'They will have a mess in France if they are not careful. If they fix railway troops' hours of duty they will have to fix Army Service Corps and Ordnance Staff and other line of communication hours as well.' On 3 February there were threats of strikes by railway and electrical men in London, over the eight-hour day. On 5 February, a strike by London Underground men. 6 February: South Western and Brighton railway drivers out on strike. Drivers and Firemens' Society threaten to call out all steam drivers if the Government does not give way to the Underground men that their eight-hour day is inclusive of meal hours.

On this day also, a General attached to the Belgian Legation came in to tell Fay that the King of the Belgians had conferred the Commander of the Order of Leopold upon him, for which he was thanked. Decorations from Allied Governments sometimes came in batches to be distributed by the War Office, and Cowans suggested to Fay, *a propos* a selection sent from the Japanese, that he ought to accept one, which he declined.

---

221 Quoted from Matthew, Chapter 24, verse 40.

Three days later he saw Robertson[222] at Horse Guards and suggested that trains run from northern centres should go direct to Folkestone and other ports without bringing them to London. On 11 February, Fay was invited to lunch at Claridges by Lord Peel, Under Secretary of State, to meet American Officers there for clearing up affairs. General Harbord[223] was the principal officer. 'Quite an interesting meeting. His language and accent exactly like that of a Hampshire or Dorset farmer.' It quite confirmed Sam's view that 'the American accent came from the South-West of England'. The next day, he was invited to dine at the Athenaeum. Among other legal men present were the new Lord Chancellor, F.E. Smith,[224] and H.S. Chilcott, MP.[225]

During dinner the latter said he knew something about railways: when he was 15 or so his father told him and his brother that one of them would have to go on the South Western and the other on the Great Western Railway, because the managers of those railways got £5,000 a year, and there was no reason why they should not get such a salary. He went on the LSWR and started at Waterloo sorting parcels. These stank of fish and other things, the work was monotonous and he hated the job, so he told his father he could not stand it, and wanted something more interesting. His father appealed, and was referred to the Superintendent of the Line (Verrinder). He did not see the latter, but saw his next in command whose name was Sam Fay. Sam recorded that he 'had no recollection of this episode'. F.E. Smith told him afterwards that Mr Chilcott MP's income was 25,000 to 30,000 a year; 'rather more than that of any railway manager', thought Sam.

On 15 February Fay received from the Secretary of War's Office a copy of a proposed bill by Geddes for the establishment of a Ministry of Ways and Communications, for a report on it. It provided for a Ministry to take over the powers of the Board of Trade and to operate the railways, on the passing of the Act. Further, that by Order in Council, the Ministry may

---

222 By this time commanding the British Army of Occupation on the Rhine.
223 Major General James Guthrie Harbord (1866–1947). He was charged by President Woodrow Wilson in August 1919 with investigating the feasibility of the Balfour Declaration of 1917: the establishment of a Jewish State.
224 Frederick Edwin Smith (1872–1930), First Earl of Birkenhead, Winston Churchill's greatest personal and political friend.
225 Harry W.S. Chilcott (1871–1942), MP for Walton, Liverpool.

purchase on terms to be settle by a Commission. Names not stated. Fay does not record his opinion.

Six days later, he was 'summoned' to see Churchill at 10.30 am. It was a question of sending stores to Denekin,[226] who for the time being was fighting against Bolshevism in Southern Russia. The shipping people were objecting to finding ships. Churchill turned up at 11.10 am, very restless, walking about the room. Fay felt inclined to tell him to perch somewhere, if only on the mantelpiece. He got out a map of Russia and demonstrated what would happen if we supported Denekin, and the dire results which would follow it. Apparently, commented Fay, his idea was to do 'Something': 'Anyhow – jump in and splash about.'

On 24 February Sam was surprised that *The Times* had notification that he was leaving the War Office. He rang them and asked what they meant, but no one he spoke to would admit responsibility. He noted that on this day, from 11 November 1918 to noon on 23 February 1919, 41,810 officers and 1,633,023 other ranks had been demobilised. But there were still delays because of shortage of ships.

At an Army Council meeting, Fay saw Churchill and General Harrington, Deputy Chief of the Imperial General Staff, about the refusal of the Shipping Controller, J. Maclay, to provide ships for troops from Rotterdam to Richborough. 'Churchill used strong language about profiteering from ship owners, and later requested that the three of them went to see Maclay, [227] who raged at Churchill's "impertinent remarks".'

'His explanation seemed to prove Churchill's case,' confided Fay to his diary for 25 February: 'The small ships were wanted off Channel Troop Service to… take up services from Liverpool to the Isle of Man and down the Clyde.'

Two days later, he had to tell Lord Peel that he could not go to France, as requested, to look around American lines and depots, much as he would like it, and on 4 March he attended the Railway Executive Meeting to discuss Geddes's bill for the Government the take over of railways: 'Long discussion, but nothing definite. There was a meeting in the afternoon of the Railway Companies' Association. Chairman of railways talked rot; some for downing Bill, others for accepting it anyhow, on the ground that if it were

226 Anton Denekin (1872–1947), Lieutenant General of the Imperial Russian Army.
227 Sir Joseph (later Baron) Maclay, 1916–1921.

left over we might get something worse.' He went on to Whitehall Gardens, where he met Geddes and Shortt,[228] the Home Secretary, in charge of the bill. At another meeting that day, concerning some regulations involving several departments:

> There descended upon us three young men who proceeded to strike out 'the's' and 'and's' and reconstruct sentences with an air of authority that was not to be questioned. They were evidently very busy men; they came in hurriedly, they departed with precipitation... my neighbour informed me that they were purists in official language, probably from the factory to which we owe Income Tax Regulations.

On 2 March, he attended a meeting with the Shipping Controller, Churchill in the chair. 'Managed to get 9,000 more railwaymen released.' He saw Churchill after the meeting, and he suggested that Oliver Bury be made Sam's deputy for a few weeks, as the GCR was pressing for Sam to attend Boards, etc. The Quartermaster General would get gradually acquainted with the work, and take over. Fay saw him (Travis Clarke),[229] who wanted Major General May as Director of Movements. 24–26 March, routine: 'Getting fairly fed up with the War Office. It gets worse and worse. The fact was I had become tired, bad-tempered, and out of my usual health.'

2 April 1919: 'To Grimsby and Immingham with Sir William Hay, General Manager, South African Railway.' 12 April: 'Fit of laziness – too tired to write up diary for some days.' 17 April: 'To Woking to look over "Beechcroft": found little done to put place right by Red Cross people to whom I had let it during the War.'[230] 24 April: 'Major-General [Reginald] May, until now Deputy QMG (France), turned up to become Director of Movements and take over the work at the War Office. To Richborough on the 28th with May to show him round.' April 29th and 30th: 'saw Churchill and went the rounds to say goodbye'.

---

228 Edward Shortt (1862–1935), Home Secretary, 1919–1922.

229 Lieutenant General Travis Clarke (1871-1962), QMG (succeeding General John Cowans).

230 'Beechcroft', let to the Red Cross as an emergency hospital, one of many, during the War.

The CIGS and Sir Charles Harris[231] were away. The latter wrote to me on 29 May:

'My dear Fay, I have been intending for some time to write and say how sorry I was to find you demobilised when I got back from sick leave, and to express my sincere thanks to you for the pleasantness of our official and personal relations during your term of office here, when the nerves of most of us were (as you well know) were rather raw... Wishing you all best of luck, C. Harris.'

Sam wrote a note to Wilson telling him:

he would not be disturbed in future by seeing my bearded face enter his room. He had in facetious mood told me, more than once, that a beard was not to be tolerated in the War Office, that he would put me into uniform, and have me properly shaved, or as an alternative send me over to the admiralty, where any sort of face was welcome. He replied, 'My Dear Sir Sam, it was always a real pleasure to see you come into my room, and I never got anything but full help from you on all occasions. "Happy go you", as the Dutch say. Ever, Henry Wilson'.

On 30 May, Sam gave a dinner at the Argentine Club to principal members of the staff, Movements, Railway and Roads, and Inland Waterways and Docks directorates. Guy Granet came and spoke well of assistance given by everybody in the department in his time, often under discouraging conditions:

His thanks and mine were the only signs of recognition received by the Directors, Generals Osborne, Manse and Cooper, for their excellent work. The powers responsible for recommendations in the Victory Honours list knew little of their efforts upon the defeat of the enemy. The dinner was a great success and we

---

231 Charles Harris (1864-1943), Senior Civil Servant at the War Office; KCB 1913, KGBE, 1920.

dispersed to take up new problems and face a new life. And thus – and thus ended my connection with the War Office.

It could be said, with full justice, that Sam Fay was never rewarded for his own contribution, at the highest level, to the work of the High Command, in the equivalent of the rank of Lieutenant General. Others of equal importance were given the honour of a Barony or at least a Baronetcy; but it has to be admitted that all along Sam refused any kind of such honour, being simply content, at every opportunity, to offer his great gifts of insight and administration to the service of the nation. As early as June 1917, Granet had approached him on the subject, as was normal. Sam asked him not to put forward his name, but agreed to send up his list of officers for inclusion, and similarly on subsequent occasions.

However, Fay goes on to record that subsequent to his War Office accomplishments, he received verbal accolades at the highest level. During his command, he had submitted a quarterly report on the operations of the Transportation Department to His Majesty the King, and attached to the reports some fifty sheets of statistics, showing in detail the various activities of the three Directorates: Movements; Railways and Roads; and Inland Waterways and Docks. Acknowledging the 18 September 1918 report, Lieutenant-Colonel Clive Wigram,[232] the King's Assistant Private Secretary, replied from Buckingham Palace on 16 November 1918:

> My Dear Sir Sam, I am sorry not to have thanked you before… the King was much pleased to see this Report, and is full of admiration for the wonderful work carried out by your Department, the development of which his Majesty has followed with the keenest interest from its foundation to the great structure of today The King hopes that the inland services of this country will now reap the benefit of the experience of your Department, and the stocks which have been collected by it. Yours Sincerely, Clive Wigram

In May 1919 came the letter following the report of the quarter ended March 1919:

---

232 Clive Wigram (1873–1960). Promoted to Secretary, 1931–1936. Created Baron Wigram in 1935.

Windsor Castle, 2 May 1919

My Dear Sir Sam, I write to thank you for the Quarterly Report of the work of your Department, which I have laid before the King. His Majesty has been much interested in these reports, and the work carried out under the direction of Sir Guy Granet and yourself. The King hopes to see you on his return to London, and to thank you personally. I will return the report when his Majesty has had time to read it. Yours very truly, Clive Wigram

Sam was received at Buckingham Palace on 14 May, and 'the King was in happy mood. He was exceedingly complimentary on the work of the Department, and by his comments on some of the more interesting features of the reports, indicated clearly that he had bestowed upon the figures no cursory glance; he had studied them in detail.' After dealing with the Report, the King spoke of other things: 'He wanted to know when the railways would get back to normal.' Sam told him that they would quickly pull round, and explained how exceptional had been the strain on all the home railways by giving help to the war transport overseas, whilst at the same time they were subject to intensive traffic here. The maintenance of rolling stock had been held in abeyance for four years:

> The King, accompanied by that almost boisterous laugh of his, quoted the story of a friend of his who travelled from the West of England to London, with fifteen people in the compartment, plus a baby. He hoped, for the comfort of the people, such over-crowding would not long continue.

He asked Sam's opinion on a Member of Parliament who subsequently became a Cabinet Minister: 'I've seen him two or three times,' said the King, 'I believe him to be an honest man.'

'When I left,' reflected Fay, 'there came to me what so seldom happens in life: a sense of complete satisfaction and well-being.' He felt that 'the King's thanks, and not least the manner of giving expression of it, was worth all that we had been able to do – and more.'

In Chapter 26 of his *War Office at War*, he wrote on:

the War Transport of the Future, that as the call upon transport during the late war was of a magnitude and character differing from any previous war, so in the next conflict, demands for movements of armies, with all their needs of maintenance, the construction or extension of railways, roads, aerodromes, docks and waterways, may be expected to assume a distinction altogether foreign to our experience in the years 1914 to 1919

In his final dispatch, Earl Haig wrote:

The wonderful development of all methods of transportation had an important influence upon the course of events. No war has been fought with such ample means of quick transportation as were available during the recent struggle.

Despite the huge increase in the size of armies, it was possible to effect great concentration of troops with a speed, which having regard to the numbers of men and bulk of material moved, has never before been equalled. Strategical and tactical mobility has been the guiding principle of our transportation arrangements; but this was at all times vitally affected by questions of supply, and by the necessity of providing for the evacuation and replacement on a vast scale the sick and wounded. The successful co-ordination and economic use of all the various kinds of transportation requires most systematic management based on deep thought and previous experience.

Fay continued:

The United States' experience in the war was, in many respects, curiously like that of Great Britain. With us it took over two years to realise that peace-time transport organisation would not meet the requirements of modern warfare.[233] With them, a year and seven months after the USA declared war, transport to the American Front all but came to a standstill. American peacetime organisation

---

[233] This is the explanation of why it took two and a half years for it to be realised that someone of the calibre of Sir Sam Fay was needed to be the organiser of the transport operations..

placed responsibility upon the Quartermaster Corps, but in the war, the Corps of Engineers, acting under the Commander of Line of Communications, was charged with operation and construction of railways. In June 1917, a small committee studied the transportation system in England and France, and in September a Director-General of Transportation, in the person of General Atterbury, Vice-President of the Pennsylvania Railway, was appointed. His headquarters were set up in Paris, and throughout the war he does not appear to have been in direct touch with the Commander-in-Chief… The pressure of the British and French Governments on the authorities in Washington, after the German breakthrough in March 1917, to send over infantry and machine-gun units only, resulted in the holding back of transport staff, together with locomotives and other rolling stock… multiplying the difficulties of dealing with an army of two millions… The situation, due to the cumulative effect of absence of necessary locomotives and staff, plus faulty organisation, became so bad in the latter months of the war that serious consideration was given to marching troops from the ports to the Front… Notwithstanding the hundreds of locomotives and tens of thousands of wagons sent from England… it was declared that if the armistice had not come as it did, it would have been necessary before all else to furnish additional resources to the railways, even to the extent of taking men from the army in order to ensure its life.

Reflecting on all this experience, Sam records that it 'proved that in order to avoid failure in meeting what could be an emergency calling for [future] immediate action, there should be an organisation *in being*, ready at any time, as the Railway Executive Committee was ready in July 1914, to function upon the declaration of a Precautionary Period'. He goes on to give details of such a requirement: 'War demands that all effort should be directed towards the Front Line; that is where victory or defeat lies.' Drawing intimately on recent events, he continued 'Anything in the shape of friction or indecision, leading to delay in giving the Commander-in-Chief all he demands, jeopardises his army.' Sir Douglas Haig stressed this in his letter to Sam on 17 August, when he wrote 'It was in [Crookshanks'] power to have wrecked our whole plan of operation.' 'That was a case', commented Fay, 'of friction and change of system in the face of the enemy, at what Haig termed "A singularly inappropriate moment".' Fay added, 'No opening should be left for a second mishap of such a character.'[234] He added further details of the duties and responsibilities of a Director General of Transport *vis-à-vis* the General Staff and Administration. 'All should be directly responsible to the Commander-in-Chief, with no intermediate authority capable of delaying operation or provoking indecision. Responsibility and Power should go hand in hand.' All in all, he recommended that, under the primary objective, all departments should cooperate to ensure smooth working.

In 1920 he received the Territorial Decoration,[235] and resigned his Commission in January 1924.[236] The Company's Memorial to its fallen officers and men during the conflict was erected on 9 August 1922 at Victoria Station, Sheffield: the heart of the Great Central enterprise. It was unveiled by Field Marshal Earl Haig. Painstaking arrangements for the invitation of relatives and friends of those named on the Memorial were made by the company, and special trains were run from London, Manchester and Cleethorpes. The train from Manchester was hauled by 9P Class locomotive 1165, *Valour*, the company's official Remembrance engine, and the one from London was hauled by *Earl Haig*, no. 1166 of the same class, which was the usual 10 am from Marylebone. The Directors' Saloon was attached to accommodate the Field Marshal; the Chairman, Lord Faringdon; the Director; and the General Manager, Sir Sam.

Appropriate addresses were given by the Chairman and Earl Haig, and the latter unveiled the Memorial, which was of an unusually impressive design. Dedication prayers were offered by Canon T. Haughton, Rural Dean of Sheffield and Vicar of Ecclesall. The Last Post was sounded, and wreaths of Remembrance were laid by Walter Burgh Gair for the Board, and Fay on behalf of the staff. The ceremony concluded with the National Anthem and the Blessing.[237]

The presence of Field Marshal Haig might be assumed to be due to his

234 *The War Office at War*, op. cit., pages 242–251.
235 *London Gazette*, No. 3275, 3 October 1920, page 7203.
236 Ibid., No. 32903, 1 February 1924, page 70.
237 Dow, op. cit., Volume III, pages 342–345.

closeness to Sir Sam during the most tense years of the conflict. Certainly, Fay's personal and almost daily contact with him, and with the topmost politicians of the time, testify, in his own openly honest account, to a much modified and balanced view of Haig's responsibility and judgement of the conduct of the War from that which we have received from some armchair post-war commentators. The German verdict on him was that 'Haig possessed strategic ability and that in the end he remained "Master of the Field".' Major General Sir John Davidson, in his book of that title in 1953, recorded the highest regard in which the British troops held him, especially in the way he constantly maintained personal contact with them: at the Front, behind the lines, and visiting them in hospital.

Nine-car ambulance train No. 2, converted from vestibuled stock
in March 1915, headed by *Sir Sam Fay*.

Sir William Robertson, Field Marshall, C.I. G.S.

Railway operative department (ROD), GCR 2-8-0

G.C.R. War Memorial, Sheffield – 9 August 1922
The unveiling of the Great Central War Memorial
at Sheffield Victoria Station, 9 August 1922.
Relaxing after the ceremony are Sir Sam Fay,
Field Marshall Haig, and Lord Faringdon

Memorial Locomotive 'Valour', G.C.R. Mobile War
Memorial, Manchester London Road Station, c.1921

11

Endgame

CHAIRMAN'S ADDRESS AT THE MEETING OF THE SHAREHOLDERS OF THE GREAT CENTRAL RAILWAY COMPANY, FEBRUARY 1918

Fay's eventual return after his war duties in 1919 was to a company which was still, within the limitations of the Government's control, operating in good order. The yearly meeting of the shareholders of the GCR was held in Manchester on Friday 22 February 1918; the Chairman, Lord Faringdon,[238] said that:

> The Statement of Accounts showed a Net Revenue of £2,104,311, which compared with £2,087,524 in 1916... To this figure must be added our Miscellaneous Net Receipts, amounting to £134,639... We have therefore £2,238,950 to deal with, together with the balance of £8,367 brought forward from the previous year, making a total of £22.247,317 available for interest and dividends. Deducting the fixed interest charges of £1,356,861 – £2,819 less than at the corresponding period – we have left the sum of £890,455, which permits the payment of all Preferences down to and including the 4% Preference Stock of 1891, and 2½% on the 1894 Preference Stock, carrying forward a balance of £8,879.

---

238 Henderson had been elevated, in the New Year's Honours list, to the peerage.

'Many companies,' he continued:

have been placing considerable sums to General Reserve and I think
we are almost the only undertaking whose dividend payments are of
larger amount this year than in the pre-war period... Our position
now and before the war [is that] until our Preferences are all paid in
full, no General Reserve Fund can be set up.

But he assured the proprietors that an ample sum for maintenance, renewal,
and the security of their enterprise was provided.

He thought they would be surprised to learn that:

excluding Excursion Traffic from the 1915 figures, and apart from
the free traffic for the Government, we have carried upwards of
800,000 passengers more than at the corresponding period of 1913,
and our Season Ticket holders have increased by 2,831.

The total of ordinary passengers carried was 22,069,508 against 21,216,847
in 1913. In respect of goods traffic, he informed the meeting that:

excluding all tonnage carried on Government Account – which
amounted to a very large figure – our tonnage of merchandise
and coal traffic originating on our own railway has amounted to
20,238,132 tons against 21,015,543 tons in 1913. These figures are
rather remarkable, and tend to show the enormous burden that the
Railways have had to bear during the past year.

He added that this satisfactory movement of traffic had been worked well
by the staff. Skilled men had left, but those remaining had coped well and
willingly, 'Ably seconded by a large army of women. The total number of
women now employed was 5,409.'

Regarding Receipts and Expenditure on Capital Account:

we have expended during the past year the sum of £47,423. The
principal items were: On lines open to traffic, £24,000; Subscriptions
to Joint Lines were £600 to the Cheshire Lines Committee; £11,500

to the Hull and Barnsley and Great Central Joint Committee; £1,600 to the West Riding Joint Committee; and £10,971 to the Metropolitan and Great Central Companies. A further subscription of £2,000 has been made to the North Lindsey Light Railway, and sundry sales have given a credit of £3,266.

The General Balance Sheet showed that indebtedness on Lloyd's Bonds had been further reduced to the extent of £250,000. The total of Reserves was £1,606,469, or £263,604 more than in December 1916. This figure should cover all liabilities arising from arrears of repairs and renewals.

The Chairman referred to the heavy strain on Gorton Works in the repairs and renewals which had been undertaken, and in meeting the Government's urgent requirements for munitions. Over the last two years these had amounted to 56,000 six-inch high-explosive shells, replenishment of five and a half million eighteen-pounder cartridge cases, a number of large howitzer and gun carriages, anti-aircraft gun mountings, 360 General Service vehicles, and many other smaller items. Coaching stock had been converted to form three Ambulance Trains, which had already run over 560,000 miles and conveyed 210,000 wounded men to the principal towns in England and Scotland. Last November a new Ambulance Train of 16 coaches was constructed, weighing a total of 442 tons, for use of the United States Medical Service in France. 9,500 employees – 27% of the staff as in July 1914 – had joined the Colours, 'but with deepest regret we have to record the fact that casualties amounted to 2,441, 25.69% of the 9,500. 772 were killed, 1,475 wounded, 61 were missing, and 133 are prisoners. Twenty-three of our Seamen who were on ships in the Elbe at the outbreak of the war and imprisoned at Ruhleben have been released and returned home.' He was proud to announce that 'over 100 of our staff have been decorated for distinguished conduct or mentioned in dispatches'.

In reply to a question, the Chairman said that well into the fourth year of the war it was still quite impossible to know when it would end. What the railway position would be when hostilities ceased he was unable to prognosticate, but what the railways had done during the past three and a half years had demonstrated their immense power and usefulness. Many organisations essential to a great campaign had broken down under the stress and strain, but the railway service had carried on with hardly a hitch, and with comparatively small inconvenience to the general public. Many hundreds of engines, tens of thousands of our wagons, have been taken from us and sent abroad, and many of our most efficient officers and employees, and yet the machine has worked smoothly and dealt with a colossal traffic.

'These facts,' he said, 'Must be borne in mind should any proposals for the acquisition of the Railways be brought forward.' He quoted the *American Railway Age* newspaper as recording the previous month that 'Industries in the busiest and most populous part of the US have been shut down for five days because the Railways could not haul the coal the mines could produce and the industries could consume.' He also drew comparison with problems of breakdown on the German system. With due modesty he thought 'our Railway record bore favourable comparison with that of other countries.'

PROPOSED NEW FISH DOCK IN GRIMSBY

From 1919 the railways were recovering their normal basic operations, but understandably, with the massive reorganisation pending, no further new capital developments were being undertaken. This was made clear on the Great Central when the Fishing Vessel and Owners of Grimsby and local authorities requested in 1921 the building of a new fish dock. The need for it had been mutually agreed in February 1912, the GCR had presented a bill to authorise the work, and the Act was obtained before the end of that year. Tenders for the construction were received on 30 July 1914, but the scheme was put on hold because of the outbreak of the War.[239]

On Friday 28 October 1921, deputations from Grimsby Corporation, the Cleethorpes Urban District Council, the Trawler Owners' Association, and the Chamber of Commerce met the Chairman and Directors of the Great Central in the Boardroom of Marylebone Station. From the GCR were Lord Faringdon; W.B. Gair, Deputy Chairman; E.A. Beazley; Eric E.B. Butler-Henderson; the Earl of Kerry; R.N. Sutton Nelthorpe; Berkeley G.D. Sheffield; Lord Stuart of Wortley; H.W. Worsley-Taylor; Sir Sam Fay; and the Secretary. Grimsby was represented by the Mayor, F. Thornton; Town Clerk, J.W. Jackson; Chairman of Cleethorpes UDC, Councillor

---

239 Dow op cit, Volume III, pages 264 and 265.

Bannister; for the Trawler Men's Association, G.H. Moody; F. Barrett, Chamber of Commerce; R. Sleight, Exors of Sir G.F. Sleight (the largest individual trawler owner, and largest landowner in Lincolnshire); and Captain F.M. Barwick, GCR Portmaster at Grimsby.

The deputation said it was essential that a new fish dock be constructed as early as possible: 6,000 people were out of work, and £5 a week was being paid out in doles. The Chairman said he realised fully the need, and pointed out that tenders had actually been obtained in 1914, but not let because of the War. At that time it would have cost £0.5 million. Now it would cost £1.5 million. It would bring in more revenue, he continued, but for every £1 received [in catch rates] the Company spends £1 1s.0d – it is costing the Company 21 shillings to earn £1.

It was asked whether the company could approach the Government to assist. Lord Faringdon replied that if the Government would grant £1 million (the difference between the two figures) it would be different, but the GCR was not going to borrow money from the Government. However, the Directors would see what could be done in such a scheme. The representatives pointed out that in 1890, 71,382 tons were landed, and in 1910, 179,792 tons, indicating a greatly increased catch in the coming years.[240]

It appears that Sir Sam was eventually delegated to deal with the subject. He wrote on 4 November 1921 to the Grimsby Town Clerk to say:

> On condition of appropriate rates to the Company, the Treasury could be asked to advance £1,500,000 at, say, 4% interest. A revenue of £84,000 per annum on the expected tonnage increase of 50%, in four years the £60,000 per annum of interest would be sufficient for the redemption of £1 million of the advance and the GCR would be willing to provide [the £500,000]. The non-payment of interest during the construction period would amount to only a fraction of the doles now paid. The plans and estimates were prepared in 1914: the work could be proceeded with almost at once.

---

240 In 1911 the figure was 190,000. The peak, in 1951, was 198,000. In 1855, when the Manchester, Sheffield and Lincolnshire Railway, under Edward Watkin, took Grimsby into its development, the figure was 188 tons.

He concluded by urging the Grimsby Corporation to take steps '*very early*' to take this proposal to the treasury'. The file ends there.[241]

NATIONALISATION

In 1919, the Government, having controlled the railway system as one unit, was not inclined to see the Railway Executive return to the 123 or so separate companies, in varying states of economic viability. Nationalisation of some form or other was under serious consideration, supported in March 1918 by the Prime Minister, Lloyd George, and in the December by Winston Churchill. The subject was not new at that time; a canter through the history shows the notion of Government control of the railway system had appeared very early: Gladstone in 1844 had promoted a Regulation Act giving powers to the Government to purchase railways authorised from that date, though it appears not to have been implemented. The Regulation of the Forces Act of 1871 authorized the taking over of the railways for the duration of any national emergency.

It was under the powers of this Act that the Government, 'without reference to any railway nationalisation propaganda whatever', took over in September 1914.[242] Trade unions urged debate of the idea of state ownership in 1894, and the Labour Party of 1908 gave support. Lord Claud Hamilton, Chairman of the Great Eastern Railway, in his address to the half-yearly meeting of the proprietors in February 1906 gave voice to a complaint against 'irrational' competition on the part of other railway companies which was affecting adversely the Board's efforts to keep down expenses.[243] In May of that year, however, in the conclusion of the report on the Post Office Pay Committee's findings, the case for avoiding Government monopolies and emphasising the virtues of competition was very strongly put.[244]

Towards the end of the war, animated exchanges in the Letters page of the *Journal* showed how the subject of nationalisation versus private

---

241 National Archives 226/625. The New Dock was not completed until 1934.
242 The *Railway Magazine,* September 1914.
243 GCR *Journal,* March 1906, page 212.
244 See Chapter 5 in this book.

ownership had become more heated. One letter from 'Immingham Dock' was quite caustic on the failure of nationalisation in other countries, listing the railways of eight European countries and Japan as being 'economically unsound', and mentioning Belgium in particular as having 'Excessive Red Tape, ill-disciplined staff, and a lack of initiative and responsibility among the Heads of various Departments.' The writer admitted that the Prussians had the best-managed and most profitable state railway system, but it had failed completely to extend its mileage, or increase the rolling stock to meet the demands of traders. And even there, just before the War, competent authorities agreed that 'A Day of Judgement for the State system was imminent.'[245] The October 1917 *Journal* carried further pieces on the subject, engaging salvos from both sides.

An article in the February 1918 *Journal*[246] by Charles Travis, author of several books on railway economics and practice, stated that the question of state ownership was the most important issue considered by the Royal Commission on Railways, the deliberations of which were interrupted by the outbreak of war. He quoted Sir Herbert Walker, the Chairman of the L&SWR, as saying to an interviewer: 'Our Railways will never revert to the independent and foolish competition which obtained [before the War].' Apart from wasteful competition, there were stark financial difficulties in the operation of independent companies. Costs had risen enormously since 1914, and covering them by increased receipts was very problematic: 'The amount distributed in railway dividends in 1913 was £35,000,000, where incremental wages now amounted to £40,000,000.' But the Commissioners were by no means convinced of the benefits of nationalisation; only three witnesses gave evidence in favour, though many expressed their belief in the necessity for some scheme of merging Railways' interests... bringing about increased traffic facilities, economising the means of transport, and possible reductions in rates and fares.' 'All indications,' the writer thought, 'appear to point to the fact that there will be no nationalisation in the general acceptance of that term, but in a compromise plan of "Districting".' By this he meant that the privately owned companies of Britain should be permitted to effect amalgamations in certain defined areas. There should be six areas: in the South East (the South-Eastern and Chatham, London

245 August 1917, page 38.
246 Pages 137–140.

Brighton and South Coast), the West and Wales (Great Western and London and South Western, as far as Shrewsbury) the North West (London and North Western, Lancashire and Yorkshire, Manchester to Carlisle;), and the Great Northern, the Great Central, and the Great Eastern cover the rest of England to the Humber; plus the North Eastern Railway as at present. The five Scottish companies would be combined in a single system to form the sixth area. This would establish wholly non-combatant organisms.'

In December 1918, Sir Sam Fay submitted to the Prime Minister a plan for a Transport Authority, composed of representatives of the Board of Trade, the railway and canal companies, the trade unions, and commercial, industrial and agricultural concerns.[247] This was to be administered in five regions. His plan was a forerunner of both the eventual formation of a Ministry of Transport in 1919, and the four-company 'Grouping' scheme of the Act of 1921 which on 1 January 1923 saw the establishment of the London Midland and Scottish, the London and North Eastern, the Great Western, and the Southern Railways.

FAREWELL TO THE GREAT CENTRAL

A communication from the Railway Companies' Association dated 9 December 1920 was received by all Company Secretaries. It was entitled 'The Future Organisation of Transport Undertakings in Great Britain and their Relationship with the State'. The Secretary of the GCR, J.A. Campbell, replied to it on 10 December. Sir Sam made sure that a copy of this memorandum was sent to all Great Central shareholders, and also to the General Manager, F. Tatlow, of the Midland Railway at Derby.[248] In addition, a copy of the Government White Paper, on 'The Future of Railways', was issued to shareholders. It outlined the provisions of the Railways Act 1921, Sections 11 and 12. A letter from the GCR Secretary was written from Manchester London Road Station on 23 December 1921 to the shareholders, declaring that the Great Central's Gross Revenue for the year 1913 (the basis for the Government's calculations) was £6,625,664.

---

247 Philip Bagwell, *The Transport Revolution, 1770–1985*, Chapter 9. 2002, Routledge.
248 National Archives, RAIL 226/624. The full text of the memorandum was not enclosed in the file.

The contribution (recompense) at 1 shilling per £1,000 of gross revenue to each shareholder amounted to £334.5s 0d.[249]

An article in the *Financier* of Saturday 19 February 1921 reported the severe criticism by the GCR Chairman in response to the Colwyn Report of that date. This report, chaired by Lord Colwyn, concerned the taking over of the railways by the Government under the powers of the Regulation of the Forces Act of 1871. It was prepared by a Departmental Committee on Railway Agreements.[250]

Lord Faringdon, speaking at the Annual Meeting of the GCR in Manchester, said he saw, from evidence given before the Conway Committee by a representative of the Ministry of Transport, that if it found that the agreements entered into by the railways were not in the interests of the State, it would have to consider whether those agreements should be carried out.

[He] had never heard a more monstrous suggestion. Calmly to discuss whether solemn agreements entered into by the Government should be carried or repudiated, as might suit the interests of the State, was so opposed to British senses of justice that one could not help thinking that some modern Russian ideas had found their way into official circles.[251]

Clearly, the negotiation of the reorganisation of the railways did not go altogether smoothly!

A meeting of the Great Central Board took place on 15 December 1922, when certain financial settlements were made. Under Minute 7532, the Chairman reminded the Board that under a Minute of the Meeting dated 7 February 1919, it was agreed that Sir Sam Fay should become entitled to a Superannuation Allowance of £2,000 per annum:

He has agreed to continue in office in an advisory capacity for the year 1923 at a salary agreed by him with the London and North

---

249 Ibid.
250 National Archives, RAIL 1057/40.
251 National Archives, RAIL 226/624.

Eastern Railway. That Company leaves to the Great Central Railway Board the question of settling with Sir Sam Fay the amount of Superannuation to which he will become entitled after 1923. It was resolved that the amount should be fixed at £3,000 p.a. subject to the approval of the London and North Eastern Board. If Sir Sam Fay should so desire, the said Annuity be capitalised on the basis of the expectation of life on 1 January 1924, viz., 9.86 years.

Minute 7529 of the same meeting recorded that following the Resolution of the Shareholder Proprietors on 17 November 1922, the sum of £20,000 be given to the Directors... the allocation to each Director as followed, starting with Lord Faringdon at £6,248, and pro-rata thence for length of service, the lowest being Butler-Henderson at £304.[252]

One last development for the GCR was the application for 'Tenders for the Proposed Electric Third-Position Signalling between Marylebone and Neasden', at the estimated cost of £13,300, 1922–1924. (The actual cost was £15,955.) In March 1922 the Board gave authority for this work, to be done in connection with the forthcoming British Empire Exhibition at Wembley. This was undertaken by letter in May 1922 by the Engineer, Harry Blundell, from his office at Marylebone. The extra cost and the whole project was ratified by the LNER in November 1924.[253]

The Final Annual General Meeting of the Great Central proprietors was held in the Board Room at Manchester London Road Station on 16 February 1923. Lord Faringdon explained at the outset that as there were no Great Central shareholders, because their interests had merged into the London and North Eastern Railway, this was 'A meeting of those whose names appeared on the Great Central Register on 31 December last.' He said it was a pleasure to submit Accounts that take us back to pre-war days for comparison with the 1922 figures – those for 1921 having being still for a period under, for a large part, the control of the Government. He proceeded to give in detail the financial figures for Receipts and Expenditure for comparison of the two years, showing, in summary, that Receipts in 1922 were £11,874,769, compared with £6,549,053 in 1913, an increase of £5,325,716; an Expenditure of £9,715, 617, in 1913 of £4,467,443, an

---

252 National Archives, RAIL 226/11.
253 National Archives, RAIL 226/631.

increase of £5,248,574. Deducting the expenditure from the gross receipts there was a net sum, including subsidiary receipts, of £2,376,208. This was sufficient, after providing for interest, Rental Charges and Preference Dividends, to pay 4.5 per cent on the 1984 Preference Stock, and leave a balance of £13,367 to be carried forward. Last year [1921] we paid only 2.5 per cent on the 1894 Stock, although in 1922 we received nothing from the Government Compensation Account. He noted that the whole improvement in net revenue from 1913, as compared with the pre-war year, came from our Joint Lines, which gave an increased revenue of £114,134.

From the General Balance Sheet he quoted the principal items on the Debit side:

Savings Bank Deposits, £789,875 – an increase of £22,710 on 1921;

Pension Fund, £858,631 – an increase of £85,906; Compensation Account under Section 11 of the Railways Act 1921 – greater by £1,005,831;

Depreciation Funds for Railways, Steam-Boats and Docks, £2,627,939 at the end of 1921, and now at £3,162,221 – an increase of £534,682.

On the credit side, he listed:

Cash, £1,372,856, compared with £358,000 in 1921;

Government Securities £1,083,059 compared with £92,000. A further sum from the Government for 1921 of £934,142 has been received since 31 December.

Finally, he declared that the tonnage of principal classes of Minerals and Merchandise carried by Goods Trains, originating on our Company's system was, in 1922, £17,780,025, compared with the 1921 figure of £11,639,421.

Lord Faringdon concluded: 'I think you have there direct evidence of trade revival.'[254]

---

254 National Archives, RAIL 226/754.

12

Presidential Address To The Institute Of Transport, 1922

Sam Fay was elected the President of the Institute of Transport in 1922, and the outgoing President, Sir Henry Maybury,[255] said it was gratifying to him to be succeeded in the Chair by his friend Sir Sam Fay, whom it had been his good fortune to know for a longer period than either had cared to remember:

> Sir Sam Fay's name is a household word in the railway world and indeed in a far larger field of usefulness. Commencing his career at the foot of the ladder he had achieved great distinction and will retire from active service as General Manager of one of the great trunk railways. While occupying these important positions he had found time for service to the State on questions amongst many others relating the Post Office, the Board of Agriculture and Fisheries... and as Director-General of Movements and Railways in the great war. In the last capacity, Sir Sam Fay was a Member of the Army Council, and no doubt he could, if he

---

255 Henry Percy Maybury (1864–1943), civil engineer; worked on the Shrewsbury to Hereford Railway (LNWR and GWR), the Ffestiniog Railway, and others. He was appointed Brigadier in Charge of Military Roads in France during the Great War, for which he received the Order of the Bath and Knight Commander of the Order of St Michael and St George, plus the French Legion of Honour. See p.36.

were so disposed, relate something of the inner workings of the great war machine.[256]

He was sure that he would add lustre to the position of President of the Institute.

Sir Sam began by quoting the subjects of the Presidential Addresses of his three predecessors – Sir Eric Geddes, Lord Ashfield,[257] and Sir Henry Maybury – 'Hope', 'Education' and 'Development': 'Hope has given way to realisation; Education is evidenced by the students of our Institute; and Development is marching on. It is, I think, proper in order of sequence, that I should select Management'. Referring to a changing world:

> the Government has from time to time wanted to reform railway management on the Whitehall pattern, but public opinion in the light of the recent control during the war has not been convinced by the arguments for State Ownership… They have returned to private ownership but under a large measure of State control… It should be capable of demonstration that *controlled* private ownership is preferable to *uncontrolled* State ownership, and it will be upon future management that proof of this will lie.

After quoting some salient words of Sir Rowland Hill,[258] Fay observed that 'in war as well as peace, civilisation depended on transport… Our complex civilisation is held together by its manifold services.' In his further consideration of the issue of state control, Fay made some characteristically pungent observations:

> Statistics are compulsory under certain heads… [but] figures may be made to represent facts or become the finest and easiest form of

256 Which Fay did in 1937, in his *The War Office at War*.
257 Albert Henry Stanley (1874–1948), was born in the USA and came to England in 1907 as Managing Director, then as Chairman, of Underground Electric Railways of London; later Chairman of the London Passenger Transport Board from 1933. Created Lord Ashfield of Southwell in 1920.
258 1790–1879, English political economist, inventor of the penny postage stamp and reformer of the Post Office, and a Director of the London, Brighton and South Coast Railway.

camouflage. There are figures of facts and figures of deduction. An average is not always a fact, and may become a disease... They are calculated to waste the time and exhaust the patience of men who are engaged in actualities.

He described the recent (1921) Act for the formation of four large groups of railway companies as 'an asset': 'The strong and the weak... the small lines, most of them financially unsuccessful, become part and parcel of a sound organisation.' He described in full detail the subdivisions of management of a railway company, pointing out that as the present railway system has a Capital of some £400,000,000, and army of up to 300,000 employees, with steamships, docks, hotels and large estates – a vast organisation – such a method of transport management had importance to other than the railways.

On management and labour, he quoted the Quaker benefactor Rowntree, who wrote that the men who are engaged in such essential work as transport should be paid 'sufficient to maintain a reasonable standard of comfort, reasonable hours of work, reasonable economic security, during the whole working life and in old age, and a reasonable share with the companies in determining the conditions of work'.

Sam continued with the observation that: 'The railwayman, in common with the rest of mankind, will travel through this world only once. He will not pass this way a second time. He is entitled in return for his services to as comfortable a journey as the transport industry can give him.' To the argument that what constituted a railway was 'Permanent Way, stations, engines, carriages and wagons, and the financial arrangements with the stocks and shares, and balances at the bank' was only half the story. He stated that the other half was the working organisation from the Chairman down to the Lamp Boy. If a device is calculated to secure equity and to cement together in goodwill the major half of this great transport industry, it will be an asset indeed.

He concluded by saying that:

For the past fifty years I have been employed in doing – more or less – the things I ought not to have done, and leaving undone the things I ought to have done.[259] During the same period I have

---

259 A quotation from the Church of England Services of Morning and Evening Prayer, General Confession.

been a fairly keen observer of other people engaged in a similar series of operations. In fewer words, I have made mistakes and seen other people do the same. It is from that particular angle that I have ventured... some dogmatic observations... But I am mindful of the adage that a speaker who exhausts his subject exhausts his audience, so I will conclude by simply saying that in the future as compared with the past, there will have to be fewer things done that ought not to be done and fewer things left undone that ought to be done, if railway transport is to live up to and fully subscribe to Sir Eric Geddes' dictum 'efficient and economical working and management'.

Fay was also at this time the President of the Institution of Electrical Engineers, London. On Tuesday, 17 October 1922, he presided over a lecture delivered to graduates and students by a member of the Council, C.J. Selway, CBE.[260] The subject of the lecture was 'The Effect of Traffic Arrangements and Working Costs of Daily and Seasonal or Periodic Variation in Passenger Loads and Unbalanced Traffic Movement'.

---

260 Who became Passenger Manager, LNER Southern Area.

Sir Sam Fay in 1923

13

Post-Retirement Years

THE ISLE OF WIGHT

At the 'Grouping' of Britain's railways which took effect on 1 January 1923, Fay was 67 years old. The LNER offered him the choice, for his retirement, between a lump sum and an annuity. Edgar records that, knowing his temperament, 'it could not have been difficult to predict that he would take the lump sum, though if he had known that he was to live until he was 96, he might have thought differently'.[261]

Leaving the L&SWR in 1902 for the Great Central did not mark the end of Sam's connection with the area. Sir John Blundell Maple MP, son of the founder of Maples furniture business[262] asked him in that year to value the Isle of Wight Railways (the first of which was opened in 1864), as not one of the three companies there was solvent. Sir John had devised a plan for the development of the island by buying land and all the railways, and began by purchasing a majority of the shares in the Freshwater, Yarmouth and Newport Line. In the following year, 1903, when Sir John Sr died, his executors sold the shareholding to Frank Gerard Aman, a Director of the line, and holder of the hotel and land interests in the Hotel and Pier Company at Totland Bay; they took a seat on the Board, and played

---

261 Edgar Stewart Fay, Memoirs (unpublished), page 93.
262 Sir John Blundell Maple, Bt (1805–1903), the developer of the Great Central Hotel, Marylebone, 1896–1899.

a significant part that year, when the Freshwater, Yarmouth and Newport took back the running of the Isle of Wight Central Railway. In 1913, Sir Sam became financially interested in the FY&N Railway, and at the same time acquired a farm at Chale, in the south-west corner of the Island. His son Edgar assumed that he embraced farming, an occupation familiar from his youth, as a relief from the pressures of his duties at that time. He visited Chale with his father on 16 August 1920.[263]

Sir Sam played a leading role in all the negotiations, recruiting suitable management (the new General Manager came from the Great Central Railway), and arranging the purchase of locomotives and rolling stock. The company was always short of cash, and Sir Sam and Frank Aman were appointed joint receivers in 1913. It never paid a dividend, but Sam expressed himself very satisfied with the capital payment received from the Southern Railway on 28 April 1923.[264]

BEYER, PEACOCK & COMPANY LTD, GORTON, MANCHESTER

Very soon after his retirement from the Great Central, when it had become part of the London and North Eastern Railway (though he continued for a while to act as an adviser to the LNER), Sam received offers from a number of companies. The one which he accepted in 1923 was that of Chairmanship of the Beyer, Peacock Company of Locomotive Builders, whose works at Gorton, Manchester, were on the opposite side to the Great Central works on the main line from Manchester London Road to Sheffield and Marylebone. His London office was at Abbey House, Victoria Street, Westminster, overlooking St Margaret's Church and the West Front of Westminster Abbey.

Such was the pressure of work in 1922 at Beyer, Peacock & Co. that a drive for draughtsmen attracted men from the Great Central drawing office, and in fact J.G. Robinson, the GCR Chief Mechanical Engineer from 1 May 1902 to 31 December 1922, took a seat on the Board there in 1923.

An indication of the global influence of Beyer, Peacock, the self-styled

263 Memoirs, op. cit., page 60.
264 National Archives, RAIL 211/4.

'Locomotive Builders to the World', was when Fay went to Stockholm in 1924 to negotiate with a Swedish company for the British rights to a new steam turbine locomotive, the one patented by Frederic Ljungstrom in July 1922. The visit was for the first attempted design which was developed later to be built by Beyer, Peacock. On completion in 1927 it was tested for over 5,400 miles on the LMS Railway, attaining 85 mph with trains of 13 or 14 bogies, but it was beset by persistent minor troubles. Further tests were carried out in March and April 1928, in comparison with tests the previous autumn of the Horwich 2-6-0 introduced in 1926. Although minor problems were again encountered, she kept scheduled times, and water consumption was far less. But the coal consumption, on a drawbar horsepower basis, was 4% more than that of her smaller, much simpler, and far cheaper (less than one-sixth the cost) rival, and the project was abandoned.[265]

In the years 1923 to 1926 an extensive modernization of the Beyer, Peacock works was carried out,[266] and in 1925, a large number of Garratt patent and ordinary locomotives were built; but Sir Sam, in his Chairman's Annual Report, expressed his dissatisfaction with the year's financial results: the works were fully occupied but were producing ordinary engines at a greater cost than those of their competitors. He reported the same tendency in 1928, despite the fact that at no period in the company's history had a greater output been recorded. In 1927 the number of Garratts produced exceeded for the first time the number of ordinary locomotives, and this happened again in 1929 and 1930.

In a letter to Edgar in 1925, Sam mentioned that three Garratts were being built for the LMS Railway, to Order No. 1114. To the 2-6-0+0-6-2 wheel arrangement, the specification was for the haulage of trains of up to 1,500 tons on fast schedules, between Toton marshalling yards on the Derbyshire–Nottinghamshire border and Brent Sidings in North London:

At the Company's request the engines departed in several ways from Beyer, Peacock's, to the detriment of their performance –

---

265 A History of *Beyer, Peacock: Locomotive Builders to the World*, 1982, pages 161 and 175. A successful 2-8-0 version was achieved in 1930 for Swedish Railways, and the system was an inspiration for Stanier's highly efficient steam turbine 4-6-2 of 1935 on the LMS.
266 Ibid., page 162.

the inclusion of relative short piston valves and rather undersized coupled-axle boxes. Nevertheless, they fulfilled their duties most creditably, and thirty more were built, to Orders 1164 and 1165, in 1933.[267]

It is odd that Fay does not seem to have mentioned that he presided over the building of the ground-breaking production of the first Beyer-Garratt for a British Railway: the LNER 2-8-0+0-8-2 Class U1. This had originated on the Great Central in 1912, as Scheme No. 81865, based on two Robinson 2-8-0s with a special boiler. On the revival of the project on 8 April 1924, two engines of this design were ordered for a quotation of £21,000, but the eventual contract was for one, at a price of £14,895. On 31 July of that year, the design was amended to have six cylinders to accord with, instead, two of Nigel Gresley's O2 Class 2-8-0s, complete with conjugated valve gear for the inside cylinders, at an extra cost of £500. Beyer, Peacock, in the summer of 1925, had only 21 days from the laying of the frames to the required delivery date, decided by the necessity of its being displayed at the Centenary Celebrations of the opening of the Stockton and Darlington Railway, to be held in July and August. The locomotive, completed as Works No. 6209, ran under its own steam to Darlington on 2 July 1925.[268]

In 1929 Sir Sam went on business in Belgium and Spain. Later he met four or five Belgians and Frenchmen who (with his son Edgar) were joint directors of the Anglo-French-Belge Engineering Company.[269] 1930 was a good year for Beyer, Peacock, producing a dividend of 8%, and the Chairman's Report was full of optimism. But by August 1931 there was a massive trading loss of £67,000 as the General Depression began to take effect.

In 1932, the Richard Garratt Engineering Works at Leiston in Suffolk

---

267 Beyer, Peacock History, page 187.
268 Ibid., pages 179 and 180. Subsequent speculations on the use of this huge machine on mere banking duties include that on the original GCR intention: was it to have several of them hauling coal over the Pennines. Would lengthy periods of inactivity between trains to be banked would cause condensation in the long steam pipes. J.G. Robinson had a Drawing (unfulfilled) for an 0-10-2T for banking duties (Dow, Volume III, page 324).
269 E.S. Fay, Memoirs, pages 263 and 322.

went into receivership, following the failure of Agricultural and General Engineers Ltd, and was purchased by Beyer, Peacock for £27,250. Garratts had been famous for its steam traction engines and steam road lorries, as well as agricultural equipment, but because of the demise of steam engines for road haulage, and the rise of the combustion engine tractor on the land, it could not make similar products in sufficient numbers to compete with other manufacturers.

There was some puzzlement at Beyer, Peacocks as to why the company had been interested in this purchase. A rumour went around that Sir Sam had a lady friend at Thorpness, near Aldeburgh, and that by having a subsidiary company nearby he could combine business with pleasure.[270] At first, the acquisition of the Richard Garratt business did not help Beyer, Peacock's financial position, but it began to produce a small dividend by securing orders for Elliott Shaping Machines, and then for war munitions. In fact, the works lasted until final closure in 1981, outliving Beyer, Peacock itself by fifteen years. In 1933, Sir Sam retired from the chairmanship of Beyer, Peacock. Edgar Fay recorded that his father had been 'encouraged' to resign because of the rumour. Sam's son (Samuel) Ernest had become a director of the company, and felt he had no option but to resign also.

Charles Frederick Beyer (1813–1876), born in Saxony, the son of a weaver, started work for 3 farthings an hour, and by his own efforts, winning a scholarship to a German Polytechnic, became a very wealthy man, rising to the status of a great engineer. He was a large-scale benefactor of education establishments and churches in Manchester, donating the sum of the present-day equivalence of £10 million to the university of his adopted city. A devout Anglican churchman, it may be possible that a Puritan ethos had survived in the business until the 1930s.

AUSTRALIA

In 1924, Sir Sam, with Sir Vincent Litchfield Raven, late of the North Eastern Railway Company, was appointed as a Royal Commissioner on the railways of New South Wales, Australia. The Australian railways

---

270 Beyer, Peacock History, page 176. The lady was Daisy Yeo.

had a different genesis from those built in Britain. The first Governor of Australia, from 1851 to 1855, was Sir Charles Augustus Fitzroy,[271] who with encouragement from Gladstone and strong support from Earl Grey, the Secretary of State for War and the Colonies, advocated the building of railways rather than roads in the Colony.[272] The building proceeded steadily during the nineteenth century, so that from 1870 to 1919 successive governments in Australia had invested over half of the total public capital expenditure in new or replacement railway works. Sir George Fuller, Prime Minister of New South Wales, could say in 1920 that Australia had already laid down more miles of railway per head of the population than any country in the world.[273] 'Unfortunately, this meant that many of the lines hardly paid for themselves, and the system was being subsidized by profits on suburban lines'; so commented *The Daily Telegraph* in 1922.

In January 1917 new railways had been transferred from the Public Works Department to the Railway Commissioners, a body established in 1857, and the Chief Commissioner, appointed in 1907, was T.R. Johnson, formerly Assistant Engineer of the Great Northern Railway of England. During 1917 a strike of railwaymen, 'bordering on civil war', was joined by other unions; the strike ended, with concessions on both sides, in September of that year, but there was a chronic shortage of labour. Sir George Fuller said, 'Here we have this great empty continent of ours, and we need to fill it up.' Filling up the empty spaces meant a policy of even more railways. Management of railways and labour strikes, interference by government and illegal pressure from outside authorities and investment adventurers, coupled with rapidly decreasing business in the 1920s, became a complicated economic and social problem.

The successor to T.R. Johnson was James Fraser, and as his term of office was, in 1923, nearing its conclusion, amid accusations of serious laxity and unbusinesslike management being made in Parliament, all these problems were beginning to be addressed more urgently. In September 1923, the new Government decided upon a full enquiry into the management of the country's railways. George Fuller told the House that two English experts were to be engaged and given full powers of a Royal Commission, with

271 1796–1858.
272 John Gunn, *Along Parallel Lines*, Melbourne University Press, 1989, pages 2 and 16.
273 Ibid., pages 283 and 291.

six months to carry out their task, prior to the introduction of a General Railways Amendment Bill.[274]

The terms of the Royal Commission were laid out in some detail:

> George the Fifth, by the Grace of God, of the United Kingdom of Great Britain and Ireland, and of the British Dominions beyond the sea, King, Defender of the Faith, Emperor of India. To our Trusty and Well-beloved, Sir Sam Fay, Kt, JP, Sir Vincent Raven, KBE, MInstCE, MIME, MIEE –
>
> Greeting: Know Ye, that We, reposing great trust and confidence in your ability, zeal, industry, discretion, and integrity, do, by these presents, with the advice of our Executive Council, to inquire into the management, equipment, and general working, including the finance, administration, control and economy of the Railway and Tramway Services in New South Wales[275]

One week later the Australian press reported the engagement of two Englishmen, Sir Sam Fay and Sir Vincent Raven, to conduct the Railway Enquiry. A brief resumé of their qualifications was given, that for Fay concluding, oddly, with his becoming Superintendent of the Line on the London and South Western Railway in 1898 – thus omitting mention of the whole of his main career. Raven was described as serving under four Chief Mechanical Engineers on the North Eastern Railway, before becoming Chief Mechanical Engineer himself in 1910.

The two Royal Commissioners faced a considerable challenge. The organization that they were charged with assessing was large and complex. *The Daily Telegraph* wrote that:

> A service so comprehensive, which touches in some way more or less intimately the business, pleasures, and convenience of nearly every member of the community must inevitably move in the full glare of pitiless publicity. The [Australian] Railway Commissioners are mighty employers of labour, and it is not in the nature of things that they should be exempt from adverse comment in an age when

---

274 Ibid., pages 291–199.
275 See Appendix 5 for the full continuation.

labour is so resolute in fighting for what it deems its rights and interests... The railways and tramways together comprise a huge concern, demanding for their successful conduct the very highest technical and administrative ability.[276]

The 'two English experts' arrived in New South Wales on 9 May 1924, and held their first formal sitting as Royal Commissioners in the office of the Chief Secretary on 2 July. On the same day, J.T. Lang, the labour leader, soon to become the Prime Minister, gave them a taste of state railway politics: 'In regard to the railway experts', he said in an address to the Legislative Assembly, 'these gentlemen know nothing at all about Australian conditions... their Report will be nothing but a laudation and whitewashing of James Fraser... they are merely being led around New South Wales by the Chief Commissioner.'[277] In fact, Fraser's Annual Report for the year ended 30 June 1924 to Parliament in August showed impressive results. The Commissioners had paid net earnings to consolidated (Government) revenue £4,699,086, an increase on the 1923 figure which was £4,571,359, and a return on capital of 5.2%.

The 'Two Knights' presented their report on 3 October 1924. In their Report, Fay and Raven, after an Introductory recalling the terms of their Royal Commission, stated that they had received answers to a sixty-item questionnaire, subsequently amplified, through the Minister for Railways. Statements had been received also from the various chief officers, the general organization, and administration of their branches. They had called for and perused the minutes of the Board Meetings of the Commissioners, the Committee Meetings and the various Officers' Conferences, and had also analysed the complaints, numbering some hundreds, addressed to the Railway Commission by the public, over a period of six months:

We travelled over the whole of the main lines, and with a few exceptions, the branch lines of the New South Wales State railway system. We devoted thirty-six days to the tours of inspection, travelling 9.580 miles in that period, and inspecting plant and facilities... We became acquainted first hand with the location,

276 Quoted, ibid., page 300.
277 Ibid., pages 300 and 301.

general layout and equipment of the track, stations, and buildings; the traffic conditions of the lines, the facilities provided for the various classes of traffic, the nature of the country served by the railway network, and the methods of local supervision and working... Inspection was made of passenger and goods stations, refreshment rooms, locomotive and electrical workshops, sheds, and manufacturing establishments, stores, yards and signalling equipments and the permanent way, together with other essentials of railway service, while conversations with the local supervisory officials helped us to appreciate the nature of the problem in this state... Almost throughout we were accompanied – at our own request – by Mr James Fraser, Chief Railway Commissioner. The Chief Traffic Manager, the Chief Mechanical Engineer, and the Information Officer also accompanied us, while traffic and locomotive officers were present in their respective districts for the purpose of explain the various features of the railway system in their areas. The tours of inspection were completed on 11 July... Regular sittings began in Sydney on 15 July, and a one-day hearing took place at Newcastle on 20 August. Evidence was taken on twenty-eight days. In all, twenty-eight departmental officers and twenty-five representatives of public bodies and associations were heard.

It became evident at any early stage of the inquiry that the system of financial control under which the railways and tramways were dependent upon the yearly budget of the State, coupled with the fact that no resources exist to meet wasting assets, dominated the organisation, and through it the efficient and economical operation of the transport services. We have, therefore, placed Finance and Financial Control at the forefront of our report. Practically from the inception of the railways, the Government has managed and operated the railway transport services and now, except for a few short, private lines, the whole of the system in New South Wales is State-owned. Under the various Acts, Commissioners were appointed as a corporate body under the name of 'Railway Commissioners of New South Wales,' in whom were 'vested absolutely' the railways and tramways, including equipment and lands. They are authorized to work and manage the railways, but their powers are circumscribed in several important respects. Expenditure is limited to moneys appropriated by Parliament, and all receipts are paid into the Consolidated Revenue of the State, day by day. Moneys for additional stores, plant, rolling stock, stations or other accommodations considered necessary to meet traffic requirements have to be sought by application through the Minister of Railways. Approval by-laws must be obtained and as rates and fares are imposed by by-law, this entails a submission to the Government of any proposed increase or decrease in charges.

The report, containing a multitude of carefully researched lists, charts, and financial earnings and expenses for the years 1914 to 1924, drew attention to the fact that the interest on the state debt had increased in those years from 3.7% to 5.2%, and this was applied to the railways, irrespective of the actual rate at which at which money for railway purposes was raised. 'The trail of ineffective and hampering finance is in evidence throughout the railway administration', wrote the Royal Commissioners: 'That a drastic change of method is imperative needs no elaboration... [It is] the belief of many people in Australia and elsewhere that a government cannot successfully manage an industrial undertaking.' They stated that it reflected great credit on those who had been responsible for managing the railway system that they had produced large net revenues while providing cheap, speedy and adequate transport throughout the state. But unless they were given control over their own funds the system could become ineffective as a development agency in the rapid progress of the country.[278]

This was a proposal unlikely to find favour with politicians, for it meant removal from consolidated revenue (including tramways) of £110,000,000, and the setting up of a separate finance department under the Railway Commissioners, plus future requirements for another £35,000,000 in the following seven years. 'This is a large sum', admitted the Royal Commissioners, but as well as power to control budgeting, their other recommendations were that the Railway Act should be amended to place the direction of the railways in the hands of a board with complete freedom from political control, and that the decentralization

278 Ibid., pages 303–306.

of railway management on an area basis was desirable. They even went on to recommend in detail the structure of command under the Chief Commissioner, who should be free to appoint his own assistants 'to secure and keep the best men in the world', and the salaries of such appointments. It was, however, 'A remarkably lucid and comprehensive report.'[279]

The report was also specific in its comments on city and suburban railways: 'The New South Wales Railway system around Sydney lends itself in a most remarkable way to electrification, from its dense and congested traffic, its steep gradients, and the proximity of coal fields.' The *Sydney Morning Herald* commended their emphasis on the prompt construction of the city electric railway, and, complimenting their 'splendid vindication of the methods of the Railway Commissioners and their observation that the political system under which they are obliged to work is responsible for any failure of the railways to function as they ought.' *The Herald* continued 'Obviously the Commissioners… are not men of little faith. They ask for a measure of self-abnegation on the part of politicians.'

The Royal Commissioners caused a temporary flurry of speculation and speculation when it became known that they had written a private and confidential letter to the Premier, Sir George Fuller, who was quick to get their permission to release its contents, which were highly flattering to the Chief Commissioner of Railways. The whole report bore the impression of the views and character of the Royal Chief Commissioner. Such a thorough and ruthless examination of all the evidence assembled, and the fearless conclusions and recommendations drawn from the enquiry, could have been foreseen by anyone familiar with the Great Central Management, or from the War Office and High Command in England. John Gunn commented that:

> The Royal Commissioners' terms of reference had not included details of the personality or achievements of the Chief Commissioner, and Sir Vincent Raven had obviously been impressed by both. Their report was lengthily discussed in Cabinet, in several debates, on its recommendations, centering on the radical financial proposals, driven by the urgency of some decisions before the expiry of the term of the existing Railway Commissioners. The proposal to give

279 Ibid., page 307.

them full control over the Treasury… involved very important considerations affecting the finances of the State as a whole, and a full discussion was postponed until the next session.

Part of the eventual debate was reported by the *Sydney Herald* that '[James] Fraser, with his re-appointment for a further seven years, and his salary increased by 66%, has had his prestige as a public servant greatly enhanced.' There can be little doubt that Fay's Royal Commission had stimulated a wider debate about the State's administration of its railway system, as well as fulfilling the original remit.

NEW ZEALAND

In consequence of this Australian commitment, Sam was invited in June 1924 by the Government of New Zealand, after he had finished in New South Wales, to report on their railways. He returned home on 7 February 1925. Samuel Ernest Fay, his eldest son, had acted as Secretary to the Australian Royal Commission, and he was offered a post on New Zealand Railways, which he accepted.

ARGENTINA

Sir Sam held directorships in two Argentinian railway companies: the Buenos Aires Great Southern, and the Buenos Aires Western Railway. There was family tradition that he attended the monthly meetings in London 'without saying a word', but his visits to the country were highly influential. On 5 January 1927 he sailed for a term of inspection of the two railways. Unfortunately he contracted food poisoning on board and 'arrived a wreck' in Buenos Aires.

But on the return journey in March he recorded that he had had a very instructive and interesting time there. 'We travelled over 7,000 miles of line and saw a great country in the making, in which the hard-bitten Britisher is taking a great part.' He expressed great admiration for 'these men who go out into the wilds and live practically alone for the best years of their lives, and turn a wilderness into a garden'. He added that 'the more one sees of them the more one is thankful for being of their race'.[280]

His son Edgar was with him on that visit, and recorded his 'astonishment at his father's influence: he was treated like the Prince of Wales, and even given a pass on the Chile State Railways to which Sir Sam's fame had spread – a privilege which even General Managers did not receive'.[281]

In April 1927, Fay was privileged to unveil a memorial at Bowen Railway Station, which was erected in honour of Sir Albert Edward Bowen, Bt (1858–1924), an Englishman born in Hanley, Staffordshire who became highly successful in business in Argentina. He was Chairman of the Board of the Buenos Aires Great Southern Railway from 1916 until his death, as well as a Director of the Buenos Aires Western Railway and several other Argentinian companies.

Aregentina – Bowen Memorial
Sir Sam is 9th from the right

280 Edgar Stewart Fay, op cit, p.288.
281 Edgar Stewart Fay, op cit, p.280.

Beyer, Peacock Works Manchester – Garratt Locomotive 2395

Beyer, Peacock Works, Manchester

14

Private Life

> I desire you would use all your skill to paint my picture truly like
> me, and not flatter me at all; but remark all these roughnesses,
> pimples, warts and everything you see in me. (Oliver Cromwell, to
> a portrait painter, Sir Peter Lely)

George Dow records that Fay was a decisive martinet, both in his office and at
times at home, and gave utterance to short outbursts of temper. One occasion
was when he had to go before a Parliamentary Committee in connection
with the takeover of the Lancashire Derbyshire and East Coast Railway. His
Parliamentary Assistant, Pierce, very assiduously drew up a comprehensive
brief, which included a great many statistics and charts, working the staff at
Marylebone until midnight. Fay read the first few lines of the brief, asking,
'What is this damned rubbish? This is no use at all.' On his return to the
office, Pierce was asked how they had fared. Looking anxious, he replied:

> The G.M. acquitted himself extremely well in the witness box, and
> so far as I know, there will be no hitches. But on the way there in the
> taxi he got more and more worked up over the brief, and in the end
> he tore up the lot and stamped his foot on them as we left the cab.

Fay could also be unnecessarily ill-mannered. After the company's HQ had
been moved from Manchester London Road to Marylebone, it was the

practice for the company's Canal Agent to give to Fay a report once a year on the canals in his charge. On one occasion this junior official was kept a whole day waiting in the outer office while Fay passed and re-passed him on the way to lunch and going home. The following morning he asked the Personal Secretary, tentatively, if Fay would now see him; after consulting the General Manager, the Secretary returned with the message that Fay would do so when he came up next year. Dow added that there were 'doubtless other similar incidents, yet despite them the company's staff accepted him for fair, and when necessary, compassionate treatment'.

Dow's description of Fay's appearance and demeanour is borne out by the photographs of him:

> He was a most distinguished-looking man, although short in stature… His ruddy… impish features, his alert brown eyes, well-trimmed dark hair, mustache and beard, and his erect bearing and impeccable dress, combined to give an immaculate impression… Some of the staff found him awe-inspiring… his son Edgar confirmed this, adding that a doctor had told him in his twenties that he 'had a click in his heart,' and advised him to give up smoking; advice to which he paid no attention at all, and chain-smoked Havana cigars virtually throughout his life… He loved alcohol, but though exercising discipline in his time on the M&SWJR[282] he was cured, for good, by Beatrice.

He exuded vitality and an abounding geniality, and to some women his personality was magnetic. Dow wrote that 'Fay was not entirely immune to the fair sex, and had been described as a prodigious lover. In this respect he was no worse than many other contemporary well-to-do men of the era characterized by the King, Edward VII.'[283] Edgar was convinced that he felt remorse because he was essentially a kind[284] man, as exemplified by his feelings for his wife, and his behaviour undoubtedly caused unhappiness from time to time.

---

282 From time to time he felt pressured by events and problems. His grandson John recorded that at times Sam would plead 'My God, my God, why hast thou forsaken me?', a quotation from Jesus's words from the Cross.

283 George Dow, *Great Central*, Locomotive Publishing Co.Ltd, (Ian Allan), London 1965, Volume III, pages 81 and 82.

284 This is the word most usually used of him by his sons and grandsons.

Thus he left for posterity three families. The main one was with his marriage to his youthful sweetheart, Frances Ann Farbrother, 'Trottie', five years his junior, whom he married in Kingston-upon-Thames in 1883. She and her brother Walter were the children of a local cabinet maker and undertaker.[285] Sam and Frances had four girls, Frances (born 1884), Clarrie ('Annie'), (born 1886), Winifred (1888) and Nellie (1894); and two sons, Samuel Ernest (1891) and Vincent David (1901).

The need arose for a children's nurse, and Beatrice Charlotte Scamell[286] (born 31 January 1875) was employed in 1892.[287] Sam was 36, and she was 17, and by 1898 they had become lovers. In the summer of that year they went together on a cycling holiday to the Forest of Arques in France. Beatrice recalled the happiness of that holiday all her life, and when she built a house in Gerrard's Cross she named it 'Arques'. The association was a profound influence on both their lives, and there was never another man in her life. It was by no means a frivolous or irresponsible liaison. Despite never being able to live together except for very brief holidays, their association was one of great happiness for both of them.

The consequent bewilderment and unsettling of his family seems, on balance, to have been charitably borne. The son of their friendship, Edgar Stewart,[288] commented in his *Memoirs* that seventeen years before George Bernard Shaw's *Pygmalion*, Fay took a country girl, the daughter of a farmer,

285 She had also an elder brother, Charles, and a sister, Mary. Charles served in the second Afghan War, and retired with the rank of Major. He had a number of children, and the eldest became station masters on the L&SWR: Charles at Cosham, and William at Winchester and Bournemouth. (Bill Marvin Fay, Letter.)

286 No relation to George Scammell & Nephew Ltd, the developers of the six-wheel 'mechanical horse' vehicle, launched in 1920 and adopted by the main railway companies for local deliveries, though the families lived close to each other and were good friends.

287 She was a daughter of Charles and Mary Scamell of Damerham, Hampshire, the youngest of six surviving children, with two sisters and three brothers. Charles was tenant and miller of Hill Farm. He died in 1880, and Mary (née Bound; Arthur was the son of one of her brothers), died in 1930, aged 95.

288 Edgar Stewart Fay (8 October 1908 to 14 November 2009), QC, who became a High Court Judge, known for his 'sharp intellect'. He conducted, *inter alia*, two enquiries into the 'Manchester United' air crash in Munich of February 1958, and in 1969 he appeared for British Rail at the enquiry into the Hixon Crossing disaster, Staffordshire, on 6 January 1968. He retired in 1980. His *Memoirs*, held in copyright by his son Francis Fay, literary executor, are an invaluable source for insight into Sam Fay's character.

with only a rudimentary education, and transformed her into a proficient businesswoman. In 1897 he sent her to a school in Margate, and then for a year to a finishing school in Brussels. In 1898 she took lodgings in London to take an apprenticeship as a florist, and in 1900 she set up her own business at 84B Piccadilly, under the name of Rohan & Cie, then in 1901 opened her own fruit and flower shop on Waterloo Station. In all this can be seen the entrepreneurial hand of Sam Fay, to think of exploiting the opening for retail trade from the passing thousands of railway travellers. At that time the only widespread shops on railway stations were those of W.H. Smith's newspaper and bookstalls. Rohan & Cie later spread to other stations and it became a limited company; Beatrice recruited a female staff with whom she 'infected with her youthful enthusiasm'.[289]

Sam moved from where he had lived in his L&SWR days to Gerrard's Cross, 'Woodbank House', on the Marylebone Line.[290] Situated on the London to Uxbridge Road, at the end of the Common, the house was described in the estate agents' advertisements as a 'mansion set in ample grounds between the Oxford Road and its Lane leading to the Bull Hotel'. He lived there until the 1920s. His youngest legitimate child, Vincent David, was part of the family there. About 1913, another child nurse was employed by Beatrice: Daisy Rose Yeo (1891–1987). She was a person keen on birds and animals, and with Sam she visited the great ships at Southampton. In 1924, she gave birth to a son, John (1924–2015), the father of whom was clearly Sir Sam. Daisy Yeo had left her employment in 1919 to go to work in France, though Edgar and his mother Beatrice visited her and her family at Christmas 1921.[291] She came back to the family at that time, and when she finally left on 28 January 1922, 'It was awful without her – she is so nice.' Daisy had shared his upbringing with Beatrice, and she had inspired in him a love for reading. She died in 1987, and Edgar had kept in touch with her to the end. He appears to have benefitted fairly happily from his

---

289 Edgar Stewart Fay, op. cit., pages 11–14.

290 Gerrard's Close had three public houses, a couple of shops, a handful of dwellings, and a church and vicarage: a very small place to receive a station on a new main line. Edward Watkin in 'Metroline' mode again?

291 Edgar left it on record that he owed a great debt, and one of many, to Daisy 'Yeo-Yeo', as he called her, for teaching him to read at an early age, and encouraging in him an interest to read good books, which he enjoyed and continued to develop afterwards. (ibid., pages 62–65).

membership of his three families, despite knowing his father as 'Uncle' until 1919 or 1920, but Beatrice herself was uncomfortable with her ambiguous status. Edgar knew her for many years as his 'Aunt', and she changed her house on Census nights to live with her sister Agnes, to avoid having to record him as her son.[292]

In 1923, Sam also moved house, no longer needing to live on the Great Central Line. He sold Woodbank House, but not before he had given Beatrice a sizeable plot of the back land, fronting on Bull Lane, on which she was to build two substantial houses. About that time, a notable residential estate came on the market in the Test Valley village of Awbridge, where Sam's forebears had lived for so long. This was 'Awbridge Danes':

> A Residential sporting estate, comprising a Victorian stone-built house (of 12 bedrooms), with the proper appurtenances of a minor seat – a nine-acre artificial lake, a false-Greek temple, finely-timbered gardens, parkland and beautiful woodlands, together with a house, farm, and three cottages – 200 acres in all.[293]

With funds from his compensation money, Fay transferred his family there, and prepared to settle into the life of the country. He had been a Justice of the Peace for some years, sitting on the Beaconsfield Bench, and he now transferred to Hampshire and joined the magistrates of Romsey. Beatrice, meanwhile, had been expanding her business. She was increasingly delegating it to, by all accounts, a redoubtable manageress, and to monitoring by accountants. Sam and she had foreseen the development of air travel after the War, and that it would attract passengers with money to spend while awaiting their flights. When it was announced that the aerodrome at Waddon, south-west of Croydon, was to be developed for civilian flights, she applied to the Air Ministry for permission to lease shop premises there, But there were no shop premises, only wooden huts for staff and air personnel. If she wanted to operate, she must provide her own wooden hut. Which she did. As there were no other shops in the vicinity, she began to provide cigarettes and confectionary, and very soon cups of tea to aircrew, passengers and visitors, and in due course it became the airport

---

292 Ibid., page 49.
293 Quoted from estate agents' advertisements.

post office. When the great British Empire Exhibition was held at Wembley in 1924–1925, she opened two kiosks there, selling fruit and confectionery to many of the 27 million people who attended.

Sam had harboured notions in his youth of becoming a barrister. He had attended the Strangers' Gallery debates in the House of Commons, and had been involved in presenting to committees for and against the passing of private or local Acts of Parliament. Dating from the Marlborough and Grafton Railway Bill of 1896, he came to be examined and cross-examined by leading members of the Parliamentary Bar, and relished the cut and thrust of the contest, coming to appreciate the quickness of mind and skill of the advocates he confronted. 'This was the life for a man of keen intelligence', commented Edgar, who was always grateful for his father's guiding him into the legal profession.[294]

Sam was a loving father, and was as careful and generous in Edgar's welfare as any father could be. This was particularly true in respect of his education. At the age of fourteen, he was sent to Sutton Courtney, Oxford, to prepare for his matriculation at Courtney Lodge School in June 1923. Up to that time he was registered as 'Edgar Stewart', being brought up by his 'Aunt' Beatrice, having a 'benign uncle'. At Courtney Lodge he was to be known as Edgar Stewart Fay, and be open about his father. After Courtney Lodge he went in 1925 to McGill University, Montreal, Canada, to read history and political science; a university which Sam had prefered to the 'stuffy' English ones, though afterwards Edgar went to Cambridge at Pembroke College to read law. He was called to the Bar at the Inner Temple in 1932.[295] In 1909, after education at Malvern Cottage, Sam had subsidized his eldest son, Samuel Ernest, to McGill, to read engineering (he was the only one on his course). While in Canada, he met E.P. Stevenson, who was later to marry his sister Winifred.

Samuel Ernest took up skiing, and achieved some skill in jumps. Belonging to a team, possibly in an English versus Canadians competition, he attempted a jump too high, landing awkwardly and sustaining a serious accident, and was in hospital for six months. He had to wear an 'iron contraption' on his leg thereafter, mentioning it painfully to his son John in a letter as the 'bone in his leg', when working in New Zealand.

---

294 Edgar Stewart, op. cit., pages 99 and 100.
295 op, cit, page 144.

Unfortunately he was unable to complete his degree at McGill, but later took a Commission in the Royal Engineers, becoming a Major.[296] Later he worked at Beyer, Peacock Locomotive Builders, and accompanied Sam as his Secretary to his Royal Commission in Australia in 1924, and accepted an invitation from the New Zealand Government to work for their Railways. In 1913, he had been part of a group headed by John G. Robinson visiting the USA and Canada, travelling over 2,500 miles and meeting several railway officers and contractors.[297] This visit produced a design by Robinson for a Great Central 2-10-2 locomotive, which would have hauled 100 40-ton wagon coal trains from the South Yorkshire coalfields to Immingham, an idea of Sam Fay, who proposed opening up Conisborough tunnel to accommodate their passage. Unfortunately, that inspiration was thwarted by handling problems, both at the collieries and on the road.

Sam's letter to his son Edgar, written on the lad's fifteenth birthday (1923), recorded faithfully in Edgar's *Memoirs*, give us an insight into his character:

> My Dear Edgar,
>
> Many happy returns on your birthday... you have all the future years to look forward to and I alas can only look backward... When you get (to) my age things will look very different from today and you will have to grow up and meet the conditions of the days to come, with all the inventions and political changes that are bound to come even more rapidly than they have since I was your age. Life will be more strenuous than now, I suspect, but you will, I am sure, be able to hold your own with the best brains of your time. Anyway, you are laying a good foundation, and the more you learn while your mind is receptive the better.

Occasionally the lad was still the subject of upbrading for what Sam described as his 'aunt' Beatrice's 'cossetting'. Despite such remonstrances, Edgar related in later life how he cherished his mother's love and wisdom in his upbringing. He also recorded his appreciation of guidance from her

---

296 John Samuel Fay, letter to the author.
297 George Dow, op. cit., Volume III, pages 324 and 325.

cousin Arthur Bound, the GCR's signals expert.[298] He and Beatrice were close friends throughout their lives. Edgar spent his first half-term break with his 'Aunt' Beatrice at the Great Eastern Hotel in London,[299] and for his first holiday, at Easter, with both his parents, the first of many such. It was at the Felix Hotel, Felixstowe.[300]

On Easter Tuesday, 22 April 1924, Edgar went to see old friends in Hove, returning on the following Friday to London on the Brighton Pullman, 'The Southern Railway's crack train', timing it as attaining 75 mph on its way to Victoria. About this time he recorded that Beatrice was 5 foot 7 tall (making her 3 or 4 inches taller than Sir Sam). On holidays with his mother they went each Sunday to church (though, unlike his father, he does not comment on the quality of the sermons). In August 1924 his relationship with his 'aunt' changed from that of a parent and child to one of friend and relation, a real bond of mutual tolerance and affection. Also in 1924 he mentioned that 'Yeo-Yeo' was in London, 'and had visited us'.

By this time Sam was giving his son Edgar a practical education across a broad spectrum. He took him on a visit to Beyer, Peacock's Works,[301] and later to a sitting of a Parliamentary Committee which was examining a proposal by local authorities for a road tunnel under the River Mersey, connecting Liverpool with the Wirral. Sam had been required by the committee to give evidence against the necessity for such tunnel (a tunnel for the Mersey Railway Company had been built in 1886). Nevertheless, the project was authorized, opening in 1934.[302]

On their journeyings, Sam gave much fatherly advice: 'Don't contradict directly; say 'Is that right?' rather than a positive statement like 'That is not true.' 'A spoonful of sugar is worth a hogshead of vinegar any day.[303] This isn't a sermon, but an essay on tact: wonderful thing is tact! Anyway, you can

---

298 During the Second World War, Bound took refuge from the London Blitz in Edgar's country house.

299 Designed for the GER by Charles E. and Edward, the sons of the architect Sir Charles Barry, in 1884. Edward Barry also designed Cannon Street Station Hotel (1861), Charing Cross Station Hotel (1864) and Crewe Hall, Cheshire (1866–1871).

300 Built 1903; purchased by the Great Eastern Railway in 1920.

301 They stayed at the Midland Hotel, opened by the Midland Railway in 1903, opposite the Manchester Central Station.

302 It was the longest underwater road tunnel in the world, a title held for 24 years.

303 Hogshead: an English ale cask size, the largest (54 gallons) in normal commercial use at that time.

be trusted to use your brains.' One letter suggested that Edgar might write to him, telling how he was getting on, giving him the address as 'c/o Beyer, Peacock & Co. Ltd, Abbey House, Victoria Street, Westminster.' 'I am there three days a week at least and shall be for some time.'

On Friday 3 June 1925, Sam took Edgar to 'Awbridge Danes', his retirement home in Hampshire. On the following Monday they went over to the Isle of Wight to visit a farm he owned at Chale, returning to 'Awbridge Danes' on Friday the 31st to meet Sam's (legitimate) family. Edgar went home on Friday, 1 August, having met them all except Ernest, the eldest son, who was in New Zealand. In his *Memoirs* he recorded his impressions of his half-sisters: Frances ('Francie') he remembered well; she was 'competent, kind, helpful, good-looking, a fine face... her hair shaped in the current attractive shingle'.[304] 'Annie ("Clarrie") appeared for short weekends: she seemed a little on the sharp side. She had a millinery business in Duke Street, near Selfridges in London. The third daughter, Winifred ("Winnie") was married to E.P. Stevenson, an engineer... a pleasant, friendly couple'. Sam had given them, too, a plot of land on the Gerrard's Close estate, and they built a house on it, fronting the Oxford Road. 'Nellie, the youngest, must have been there, but I have only the faintest shadow of her.' He thought she was in 'ill-health, and she died only twelve years later'. The second son, and youngest child, David (1901–1975), appeared one weekend. He worked in Dean & Dawson's, the Great Central travel subsidiary, of which he became the General Manager. He said to Edgar, 'Oh, I heard about your advent.' It was the only time the two ever met. David was the only member of the family to take extreme exception to Edgar's existence, refusing to visit Awbridge, much to Lady Fay's disappointment, as she could not see David's children.

Sam Fay included his daughters in his managerial capacity on the GCR. The new steamship *Dewsbury* was launched by Frances Mary on 14 April 1910, the first steamship to leave from the future Immingham Dock complex. On 7 June 1910 Annie Clara launched the *Accrington*; Winifred

---

304 Frances married, in January 1935, the Vicar of Awbridge, the Revd Albert Orton (1879–1952). After ordination in 1929 and two curacies he became the Vicar there in 1933, leaving in 1935. He served a further six appointments in six different Dioceses until retirement in Ludlow, in Shropshire, in 1947. An average of only two years in each place suggests a problem of some kind. The marriage appears not to have lasted long, and there were no children. (Indeed, not one of Sam's daughters had any children.)

May officiated for the *Bury* on 10 November in the same year; and Nellie Beatrice did the same for *Macclesfield*, the GCR's last ship, on 22 May 1914.[305]

Edgar's visit to 'Awbridge Danes' for the first time made a deep impression on him. He said it was of the doomed breed of English country house with the appropriate establishment of butler, housekeeper and chauffeur, and still carrying on the traditions of tea on the terrace, and 'Anyone for tennis?', 'portrayed in a thousand novels from P.G. Wodehouse to Agatha Christie'. The butler 'was a disappointment' – quite unlike Jeeves and company. He was a young man, very nervous, and clearly terrified of Sir Sam. Sartorially, Edgar started off on the wrong foot: he had not brought his dinner jacket, not having realized that he would be changing for dinner each evening. Aunt Beatrice and he came from a different world. He was puzzled (permanently) as to why Sir Sam had made him known to his whole family. He was introduced as a young friend who would, with the help of Frances, catalogue the library (which had come with the purchase of the house). But he entered into the new environment with both curiosity and pleasure.

Back at Awbridge after a visit to Chale Farm, Isle of Wight, he started sorting the books, and on Sunday 5 July he went to church, pronouncing the sermon 'too high for country folk'. In the evening, he 'did books until 11.15 pm'. 3 July: 'walked around the park with father in the morning and on Sunday, the 5th, went to church, then cataloguing, but it is still rough and unfinished'. The following day, 'catalogued all morning, then joined the others on the lake for a picnic – wonderful time'. On 9 August: 'Father went early to the Isle of Wight: we, Winnie, Francie and Stevenson, played tennis: one set each – very good.' After lunch, he wrote that he 'was having a wonderful time, and was putting in 8½ hours on books today'. On 5 August, his last day there, he had two lots of cataloguing, divided by a wander round with Francie to get eggs. On 6 August, he 'worked hard with Francie from 9 am to 1 pm, and got the books done from "S" to "W"'.

He visited his half-sisters again at Awbridge during the summer vacation the following year (1926), and after that he saw them no more. The son he had not met, Ernest, he met in 1953, when he discovered that Ernest was the executor of Sam's Will, with which Edgar helped when the time came.

305 George Dow, op. cit., pages 270, 273 and 274.

Looking back, he felt it was a pity he had had no further contact with the family. Because of his 'equivocal status', he felt that any initiative should come from them. Whichever way we look at it, the friendliness between Edgar and the family was a tribute to both his sociableness and openness, and to Sam's main family, in their ability to form friendships across what might have been a difficult gap.

Of Lady Fay, he recalled an impression of 'a small, bustling person, rather overshadowed by her daughters'. One of Sam's grandsons remembered her in her latter years as being nearly stone deaf, never dressing in any clothes except black, and remaining Victorian in her outlook on modern fashions, 'She had some sort of limp (it was because of this she had always been known as "Trottie") but it did not prevent her from trotting round the house, seeing to everything: she kept the house in immaculate order.' He also recalled that 'during the War the youngsters wondered about her sanity, especially during the Blitz, when she said she could hear what the German pilots above were saying, and they used such awful swear words'.[306] Another grandson described her as a 'fairly grey, in-the-background character', and who seemed to have remained closer to her social roots than had Sir Sam.' Edgar remembered that she was 'rather overshadowed by her daughters, and one of them admonishing her mother for expressing herself in a less than middle class way'.

Edgar never discovered his father's reasons for thus introducing him to them all: 'Was it a wise move, or a piece of colossal cheek?' he wondered. He liked to think that Sam had a wish to incorporate him into his family, now that he was to be called Edgar Fay, rather than as hitherto 'Edgar Stewart'. (This seems to be by far the likeliest reason.) He was surprised that they had not 'booted him out', and he attributed their acceptance of him to innate good manners assisted by the aura of authority emanating from Sir Sam: 'He was very much in charge.' The two families, mainly through John Samuel and Edgar's son Charles Stewart, met regularly on friendly terms.[307]

Fay recorded in his diary on 7 September 1917[308] that he had received a request from his eldest son, Samuel Ernest, for £1,000 to put into his

306 John Samuel Fay, in a private letter.
307 John Samuel Fay, private letter.
308 Not all these entries in Sam's wartime diaries found their way into the publication of *The War Office at War*. Hutchinson 1937.

marriage settlement, who expressed surprise that his father refused. Sam explained that 'In the present state of uncertainty he would not put anything into a marriage settlement, but would see that he did not want. A wartime wedding means wartime conditions', he concluded. On 15 December he learned that Ernest was on the list of Haig's 'Mentioned in Despatches'. At Samuel Ernest's wedding in February 1918, he kept the parenthetic assurance by sending him £200. In Sam's Kingston days he had helped out his own father, who was having financial problems on his farm, giving him all his savings and £3 or £4 a month (40%) from his pay. About the same time he bailed out a bookstall clerk who was desperate for cash he could not repay.[309]

In a letter of 3 November 1925, Sam mentioned that: 'We (Beyer, Peacock and Company) are at present time getting more than full orders. We are building Garratts for the LMS and the Argentine[310], as well as South Africa and India; five electric engines through English Electric for Montreal Harbour have also come in.'

On 18 January 1926 he expressed concern for Edgar's well-being in a cold Canadian climate by exhorting him to keep up his 'bodily heat by good living and plenty of it. Like the Esquimaux you must eat fat, not necessarily candles.' At the end of his first year, and good examination results, his father was enquiring about eventual law courses, and the requirements for being called to the Bar.

On 5 January 1927, Sir Sam sailed for a tour of inspection of his Argentinian railways, writing to tell Edgar of his hopes for time to develop a story he was writing about a man, a woman and a dog. Commenting on his father's literary ambitions, Edgar observed that in advancing years many people engage in reflecting on the origin and meaning of life, but few commit their thoughts to paper, let alone in such an ambitious form as he was attempting. In March, writing on the return voyage, Sam reported that he had had 'an instructive and interesting time in Argentina'. At the age of 71 he was in full vigour, looking much the same as he had ten years earlier. Sam was generous by nature, as long as his finances were secure, but always

309 William Charlton Fay, op cit, (unpublished).
310 The first Garratts for Argentina were built in 1925 for the North Eastern Railway there, and a repeat order for four more followed in 1927. Also in 1927, five to a similar design were supplied to the neighbouring Entre Rios Railway (*Beyer, Peacock' Locomotive Builders to the World*, R.L. Hills and D. Patrick, Transport Publishing Company, Glossop, Derbyshire,1982, page 182).

with a warning about living above one's income; a disciplinarian in this sphere, as in others: It was easy to increase one's standard of living, but very difficult to reduce it.'

In his early twenties, Edgar was preparing to get married, and in order to give a clear picture to his in-laws, he questioned his father and Beatrice (separately) about his status. Sir Sam was, surprisingly, discountenanced, 'taken aback as to what to answer, muttering something about people arriving uninvited, seeming embarrassed and ashamed'. They went on to discuss Edgar's proposed marriage, and Sam gave him some advice which seemed to arise from his own experience: '(i) The danger of an attraction of someone of superior intelligence, and (ii) The necessity of a man's wife being socially able to cope with one's friends and associates.

About this time, Sam had sent to Edgar the manuscript of the story he had written, before sending it to a publisher. Entitled *The Soul of the Dog*, It was an allegory expressing views on philosophy and religion. Edgar recorded that it was 'A very great thing – absolutely original in its form. Part of it was written in Biblical English', but he quoted in precis from the 'Secular' section: 'A young countryman marries a girl of his mother's choosing to soothe her last days – she having set her mind on it. Later, her cousin comes along. The young man falls in love.' There follows, more simply and beautifully, and more realistically than any other episode in the book, the story of their love, their determination to part, their failure to do so, and the inevitable result. Edgar was sure it was autobiographical. He added that 'unfortunately the manuscript had not survived.'

Lord Birkenhead, in his Rectorial Address to the students of Aberdeen University, expounded on 'The ambition and the glittering prizes of material success', and a copy was distributed to every McGill student. But Edgar was redirected by this message. In two leading articles for the *Montreal Star*, he argued that 'getting on in life' was not the 'be all and end all' of life. He wished that Lord Birkenhead had 'stirred a drop of two more of the milk of human kindness into his address'. It is not difficult to assume that he had learned this point of view from Sir Sam and Beatrice.

His father wrote to him in October 1928 to say that he was trying to get him into Cambridge in 1929, warning that 'he would find a very different crowd from McGill... some rich, some poor, some bound to succeed in life, some who will never be any good to themselves or their friends'. He went on to say that 'I shall treat you exactly as I have treated my other boys, viz: I give them as good an education as possible, and after that shift for themselves. It is the best way to make a responsible citizen.' On 19 November 1928 he wrote to advise: 'There is no reason to hesitate to say that I am your father. My family do not know it, though some of them may think so.' 'At the same time,' he added, 'it would be cruel to disturb the mind of my wife, who is a very dear and simple little woman.'

With reference to financial assistance after Cambridge he warned that there might be difficulties, as he was dependent mainly on earnings, and not on investments. He had three daughters to provide for, and the fourth was not too well married. He pointed out that his income would cease on his death. Further fatherly advice came late 1929, which was 'In attack upon anything, try to put yourself in the skin of other people who hold different views, and try to anticipate what you would think and do if in their place. That's a good principle in business as in all social intercourse.'

About this time, Beatrice's health was giving cause for concern. Sam urged Edgar to visit her. She was suffering from neurasthenia, leading to fancies caused by her lonely lifestyle. During the spring she found a satisfactory companion-housekeeper and her health improved. She had reacted with sadness to a meeting with Edgar's fiancée, and he realized that all along she and Sam might have married, and failing that, he – Edgar – had been the man in her house. Beatrice and Edgar did their best, but understandably never achieved terms of real closeness.[311] As an aside, in 1930 Sam compared Boat Race nights to modern accounts of football hooliganism, and commented 'plus ca change'.

By 28 June 1930 Edgar Stewart was back in Montreal to meet up with his fiancée Kathleen, and where his cousin Arthur (Bound) sought him out. Bound was on a term of inspection of North American Railways, with the LMS General Manager and its Chief Mechanical Engineer. In the December of that year the economic Depression had set in, and Sam felt the need for drastic cuts at 'Awbridge Danes', and having to review his subsidies to Edgar. Sir Sam wrote to Edgar in July 1931 that there were hundreds of rich men walking about without an income: their stock and their possessions bringing in nothing, and they cannot sell their wealth.[312] He mentioned in

311 *Memoirs*, op. cit., pages 314–323.
312 In September of that year Britain was forced off the Gold Standard.

passing that he had only once applied for a job – his first. The rest had been offered to him.

In 1932, Edgar was qualifying for the Bar. He had to borrow £50 from Beatrice. He was struggling to earn money, mainly from journalism; the pound had devalued steadily over the years. The publication of his examination results showed: 'Classics 1, The Hon Quintin Hogg, [313] Lincoln's Inn; E.S. Fay, Inner Temple.' His Class 1 bought Edgar a Certificate of Honour, and a £50 prize.

In 1933, Sam wrote to Edgar to say that he was 'full up for the work with engineering works, old ones, Russian contracts, ditto India, ditto French; pulverized coal locomotives – an old flame come to life (no details); various other ideas, ghostly and substantial'. Edgar commented that the financial Depression had not stemmed his flow of ideas, despite his age of 75 years. Sir Sam retired from Beyer, Peacock in 1933. For the first time in his life he had no office to go to, and no daily work to take him up to London from Hampshire. He kept several chairmanships, principally those of the two Argentinian railway companies, but they required a journey to London only once or twice a month. For those meetings he would sometimes stay with Beatrice at Hampstead, where she was then living. He also continued to correspond frequently with Edgar.

In the autumn of 1933, Sam had a serious microbiotic attack on his face, causing a disfigurement. He got Lord Horder, [314] the Royal Physician, to come to him, who had been consulted on his 'desperate illness' thirteen years earlier. But Sam made a speedy recovery, and vowed he would live to be 100. He resumed his literary enthusiasm, and though no more was heard of *The Soul of the Dog*, he wrote of his time at the War Office, and this was published by Hutchinson in 1937, as *The War Office at War*.[315] He also made a pilgrimage to La Rochelle, on the Bay of Biscay, to trace his Huguenot ancestors, and a result of this was the commissioning of two large paintings, to commemorate the departure of the Protestant exiles from France.[316]

---

313 1907–2001. Later Lord Hailsham.
314 Thomas Jeeves Horder (1871–1955), 1st Baron Horder of Ashford, Southampton (he lived in Petersfield), 1933.
315 Republished in 1973 by E.P. Publishing Ltd.
316 One of *La Rochelle Harbour* (bequeathed to Daisy Yeo), and *Richelieu Watching the Attack on La Rochelle by the English Fleet*, by A. Grimaud, after Henri Motte (left to Southampton Corporation) (William Charlton Fay, by letter).

Beatrice's business affairs, meanwhile, were flourishing. The profits at Croydon Airport now outstripped those at Waterloo, and she enlarged her house at Gerrard's Cross. In 1936 she took to visiting friends around the world, and bought another house at Southbourne, a suburb of Bournemouth, which afforded easier visiting for Sir Sam, by train from Southampton.

By 1944, Fay was 87, and becoming frail. His legs were giving him trouble, and on a visit to Beatrice in June of that year his condition so alarmed her that she accompanied him back on the train to Southampton. On arrival there, she assumed that the car from 'Awbridge Danes' would be awaiting them, but unknown to her (and to Edgar), Sir Sam had been associating for years with another lady, and a son had been born to them in 1924. It was this lady who met the train. The shock was the greater in that she was known to Beatrice and Edgar, being none other than the former childrens' nurse Daisy Rose Yeo, who was so revered by Edgar from his childhood.

Beatrice returned to Southbourne and was admitted to a nursing home. She had a nervous breakdown and was 'in a pitiable state'.[317] She burned all Sam's letters. After a while she recovered and returned home, on 6 June 1944. 'The effect on her was cathartic', wrote Edgar. 'She had been living in an illusory land where one day she would live openly with Sam, and tend him in his old age. Compelled to face reality, she had the strength to return to the real world, and found it bracing. Apart from overseeing her business into a Limited Company' it was by then concentrated on Waterloo, the Croydon shop had been closed at the outbreak of war,[318] and the one on Marylebone Station had been closed as uneconomic.

She wrote to her son on New Year's Eve 1956–1957, concluding, 'May God's blessing be on all you do', and enclosing a card bearing words which Fay had copied into his diary each New Year: 'I expect to pass through the world but once; any good thing, therefore, that I can do, or any kindness that I can show to my fellow creatures, let me do it now. Let me not defer or neglect it; for I shall not pass this way again.'[319]

---

317 E.S. Fay, Memoirs, op. cit., pages 416 and 417.

318 When it became an RAF Battle of Britain airfield.

319 The author of these well-known words was Stephen Grellett (1773–1855), a Quaker missionary. Sometimes misattributed to William Penn (1644–1718), founder of Pennsylvania.

Beatrice died, without warning illness or signs, in her sleep on 28 July 1957.

Meanwhile, Fay had been kept busy in his writing,[320] and a little book of 44 pages emerged entitled *By My Fay*. Its dedication read, 'To all my old Railway Colleagues, Greeting, S.F.' and the facing page explains that the title was taken from Chaucer[321] and Shakespeare.[322] The book contained ten poems, and a couple of prose pieces with a local Awbridge flavour. One of the poems is worth quoting at some length, as it seems to reproduce faithfully the emotions of a lifetime of a highly practical devotion to managing very down-to-earth matters, recollected in tranquillity of a wide range of reading:

Alone
As thoughts not of our own/ Come and go, like shadows on the moon,/ Note them down, my brother,/ For the children we shall never know,/ In the days of peace and fealty (faith)/ Near to Paradise I ween (surmise, believe).

When verdue decked thy vast domain/ In unimagined loveliness,/ Thy winged songsters, ever free,/ Acclaimed thy just award * 'And saw that it was good.'[323]... All creation rejoiced and sang/ As darkness gave way to light./

But that evil spirit,/ Twin brother to the Master of the Pit,/ Mad with envy, rage, and fear,/ Burst all bounds/ And shamed the world with broken faith and terror amain (violent force)./

'Twas then we stood alone, alone, alone with God;/ Clad only in our worldliness./ Rememb'rest thou?

From out the chaos and distress/ Of the striplings and the daughter's grief,/ Came our unceasing cry – 'Lord of Hosts, Thine aid we pray.'[324]/ Now! Now!

The tramp, tramp, tramp of armed men/ Comes faintly through

320 Having had a poem published in the Romsey local paper in December 1943, though it has not been traced – poems being submitted for publishing under a pseudonym.
321 The *Canterbury Tales*, Prologue, The Miller's Tale, The Wife of Bath's Tale, The Merchant's Tale, etc.
322 Hamlet, *The Taming of the Shrew*, and others.
323 * Sam's own footnote, 'Genesis, Ch.1, v.5'
324 From Rudyard Kipling's 'Recessional': 'Lord God of hosts, be with us yet.'

the void./ The tramp, tramp, tramp of a mighty host/ Echoes far and wide.

Thus, thus, and ever thus, Thy loving kindness/ Gives us visions of a clear and better world anon...

Rejoice with me,/ Mother o' mine, O' mother o' mine;[325]/ For victory has crowned my brow/ With a soldier's guerdon (reward),/ And mine eyes have seen the splendour/ At the rainbow's end/[326] When gloriously at close of day/ The foe was swept from land, and sea and air,/ Away – and away./ Our men we mourned as men,/ Not now, not now./ Their bones whiten all ocean beds;/ Their ashes mingle with desert sands;/ On Afric's strands and Arab lands[327]/ The fig tree and the vine entangle them there./ Mountain crests have heard their tread,/ Leaving snow and ice for requiem.

Now in the twilight of my days,/ A clear call comes to me†/ Through the doorway of eternal peace,/ I hear the beat of the angel's wing[328] – lingering./ Spread my ashes on the highlands,/ From whence the river seeks the sea;/ Richer may its waters be/ For all my love and constancy,/ Flowing by town and hamlet, port and moaning bar†/ To their rest, at Thy behest, silent –/ And alone.[329]

One of the book's prose items was a romantic sketch, 'A Summer Idyll', in which a young man and a young girl called Jessica make love. The booklet contains also a series of photographs. Apart from the photo of himself at the age of four, and three of Beatrice, there are only two others. One is of his mother, Anne, and the other of his granddaughter Maryelle, who perhaps stood in his affections for the absence of children from his own daughters. One of those of Beatrice is captioned "Beatrice B" (Sam's pet name for Beatrice? As Jessica.' The book was published privately, and at least one of his grandsons expressed a certainty that:

---

325 A popular song of the Edwardian era; words by Kipling.
326 Possibly an allusion to the Children's Play of 1916, *Where the Rainbow Ends*, made famous by Roger Quilter's incidental music. It was performed every year for 49 years, excepting the two World Wars, and many times since.
327 Compare the hymn, 'From Greenlands icy mountains and India's coral strand, where Afric's sunny fountains roll down their golden sand'.
328 Possibly a memory of Ezekiel Chapter 10, verse 5.
329 Both quotations † are from Tennyson's poem 'Sunset and Evening Star'.

No publisher would have touched it – full as it was of daft articles. He seemed to have thought of himself as a literary genius. His ideas for several inventions he submitted to the *Railway Magazine*; none of them was at all practicable, and the Editor was rather scornful of them.

None of such products of a declining state of health could, of course, detract from the undeniable value of his history of the South Western Railway, his *War Office at War*, and his written contributions to the discussions on the post-1919 future of the rail network.

Fay had negotiated with the College of Heralds for a grant of arms, which he obtained on 14 January 1944. It appeared on the cover of his 'little book', painted by a noted miniaturist commissioned by Fay. The book closed with the following words, signed by him: 'As thoughts have come like shadows on the moon,/ I've noted them down/ for the children I shall never know/ In the long days of peace to come.'

The final words of John Samuel Fay and Edgar Stewart Fay on Sir Sam, were, despite the ups and downs, 'I loved him.' It is clear that Daisy Yeo did also. In 1945 he bought a cottage at Awbridge for her to live in, where, after his wife's death in 1946, he himself went to live and was cared for by Daisy. In 1948 he underwent a financial crisis: he had been living on an increasing overdraft and the bank refused any further loans. His eldest son, Ernest, with Edgar, arranged for 'Awbridge Danes' to be sold. This was a source of sadness for Sam's grandchildren, who had visited there during school holidays and during the war years, with fond memories and despite their grandfather's failings towards the end. At least one of them continued to visit Daisy Yeo's son John, and his wife Monica.[330]

The sale was completed in October 1949, raising a sum sufficient to pay the bank overdraft, and provide a small income for the years ahead. Fay was 92 at the time of the sale, and during the four years left to him, visited from time to time by his grandson John Samuel, he slipped very gradually

---

330 John Samuel Fay, private letter. John Yeo (1924–2015) was the last son of Sir Sam, and felt a certain sense of neglect by his father, compared with his other sons. But by the time of John's maturing it is only fair to observe that Sam's ability to be a competent father had waned to the point of limited aptitude, and financial resources were sadly diminished.

into senility. He died on 3 May 1953, and was buried beside his wife after a funeral service at the village church.

His life embraced two important events in the history of the express steam locomotive in Britain: he was born one year after the completion of the last GWR Broad Gauge 4-2-2 *Iron Duke*, the fastest in the world at that time, and he died one year before the appearance of the last British Rail Standard steam express 4-6-2, *Duke of Gloucester*, the apogee of the British steam express development.

Two locomotives were named after him: Great Central Class 1 4-6-0 No. 423 in December 1912, and in the twenty-first century a member of Class 66 Co-Co Diesel-Electric No. 66707 was named *Sir Sam Fay GREAT CENTRAL RAILWAY*.

A. Esmé Collings's   129. Western Road, West Brighton

Beatrice, 1900

Beatrice, 1905

Rohan and Cie, Marylebone Station

Edgar Fay, 1911, with Maidie Capron (a cousin of Daisy) and
Daisy Rose Yeo (1891-1987)

5 January 1918: Wedding of Sam's first son , Samuel Ernest Fay
Extreme left: Dorothy Foulger (later couzens), Back row: Robert Foulger,
Maternal Grandfather Harry Bevan Wedgewood-Foulger, Best Man (Name
unkown – died of flu after the war); Cecil Foulger, Vincent David Fay.
The five in the half row: Lady Fay, Sir Sam, Winifred Fay (later Stevenson);
Francie Fay (later Orton); Clarrie Fay.
Front row: Nellie Fay, Samuel Ernest Fay, Mabel Bary Foulger (now Mrs Fay);
Joyce Foulger (later Whitechurch); Mrs Lillian Foulger (bride's mother)

Edgar Fay, 1929

Sir Sam Fay, grandson Charles and Edgar, 1939

Sir Sam in 1950

Sir Sam with Lady Fay at Awbridge

Lady Fay in Awbridge

Awbridge Danes

Awbridge Danes, Garden

John Yeo (1924–2015)

Sir Sam, Lady Fay and granddaughter Maryelle

Sir Sam's coat of arms

15

Financial Summary

Railways, which made large-scale industrial development possible, combined practically all the problems – joint costs, integrated processes, depreciation and obsolescence, heavy fixed investment, and the control of a widespread organisation.[331]

The writer of the Foreword to the 1973 reissue of Fay's *The War Office at War*, could state:

> This grand old man of railways, who died on 30 May 1953, while living in a small cottage near the estate on which his father had died, and Sir Sam had bought many years later… thanks to the Government's Town and Country Planning Act, had to sell up everything, and left the world practically penniless, just as he had entered it. The wheel of fortune had turned full circle in his life; a life so rich in achievement and deserving of greater mention and respect than at present is given.

Many of the writers of the history of the Great Central Railway have, for reasons best known to themselves, presented it in a wholly distorted

---

331 R.S. Edwards, in *The Accountant*, Volume XCVII (1937), page 193. Quoted in T.R. Gourvish, *Mark Huish and the London and North Western Railway*, Leicester University, 1972, page 239.

and unsympathetic manner. It is a characteristic carried over from their assessments of Sir Edward Watkin, and as in his case, it bears little relationship to a properly researched and objective way of presenting historical fact. An example of this is in oft-repeated statements like 'The GCR never made a profit.' One of the most venerable of railway historians could declare confidently that 'The supporters of the Great Central got nothing – they never did.'[332] This was demonstrably not true. The old saw, constantly repeated, characterised the Manchester, Sheffield and Lincolnshire Railway as 'Money, Sunk and Lost', and applied it, after the Extension to London, as 'Gone Completely'. As with so many superficial soundbites, these aphorisms have been regularly restated without reflection by writers, without any research for the truth of a balanced view.

As recently as January 2013, one writer still repeated the myth that 'While the Great Central continues to be a cherished institution, those who bought its share capital would certainly not feel well-disposed – because of its lamentable performance in paying dividends – the prime reason the investors subscribed for the stock.'[333] It is true that the GCR never paid a dividend on its Ordinary Stock, but when the Chairman launched, in 1911, a new issue of Ordinary Shares, nearly £1 million pounds was subscribed (over £100 million in 2017 values): hardly a sign of a lack of solid confidence in the company's future and its policies. All history writing is necessarily selective, but there is a duty to reflect facts without distortion of a true overall picture.

Part of the Great Central's financial difficulty stemmed from it inheritance from the capital structure of the Manchester, Sheffield and Lincolnshire, which had a comparatively small proportion of its Ordinary Stock, and the working difficulties of its predecessor, the Sheffield, Ashton under Lyne and Manchester Railway. This bold enterprise, in building the first railway between those two cities, was confronted from the beginning with crossing the Pennines, and being restricted to traffic from East to West, and vice versa – against the natural flow from London to the Midlands and the North.[334]

---

332 In *Railways in Britain*, Marshall Cavendish, 1979, page 109.

333 In *Steam World Magazine*, page 17.

334 The Hull and Barnsley and the splendid Lancashire and Yorkshire were similarly hamstrung, and they were eventually absorbed by giant neighbours.

But calculations other than those of share revenue show that the MSLR was by no means a badly run or inefficient enterprise. Taking the years 1889–1890, for example, shows that its income from all traffic increased from £32,003 to £34,650; receipts per mile in 1889 amounted to £112, a figure which increased to £121 in 1890. (The mileage was 287½.) For the record, the MSLR paid out on its Ordinary Shares every year from 1846 to 1898, except during 1849–1853, and three other odd years. The highest figures, apart from 5% in 1847, were 3½% (1872), 3⅜% (1889), and 3% (1872 and 1880).[335] Further indications of its efficiency were that in 1880 it had a better operating ratio (receipts/expenditure) than the UK average; its return rate on capital was almost identical to the UK average.

Although payments on Ordinary Stock were the most frequent yardstick of financial success, they are not a good reflection of overall performance. In 1899 on the Great Central, Ordinary Shares constituted only 16.22% of total capital, where on railways generally the percentage was nearer 50%.[336] Fewer shareholders, therefore, were disappointed of dividend than on other companies, though, of course, they were the poorest financially of the proprietorial body. The company capital at that time was £33,906,309, of which Ordinary Shares represented £5,493,960.[337]

Quoting again from the school of vilification, a writer in the magazine *Backtrack* of May 1996 (page 270), reproduced a comment by a member of the Stock Exchange with 40 years' experience, who recalled that when the book *The Work and Management of an English Railway* by George Findlay[338] was published in 1891, some wag had posted a notice of a companion volume: 'The Mismanagement of an English Railway Company, by Sir Edward Watkin, Baronet.' The quoting writer commented that this was 'brutal, but true', whereas it was in fact quite brutally untrue. On the basis of his performance on the MSLR, Watkin received invitations from several companies which were in dire administrative straits due to mismanagement or fraud, or both. Most of them he was unable to accept, but the most prominent of those he did – the South Eastern Railway and the Metropolitan Railway – were transformed into 'good investments'. The former became

335 *Bradshaw's Shareholders' Manual and Guide*, 1899, pages 97 and 98.
336 *Herepath's Railway and Commercial Journal*, 20 January 1899.
337 National Archives, RAIL 1140.
338 General Manager of the London and North Western Railway, 1880–1893.

close to the average UK standard of efficiency, and the latter went from a dividend of 1% in 1872 to one of 5% in 1894. It is clear that Watkin's managerial ability was more evident to the directors of railway companies at the time than to our contemporary commentators.

The *Financial Times* of 15 April 1901 said it was 'curious that the Manchester, Sheffield and Lincolnshire, which had produced from its ranks more brilliant railway administrators than probably any other company, should have withstood all attempts to improve its position'. But with the GCR it could be argued that eventually it did: it increased its profits year on year, up to 1913. By 1914 it had become the largest carrier of freight of all the railways that served London.[339] In that year it was recorded that receipts from passengers (£14,032) were less than one-third of those from goods traffic (£44,758: 22% to 67%). In 1910, J.G. Robinson made a submission to the Board of Directors to the effect that the passenger services, as such, did not pay their way. They did not yield more than 2s 2d per train mile, as against the cost of gross passenger expenditure which was 3s 6d per train mile. The livelihood of the Great Central depended on its freight traffic, he said, and he recommended the construction of more eight-coupled locomotives.[340] He clearly received authority to proceed with his suggestion, for it gave rise in 1911 to the appearance of his Class 8K superheated 2-8-0s, which were to be so important to both the GCR and to the country in World War One, and the years following.

The *Statist* enquiry into revenue per freight train mile, 1899–1912, produced, for 28 major companies, a 45% increase, which suggested a 32% improvements in loadings. The railway industry in 1900 had improved in efficiency (receipts/expenditure), and the GCR had contributed fully to this greater efficiency, with a 64% increase in revenue, a saving of 39%. The company's performance was equalled only by that of the LNWR and the North Eastern.[341]

In 1921 the *Manchester Guardian* of Saturday 19 February, reported on a meeting of GCR shareholders in the Boardroom, Manchester London

---

339 Jack Simmons and Gordon Biddle, *The Oxford Companion to British Railway History*, Oxford University Press, 1997, page 189.

340 George Dow, *Great Central*, Locomotive Publishing Company (Ian Allan), 1965, Volume III, page 307.

341 T.R. Gourvish, *Business History, the Performance of Railway Management*, 1978, page 198.

Road Station, the previous day. The Chairman had declared the register of shareholders as numbering 45,273. Of these, 26,215 held Ordinary Shares, 15,298 holding less than £500. Net revenue was £2,125,526, an increase of £14,259 on the previous year. According to Cecil J. Allen, in his history of the London and North Eastern Railway,[342] in 1922 the GCR gross receipts stood at £11,874,720, as against expenditure of £9,715,618, a net figure, including other net receipts, of £2,363,304. This compared with the figures for the North Eastern Railway (a company with a virtual monopoly from the Humber to the Scottish Border), of £22,178,008 and £18,144,952, and a net total of £4,723,709, almost exactly double in each case. But the total number of staff – 31,456 on the GC and 63,063 on the NER – indicates that the same standard of efficiency was achieved with proportionately fewer staff.

The Great Central did not fulfil the high hopes of its promoters and financiers because it had been a vital part of a larger plan, the greater part of which could not be accomplished for politico-military reasons. The perennial payment of interest charges on its loans – the recuperation of the cost of its construction – consequently hampered its financial prospects, stunting its traffic potential for both passengers and freight. The 'fixed charge' of such repayments in 1922 amounted to £1,374,658, which despite the steadily increasing operating profit (to £2,611,498 in 1921) vitiated the operating profit and resulted in an eventual balance carried forward, after dividends amounting to £900,000, of £10,261.

But it is also undeniable that the achievements of the Great Central, in so many fields of excellence, placed it in the forefront of railway operations in this country. Such an accomplishment was due to the exemplary team work of the company. At almost every level the highest standards were to be seen, serving passengers and freight customers with efficiency and courtesy, from a first-class Chairman and Board, through one of the greatest managers in British railway history, to the men at all operating levels.

In his War Diary, Fay quoted Lieutenant General John Steven Cowans as saying: 'The duty of general staff is to think, not act, and it was improper to deal with administrative matters.' In other words, to have an overall grasp of the enterprise, leaving the detail to others. But an outstanding manager like Fay was adept at superintending both strategy and tactics: 'thinking'

342 Published by Ian Allan, 1966, pages 32 and 33.

and 'acting' were all of a piece with him. He showed all the characteristics of a successful manager, as listed by G.A. Steiner:[343] 'The major requisites of successful management are a first-rate planning system, charisma, and a sense of competitive urgency.' Fay and all the staff exhibited adhesion to the company's motto – 'Forward' – in all their work, as did, in their own way, the faithful proprietors and the trust they showed in the leadership of the company.

Fay's opinion on a mere 'balance sheet' judgement of an organisation was in one of his shrewd epithets: 'Accountants are backward-looking, studying what has happened; the boss-man should have his eyes fixed on what lies ahead.'

An official publication from the Science Museum, published by Her Majesty's Stationery Office in 1980, declared that '[The Great Central] owed its splendid achievements to a few near-geniuses... including Lord Faringdon and Sir Sam Fay.'[344]

---

343 In *Top Management Planning*, Macmillan, 1969.
344 Christine Heap and John Riemsdijk, *The Pre-Grouping Railways, Part Two*, HMSO, 1980, page 45.

Appendix 1

PROSPECTUS.

" 𝔗𝔥𝔢 𝔖𝔬𝔲𝔱𝔥 𝔚𝔢𝔰𝔱𝔢𝔯𝔫 𝔊𝔞𝔷𝔢𝔱𝔱𝔢."

LONDON, MAY 5TH, 1881.

On the 1st of next month, and on the 1st of each succeeding month, it is proposed to publish the "**South Western Gazette**," a paper devoted exclusively to matters affecting the South Western Railway. The price to be one penny.

The profits will be handed over to the **Widows' and Orphans' Fund.**

The principal features of the " **Gazette** " will be as follows :—

> A list of the promotions and appointments in all branches of the service: both in salaried and uniform staff.
>
> Short articles on matters affecting the South Western Railway.
>
> Local notes from all Stations.
>
> Personal recollections of former Superintendents, Station Masters, &c.
>
> A History of the South Western Line is also promised.
>
> Correspondents are respectfully invited from all Stations.

It has been thought that a paper such as this would be interesting to all S. W. men, and that by the exchange of ideas it would create a good feeling between all classes in the service.

May we—the promoters of the " **Gazette** "—ask you, in the interest of the **Widows' and Orphans' Fund,** to kindly canvass your clerks and men for orders, and forward the same to the Secretary of the South Western Company's Institute and Club, Brunswick House, Vauxhall, not later than the 14th inst., together with any suggestions of your own for increasing the popularity and usefulness of "**The Gazette.**"

Upon receipt of the first number we should be glad if you would collect the pence from the subscribers for the following three months, and forward the same to the Institute at your earliest convenience.

Any Local Notes from your Station for our first number will be especially welcome. If you favour us with any copy during this, or any other month, please to send it in five days *at least* before the end of the month.

W. H. GOFFE.

S. FAY.

H. DYER.

Appendix 2

								£ s. d.
The Total Salaries are	...	...	...	...	...	...	...	70 15 2
,, ,, Supplemental Earnings are			...	...	...	...	...	0 12 6
Total Income	...	...	...		...	...	...	£71 7 8

The Total Expenditure may be summarised thus :—

				£ s. d.	£ s. d.
HOUSING.—Rent and Rates				13 7 8	
Travelling				0 5 3	
Fire and Lighting				6 8 0½	
Other Household Expenses				2 7 9	
					22 8 8½
FOOD					32 15 11
CLOTHING (including Hairdresser 4/5)					6 11 3½
SUPERANNUATION, &c.					5 15 8½
HOLIDAYS					0 19 2½
RECREATION, &c.—Postage				0 5 6	
Reading				0 14 0	
Tobacco, &c.				1 6 7½	
Charities				0 13 5	
Miscellaneous				0 1 7	
					3 1 1½
Total Expenditure					£71 11 11½

The Average Expenditure under the various heads is approximately :—

							£ s. d.		
Housing	...	...	...	...	...	...	0 10 11	...	31.3%
Food	...	...	...	...	...	...	0 16 0	...	45.8%
Clothing	...	...	...	...	..		0 3 7½	...	9.2%
Superannuation, &c.	...	...	...	...	...	...	0 2 10	...	8.1%
Holidays	...	...	...	...	...	...	0 0 5½	...	1.3%
Recreation, &c.	...	...	...	...	...	...	0 1 6	...	4.3%
Average Expenditure	...	...	...	...	...	...	£1 14 11		

The Average Number in Family is 4. Of the 79 children, 71 are not over 10, 5 are over 10 and not over 15, and 3 are over 15 and not over 20. In the Family where there are children over 15, Supplementary Earnings are received from the children, and these are included in the weekly income.

The Average Weekly Income, including Supplementary Earnings, is £1 14s. 10d., which is 1d. less than Expenditure.

Appendix 3

In accordance with the National Registration Act of 1915, the Great Central Management issued a form to be filled in by every employee between the ages of 15 and 65. This form included personal details of age, address, nationality, martial state, number of dependent children, other dependents (including employees), and details of occupation and skills. This was to provide the Government, and the Company, with information in common interests.

Great Central Railway.

GENERAL MANAGER'S OFFICE,
MARYLEBONE STATION,
LONDON, N.W.

August 10th, 1915.

NATIONAL REGISTRATION.

In accordance with the provisions of the National Registration Act, 1915, all persons between 15 and 65 years of age will be required to fill in and sign a return in the following form :—

Name..

Residence..

Age last Birthday.	If born abroad and not British state nationality.	State whether Single, Married or Widower.	How many children are dependent on you?		How many other persons are dependent on you, excluding employees?		Profession or occupation. State fully the particular kind of work done and the material worked or dealt in (if any).
			Under 15 years.	Over 15 years.	Wholly dependent.	Partially dependent.	
(1)	(2)	(3)	(4)		(5)		(6)

Name, Business and Business Address of Employer. If not working for an employer, write "None."	Are you employed for or under any Government Department? Say "Yes" or "No" or "Do not know."	(a) Are you skilled in any work other than that upon which you are at present employed, and if so, what? (b) Are you able and willing to undertake such work?
		(9)
(7)	(8)	(a) (b)

In filling up Sections 6 to 8 of the form, the Company's Staff should observe the following directions :—

Section 6. State the grade of railway service in which employed.

Section 7. Write only "Great Central Railway."

Section 8. Write "Employed on a Railway which is under Government control."

As regards Section 9, if any member of the staff has any special skill that he considers might be of value to the State and is willing to place such skill at the disposal of the State, he should give the necessary information in answer to the questions, but should make it clear that he can only undertake such work with the consent of the Company.

To facilitate the preparation of the National Register and its subsequent use, it is important that the foregoing instructions should be closely observed.

Appendix 4

In the GCR *Journal* for January[1] and May 1918[2] there appeared two articles on the subject of the future of the Railways in Britain, after the change of perspective caused by the Great War. They were signed anonymously "Futuro," but from style and vocabulary that seems almost certain to be a pseudonym of Sam Fay.

The first article was entitled "Transport after the War," and the full text follows:

TRANPORT AFTER THE WAR

Among the post-war problems which are at present exercising the minds of all thinking classes of the community, indubitably the foremost place must be given to those urging increased production, which, together with decreased consumption, can alone really assist in the reduction of the enormous debt that we as a nation will have to meet.

It may be taken for granted that business will be so expanded as to throw much greater burdens upon the railways than existed in pre-war days; this point need not be laboured, for a moment's reflection on the great material wealth of the world which has been, and is being destroyed will require building up again and the sooner the wealth is recreated the better for the burdens which the world will be called upon to bear. As a manufacturing country our share of the re-construction will be great and the greater our output the lesser the burden on ourselves and posterity. In this matter of increased production the railways must necessarily play a leading part.

Prior to the War there had begun to evolve a better feeling between the Railway Companies and the Traders, due, in no small measure, to the outspoken appeals made by one or two General Managers, who made it clear that the interests of Railways and Industrial Firms were so closely interwoven that strife was prejudicial to the interests and successful development of both. The effect was good and increasingly so when the War intervened, since which time national interests have overshadowed everything else and both traders and Railway Companies, each working together under ever-expanding difficulties,

---

[1] Pages 117-119.
[2] " 189-191.

265

have endeavoured, and with undoubted success to work amicably together.   To ensure the successful handling of increased business, this good feeling, kindled before the War and fed by it, must be continued when the present upheaval is happily ended.

Presuming, as we have a right to, that this hope is justified, the question arises 'Will the Railway Companies be in a position to cater so economically as to materially assist in the building up of large volume of business?' Anyone connected with railway operation knows well that the density of traffic carried over the railway systems of this country had prior to the War reached a point which it seemed impossible to pass to any great extent. We have, however, assumed that the good feeling between the Railway Companies and the Traders will be continued but this must be augmented to at least allow the Companies to make such working or pooling arrangements between themselves as will permit of the greatest possible use being made of existing accommodation and facilities... [but] the inevitable financial strain which follow the conclusion of hostilities will not allow the Railway Companies to embark on large capital expenditure and even if this course were possible any such expenditure would be required to be recouped from the rates, a procedure detrimental to the object we have in view.

Granted then that trade will be stimulated, and allowing the point that it will not be possible , or at least desirable, to spend capital moneys, how are the railways to get through the increased business, even with the assistance of co-operation among themselves. The demands will be great, stretching far beyond anything reached in the past; on the other hand, supplies, including Rolling Stock, Railway Lines, etc., are inelastic and the problem largely turns to the one thing that in the Railway World is elastic, viz., the human element.
All of us know that relations between Capital and Labour were not of the best preceding the War either on railways or in the commercial world generally; in fact had it not been for the War it would have had to be faced before this. For another crisis to arise immediately after the conclusion of hostilities it would be disastrous. It is essential that the efforts of both employers and employees should be devoted to the achievement of the great common object for the common good. But the naked truth is that the signs of such a crisis are unmistakably showing on the horizon already. How is the crisis to be avoided? Let us return to history to see what has been recorded in the past, (a) to avoid disputes and (b) to encourage the men to give of their best. The answer to the

first part of that question is largely the history of the Conciliation Boards, where, by getting the representatives of the men and the representatives of the companies together, grievances have been ventilated and matters adjusted. The result is fixed rates of pay, scales elaborately set forth with maxima and minima in abundance. So far as point (a) is concerned they have fulfilled their mission in that they have kept the peace; but what of point (b)? Scales of the Medes and Persian-like order in that they change or vary not, are objectionable on the grounds that the human element is thrust out and is not able to give of its best; in short, scales are machines of precise measurements and tend to make men automata. Such a policy cannot be successful when these human machines are called upon to get through much more work than they have been accustomed to. Maxima are particularly objectionable; let us take the case of a youth entering the service as a clerk: he has before him on entering the service the rate at which he will be remunerated for many years to come. There is no incentive to excel, none of that healthy spirit of competition which has been responsible for so much of the world's progress, consequently when the scale comes to its appointed end the chances are that the clerk has dropped into the Slough of Despond. To lessen any determination he may have attained and to make the situation more ironical still he is faced with another maximum, operating for each position for every station on the line. Perhaps in a self-contained firm ...the staff being under direct observation of the Manager, the scale can be varied in accordance with the zeal and ability shown. On a railway, extending over three or four hundred miles, the staff, scattered North, South ,and East and West, have little opportunity of coming beneath the immediate notice of the Chief Officers, and the orthodox method of approaching these gentlemen is circuitous.

To put the position fairly it must, however, be stated that from time to time something has been done in the past to meet these difficulties. A greater tendency was shown some years before the War than had obtained previously to move the staff between the various sections of a department, enlarging their powers of perspective , and a preventive, to a certain extent, of their getting into a groove. Appeals have been made by Officers urging the staff to 'wake up' and probably succeeding in some few ambition. The Higher Grade Scheme , a bold innovation, gave an opportunity to the more ambitious of the younger men. The formation of the Debating Society assisted, as did the decentralisation of the Line, although the latter added a further link between the servant and his General Manager.

These have been productive of good, yet the scattered nature of railway employment demands something more, and harking back to the idea that Railways will be strained to breaking point after the War and that the main hope of dealing with the traffic lies with the ability to et more from the staff than has hitherto been obtained, other innovations of a far-reaching character will have to be adopted.

It is frequently stated - by the staff themselves - that higher wages will have to be paid, but while such a statement is easy to make, it has to borne in mind that many of the Railway Companies pay little or no dividends and that in any business enterprise the shareholders, as well as the staff, are entitled to consideration. Fortunately there is a scheme already in operation which in many industrial concerns has been attended with transcendent success: profit-sharing, if beneficial in industrial organisations in which the employees are congregated together, should be far more effectual on a railway, extending through many Counties, and should lead to that co-operation which is vital to the economical and efficient work of the line... [This] certainly creates a personal interest in the undertaking, but it does not gratify the ambition of the individual.

Turning to that side of the problem the obstacles seem to be the impossibility of a General Manager of a railway coming into personal touch with his staff: the line of communication from the employee to his manager is long and winding and is unfortunately is liable to be cut in three or four places. The situation would appear to be the appointment of an Officer whose duties would be to study the personnel of the railway and to make recommendations as to changes and promotions. Some first- hand knowledge would thus be gained, scales, necessarily be rigid under existing circumstances, could, when the occasion warranted, be made pliable. Energy and capacity could be rewarded. It would make a great difference to men of ambition – and they must be many - who are at present rusting in some obscure part of the country, and the resultant advantage to the Company would be correspondingly high. Given an Officer of integrity and discernment, in touch with the General Manager on the one hand, and with the men on the other, ambition would be given an added stimulus, and the interests of both better served.

A further aid to the ambitious would be the inception of an Institute of Transport, as advocated by Mr Travis recently. The widening of knowledge by contact with fellow workers on our own and other railways would be considerable and there would also be the initial study necessary to qualify for membership, which would presumably be determined by examination.

The problems which peace will bring to Capital and Labour are sure to be serious and if friction results the consequences to the country cannot be other than grave. The predominant nation of the future will not be the one with the greatest army and navy, but the one which can so reconcile the conflicting elements of the industrial sphere as to obtain the most complete sphere as to obtain the most complete benefits which science can offer.

"Futuro"

The second article dealt with Railway Motive Power of the Future , and a precis of the section on Electrification was as follows:

The writer dealt with the various systems under the broad headings of 'Live Rail, Overhead Wires, and Battery systems on Locomotives. The preferences will depend on local requirements, and on whether the line is mainly concerned with passenger or heavy mineral traffic. A main difficulty with electrification is the cost of conversion from steam to electric traction. In 1902 the paid-up capital of British railways was about £1,000,000,000, and of this, rolling stock represented some £150 million, or 15% of the total expended capital. Repairs and renewals amounted in that year to £5,750,000, and the actual working of engines, including wages, to £13,000,000. Such enormous expenditure as would be involved by the conversion requires very thoughtful consideration, as railway companies are not in a position to spend huge sums of money unless there is every possibility that the initial revenue recovered, together with the amount saved in working expenses will more than cover the interest on the necessary capital. An additional difficulty is that wear and tear on track becomes serious on electric railways, compared with that from steam locomotives. The modern steam locomotive, with its high centre of gravity, is a very easy-riding machine, but the present motor-truck , with its very low centre of gravity, results in a serious rail and tyre wear because there is no elasticity between the weight above and the weight below.

The 'Future,' is, however, wide-reaching in its meaning; it includes tomorrow, next week, next year and so on, *ad infinitum.* Whilst few doubt that the present century will see a complete revolution, electricity reigning where at present steam is so mighty, the change is certain to be accompanied by caution, rendered necessary for the enormous capital expenditure required to electrify a main line, with the multifarious matters connected with the change, likely to affect expenditure and receipts. It would appear that for a limited period steam will hold its position, and a further era will find it confined to humbler duties whilst its place for general transport will have been occupied by its newer and greater power.

'Futuro'

Appendix 5

COPY OF COMMISSION.

GEORGE the Fifth, by the Grace of God, of the United Kingdom of Great Britain and Ireland, and of the British Dominions beyond the Seas, King, Defender of the Faith, Emperor of India.

To our Trusty and Well-beloved,

SIR SAM FAY, Kt., J.P.,
SIR VINCENT RAVEN, K.B.E., M.Inst.C.E., M.I.M.E., M.I.E.E.—

GREETING :

KNOW YE, that We, reposing great trust and confidence in your ability, zeal, industry, discretion, and integrity, do, by these presents, with the advice of our Executive Council, authorise and appoint you to inquire into the management, equipment, and general working, including the finance, administration, control, and economy of the Railway and Tramway Services in New South Wales, and more particularly :

(1) The organisation and running of the passenger and goods traffic, the services rendered, the scales of fares and freights operating, and the financial returns.

(2) Matters appertaining to the organisation and conduct of the Mechanical Section of the system in relation to the respective types of locomotives and rolling-stock adopted, cost, economy of life and use, equipment, renewal, and maintenance charges.

(3) Matters relating to the construction, renewal, and maintenance of the permanent way, including station equipment and the systems of signalling and interlocking adopted.

AND WE DO, by these presents, give and grant to you, or either of you, full power and authority, with all proper or necessary assistance at all times, to call before you all such persons as you may judge necessary, by whom you may be better informed of the truth of the premises, and to require the production of all books, papers, writings, and other documents as you may deem expedient, and to visit and inspect the same at the offices and places where the same or any of them may be deposited, and to inquire of the premises by all lawful ways and means. AND Our further will and pleasure is that you do, within the space of six months after this, Our Commission, or sooner if the same can reasonably be done, certify to Us, in the office of Our Premier, what you shall find touching the premises. AND WE HEREBY command all Government officers, and all other persons whomsoever within Our said State, that they be assistant to you in the execution of these presents. AND WE DECLARE this, Our Commission, to be a Commission for all purposes of the Act No. 29 of 1923, intituled " The Royal Commissions Act, 1923."

IN TESTIMONY WHEREOF We have caused these Our Letters to be made Patent, and the Great Seal of Our State of New South Wales to be hereunto affixed.

WITNESS Our Trusty and Well-beloved SIR DUDLEY RAWSON STRATFORD DE CHAIR, Admiral in Our Royal Navy, Knight Commander of Our Most Honorable Order of the Bath, Member of Our Royal Victorian Order, Governor of Our State of New South Wales and its Dependencies in the Commonwealth of Australia, at Sydney, in Our said State, this ninth day of May, in the year of Our Lord one thousand nine hundred and twenty-four, and in the fifteenth year of Our Reign.

(Sgd.) D. R. S. DE CHAIR,
Governor.

By His Excellency's Command,
(Sgd.) GEORGE G. FULLER.

Entered on Record by me, in REGISTER OF PATENTS, No. 40, page 13, this twenty-sixth day of May, one thousand nine hundred and twenty-four.

FOR THE COLONIAL SECRETARY AND REGISTRAR OF RECORDS,

(Sgd.) E. B. HARKNESS,
Under-Secretary.

per H.D.

1924.

—

LEGISLATIVE ASSEMBLY.

NEW SOUTH WALES.

FROM: NEW SOUTH WALES
PARLIAMENTARY PAPERS
1924
4th SESSION, VOLUME 3
DC 342.91/1

REPORT

OF THE

ROYAL COMMISSION OF INQUIRY

INTO THE

RAILWAY AND TRAMWAY SERVICES,

TOGETHER WITH

COPY OF COMMISSION, EVIDENCE, AND APPENDICES.

Ordered by the Legislative Assembly to be printed, 7 and 9 October, 1924.

SYDNEY: ALFRED JAMES KENT, GOVERNMENT PRINTER.

1924.

[12s. 6d.]

28910   167—*a*

TABLE OF CONTENTS.

ROYAL COMMISSION ON RAILWAYS AND TRAMWAYS.

REPORT.

To His Excellency Sir DUDLEY RAWSON STRATFORD DE CHAIR, Admiral in the Royal
Navy, Knight Commander of the Most Honorable Order of the Bath, Member of
the Victorian Order, Governor of the State of New South Wales and its Dependencies,
in the Commonwealth of Australia.

MAY IT PLEASE YOUR EXCELLENCY,—

1. We, your Commissioners, appointed to make a full inquiry into the finance,
management, equipment, and general working, including the administration, control,
and economy of the railway and tramway services in New South Wales, and more
particularly—

(a) The organisation and running of the passenger and goods traffic, the services
rendered, the scales of fares and freights operating, finance and financial
returns,

(b) Matters appertaining to the organisation and conduct of the Mechanical Section
of the system in relation to the respective types of locomotives and rolling-
stock adopted, cost, economy of life and use, equipment, renewal and maintenance charges,

(c) Matters relating to the construction, renewal, and maintenance of the permanent
way, including station equipment and the systems of signalling adopted,

have the honour to submit the following report :—

I.—INTRODUCTORY.

Appointment of Royal Commission.

2. The appointment of a Royal Commission was announced by the Premier
on the 22nd December, 1923, the members being Sir Sam Fay and Sir Vincent L. Raven,
to whom your Commission was issued on the 9th May, 1924, authorising and appointing
those Commissioners to inquire into the above-quoted subjects.

3. The appointment of this Royal Commission was the result of discussions in the
Legislative Assembly upon railway administration generally, including the reappoint-
ment or otherwise of the present Railway Commissioners. As a temporary arrangement,
and pending the report of your Commission, the services of the Railway Commissioners
were extended until 31st December, 1924.

Conduct of the Inquiry.

4. Your Commissioners arrived in Sydney on 9th May, and immediately proceeded
to issue a questionnaire of sixty items (subsequently amplified) through the Minister
for Railways to the Railway Commissioners. Statements were also obtained from the
same source as to the duties of the various chief officers, and the general organisation
and administration of their branches. We have also called for, and perused, the
Minutes of the Board Meetings of the Commissioners, the Committee Meetings, and the
various Officers' Conferences, and have also analysed the complaints, numbering some
hundreds, addressed to the Railway Commissioners by the public over a period of six
months. In conjunction with our personal observations, these have probably given
us as much information on the subject of the New South Wales Railways as the evidence
placed before us.

5. Commencing on 13th May, we travelled over the whole of the main lines,
and, with few exceptions, the branch lines, of the New South Wales State railway system.
We devoted thirty-six days to the tours of inspection, travelling 9,580 miles in that
period, and inspecting the plant and facilities. In the course of these tours, which
were

viii

were undertaken primarily to enable us to become acquainted at first hand with the location, general layout and equipment of the track, stations, and buildings, we ascertained the traffic conditions of the lines, the facilities provided for the handling of various classes of traffic, the nature of the country served by the railway network, and the methods of local supervision and working. To this end an inspection was made of passenger and goods stations, refreshment-rooms, locomotive and electrical workshops, sheds, and manufacturing establishments, stores, yards, signalling equipments, and the permanent way, together with other essentials of railway service, while conversations with the local supervisory officials helped us to appreciate the nature of the railway problem in this State. These tours of inspection also enabled us to study the detailed organisation of the various districts on the spot.

6. With the exception of a tour to Broken Hill and an inspection of the lines in the Riverina area, we were accompanied—at our own request—by Mr. J. Fraser, C.M.G., Chief Railway Commissioner, in order that we might have the advantage of ascertaining at first hand such information upon the layout of the lines and various phases of railway working as we required. The Chief Traffic Manager, the Chief Mechanical Engineer, and the Information Officer also accompanied us, while traffic and locomotive officers were present in their respective districts for the purpose of explaining the various features of the railway system in their areas.

7. The tours of inspection were completed on 11th July, and at intervals between journeys evidence was taken on oath from the Commissioners, the principal officers of the Railway Department, and also from Mr. F. A. Coghlan (Auditor-General), Mr. E. J. Sievers (Valuer-General), Mr. J. Spencer Watts, of Messrs. Smith and Johnson, Public Accountants, Sydney, who made a report to the Railway Commissioners in 1921 upon finance and financial methods, and Mr. J. Spence, Director of Finance at the Treasury.

8. Regular sittings were commenced in Sydney on 15th July, and one day's hearing took place at Newcastle on 20th August. Evidence was taken on twenty-eight days. In all, twenty-eight departmental officers and twenty-five representatives of public bodies and associations were heard in addition to the gentlemen named above. The list of witnesses is given in Appendix 3.

9. It became evident at an early stage of the inquiry that the system of financial control under which the railways and tramways are dependent upon the yearly budget of the State, coupled with the fact that no reserves exist to meet wasting assets, dominated the organisation, and through it the efficient and economical operation of the transport services. We have, therefore, placed Finance and Financial Control in the forefront of our report.

10. Summarised, the Terms of Reference fall into five main heads, as shown below, and we deal with them in that order :—

FINANCE AND FINANCIAL CONTROL.

ORGANISATION.

MANAGEMENT.

(a) Permanent Way and Works,
(b) Signalling,
(c) Mechanical.
(d) Electrical.
(e) Stores.
(f) Operation.
(g) Rates and Fares.

TRAMWAYS.

MISCELLANEOUS QUESTIONS.

A final section contains a Summary of our principal Recommendations.

Railway Development in New South Wales.

11. The first attempt to introduce railway communication in New South Wales was in 1846, but it was not until 1848 that a company entitled The Sydney Tramroad and Railway Company was formed for the purpose of constructing a railway from Sydney to Parramatta and Liverpool, with possible future extensions to Goulburn and Bathurst. This company, however, made very slow progress with the work, which was ultimately taken over by the Government. Meanwhile, another company had been started in 1853 with the object of constructing a railway from Newcastle to Maitland. This was no more successful than the Sydney company, and shared the same fate.

12.

Index

French Control 128, 129, 130, 131, 135-137, 147, 150-152;
 Railways 158-164, 166, 168, 172, 174
French, Sir John 137
Freshwater, Yarmouth and Newport Railway 203, 204
Frevent 154
Furse, Sir William 120, 121, 125

Gainsborough
Geddes, Eric 119, 120, 122, 125, 126, 129, 130, 131, 136, (153), 163, 173, 174, 175
Gerrard's Cross 45, 221-223, 234
Gibson, Food Transport, Manchester 141
Gloucester Standard 22
Golf 3
Gorton 46, 137, 138, 204
Granet, Sir Guy 119, 120, 122, 125, 126, 129, 130, 149, 176, 177, 178
Grateley, Hampshire 25
Great Central Railway Company 25, 41-45, 47, 48, 57, 58, 59, 66, 67, 72-77, 82-88, 119, 124, 133, 138, 170, 175, 203, 204
    Audit Office 105; Directors 25, 39; Female Clerks 105, 108
    Financial Statement, 1918 187, 194, 195; 1922 196, 197, 254-259
    Hotel, Marylebone 37, 'Hospital' 136; 166
    Company *Journal* 48, 57, 65, 105, 106
    Ships Impounded, 1914 165
    War Memorial, Sheffield 181
Great Missenden 45
Great Northern Railway 41, 58, 59, 63, 72-77, 116, 194
Great Western Railway 9, 13, 21, 22, 41-44,

172, 194
Grey, Lieutenant Colonel 20, 21
Grimsby 43, 45, 82, 84-87, 89, 126, 139, 175, 190, 191, 192
Guide bridge 46, 82
Guildford and London Railway 10
Gunnislake 9

Hadjaz Army 162
Haig, Earl 119, 127, 128, 131, 137, 146, 147, 150, 153, 157, 158, 159, 166, 170, 171, 172
 179, 180, 181, 182, 230
Haldane, Richard 117, 144, 145
Halifax 43, 44
Ham, Hampshire 4
Hamble-le-Rice 1
Hamburg 45, 165
Hamilton, Lord Claud 192
Hampshire 8, 15
Hampshire Accent 173
Hand Grenades 145, 146
Harbord, Major General James, US Army 173
Harmsworth, Cecil 129
Harrington, Sir Charles 162, 174
Harris, Charles 176
Harrison, General, Light Railways 136
Harrod's Stores 80
Harrow 45
Hart, F.H. 65, 68
Haughton, Canon T. 181
Hay, Sir William 175
Hazebrouk 136
Henderson, Sir Alexander [From 1916, Lord Faringdon) 40, 47, 72, 73, 74, 84, 85, 88